BREAK DOWN THE BARRIERS THAT ARE BLOCKING YOUR HAPPINESS

Do you feel dissatisfied?
Are you depressed?
Do you feel alone or unable to cope?
Are you anxious or do you have trouble relaxing?
Do you wish your relationships with others
were more satisfying?

If the answer is yes to any of these questions, Dr. Henry Cloud has a simple four-step plan that can change your life. By first identifying the issues that we all struggle with, and offering helpful guidelines to resolve these issues, Dr. Cloud's program can help you put the meaning, purpose, satisfaction, and fulfillment back into your life.

Case studies from his practice, easy-to-understand language, and an invaluable study guide will help you recognize problems from your past and implement change in your future. By outlining how to incorporate your spiritual faith, values, and beliefs into a practical approach to healing and recovery, Dr. Henry Cloud explains how to take control of your life, heal your inner wounds, and regain the happiness you deserve.

Changes That Heal

HOW TO UNDERSTAND YOUR PAST TO ENSURE A HEALTHIER FUTURE

Dr. Henry Cloud

HarperPaperbacks
New York, New York
ZondervanPublishingHouse
Grand Rapids, Michigan
Divisions of HarperCollinsPublishers

HarperPaperbacks *A Division of* HarperCollins*Publishers*
10 East 53rd Street, New York, N.Y. 10022

A trade paperback edition of this book was published in 1992 by Zondervan Publishing House, a division of HarperCollins*Publishers*.

Published in association with Sealy M. Yates, Literary Agent, Orange, CA.

First HarperPaperbacks printing: May 1995

Printed in the United States of America

HarperPaperbacks and colophon are trademarks of HarperCollins*Publishers*

❖ 10 9 8 7 6 5 4 3

To Julie and Christi

My prayer is that the fruit of your grace can be seen
in these pages.

Contents

V. Becoming an Adult

Acknowledgments

I DID NOT SET OUT TO WRITE THIS BOOK. IT IS the product of a lot of people, without whose input this book would not exist. The ideas presented here are composites of many experiences over the last fifteen years that involve faithful servants of Jesus Christ, and I would like to acknowledge some of the persons specifically.

Dr. John Townsend, my friend and associate, has been instrumental in the development of the model presented in this book. Through many hours of dialogue and team teaching, his input and thinking have added much to my understanding of Scripture and of emotional life. I am indebted to him for the loyalty of his friendship, the discipline of his professional life, and the example of his heart, which is attuned to the hurts of others. We have taught this material together for several years, and there has never been a single presentation where some idea of his has not influenced my thinking. I am grateful for his involvement in the concepts presented here.

Dr. John Carter deserves many thanks for introducing me to the understanding of what an incarnational gospel really means, and to the understanding of the value of relationship at the center of any true scholarship. He was a model instructor at Rosemead Graduate School, and his continuing input over the years has shown me that Jesus holds all understanding in his hand.

Dr. Phil Sutherland's model of a wisdom perspective on the Scriptures gave me new lenses through which to approach the Bible, and significantly helped me to discover "new wineskins" that could contain the true miracle of therapy. Everything that I think about the ways that humans grow contains the seeds of his perspective. I am thankful for his input into the early manuscript as well.

Dr. Bruce Narramore's thinking on the concepts of guilt and conscience, as well as on a process understanding of growth, were invaluable to me in my training. His commitment to training professionals has borne fruit for the last twenty years.

I will be forever grateful to Dr. Frank Minirth and Dr. Paul Meier, who fifteen years ago encouraged me to go into the field of helping. If it were not for them, I would certainly be doing something else with my life. And I am grateful to Dr. Althea Horner for her supervision and humanity. Her thinking about how people grow has been more than helpful to me as I have developed my own thinking. She has shown me that psychoanalysis must bow to love. Dr. Doug Wilson deserves special thanks for giving me a place to begin practice and for encouraging me to integrate that practice into ministry, as do the rest of CORE: Dr. Michele McCormick, Monte Pries, Ann Huffman.

Campus Crusade for Christ deserves special thanks for the development of this book. It was under their original request that this material was developed and envisioned. Loren Lillistrand, then U.S. field director, put the original project together, and deserves much credit for its coming to fruition. In addition, other Crusade staff members have been very encouraging to the development of this work. Special thanks go to Mary Graham for thinking that this could be used in training, and Melanie Alquist for reading the manuscript.

The staff at the Minirth-Meier Clinic West have been

superior models with whom to work in recent years. Their continued commitment to healing in the lives of others has encouraged me professionally as well as personally. I love seeing the fruits of their daily gifts to others. Dr. Dave Stoop has been a constant encouragement in the writing of this book, and his input as he taught the material with me was invaluable. Thanks go to him for helping bring metaphor to life.

Thanks also go to the Friday group for their application of faith to life.

Also I'd like to thank Dr. Anita Sorenson for reading the manuscript and making some helpful observations. I appreciate the support that Jana Swanson has offered personally and for interacting with the material.

Thanks to Scott Bolinder for believing in the book and for agreeing to publish this revised edition, to Sandy Vander Zicht for her thoughtful and meticulous work in making the manuscript more user friendly, to the rest of the Zondervan team for their encouragement and welcome, and to Sealy Yates for all of his encouragement and support and for the invaluable role he plays in the lives of Christian authors.

If anything comes through in the message of this book, it is that the body of Christ is the only place in which we grow. My community of friends has been the place where I have "grown into" the concepts presented here. They deserve special thanks: Dr. Edward Atkinson for being a true friend through the years and showing me the Lord when he was not easily found; Bill and Julie Jemison for taking a new Christian in and walking through the early days of faith—their love and support will never be forgotten; Guy and Christi Owen for their supreme ability to produce a safe harbor for me; Toby Walker for keeping theology practical and being a truly giving friend; and my parents, whose early and sustained commitment to me have imparted much toward my ability to see God as good.

Changing in ❧ Him

EVERY WEEK I SEE CHRISTIANS who are suffering from a whole range of emotional problems: anxiety, loneliness, grief over broken relationships, resentment, and feelings of inadequacy. Often they have been struggling with these problems for years. They are people in pain.

The church is split on how to deal with these hurting people. Those on one side of the issue say that people who struggle emotionally are "in sin." They "don't have enough faith," "are not obedient," or "don't spend enough time in the Word." These people tend to blame the hurting person for his or her pain.

The answers Christians on this side of the argument tend to give sound a lot like the ones Job received from his friends. "God is trying to teach you something." "Look at the blessings you still enjoy." "God is testing you." "Give thanks in spite of your circumstances." The speeches of Job's three friends contain elements of truth, but do not often help the person in pain.

A despairing person should have kindness from his friend, said Job, "lest he forsake the fear of the Almighty" (Job 6:14 NASB). Job recognized, as only a person in pain can do, that simple answers not only fail to relieve pain, they can literally drive a person further away from God. The hurting person who takes this sort of advice to heart often has two problems instead of one: the *pain* she originally had, plus the *guilt* over not being able to apply the answers she was given.

The help offered to Christians in emotional pain over the years has done untold damage and has led many to reach the conclusion Job did: "You smear me with lies; you are worthless physicians, all of you! If only you would be altogether silent! For you, that would be wisdom" (Job 13:4–5).

Faced with this kind of help, sufferers either learn to fake healing to remain in the church, or leave the church, deciding that their faith provides little solace for their emotional pain.

People on the other side of the issue reach out and try to touch the pain of hurting people. Looking for answers that work, and not finding them in the church, they turn to psychology. Often psychological methods succeed, and hurting people find relief. But now these people are in a quandary. Was it God or psychology that provided the cure? They know that the relief is from God, but there seems to be no biblical system by which to defend it. They just know that "it works."

As a Christian, a psychologist, and a fellow struggler, I have stood on both sides of this fence. I have tried the "standard" Christian answers for myself and others, and have come to Job's conclusion: they are worthless medicine. I have also tried "baptizing" psychological insights so that they would somehow feel "Christian." This didn't work either.

Several years ago I found myself saying to God, "I quit. I really don't know what helps. God, if there is something that does, you will have to show it to me." Over the next few years, God led me on a spiritual journey in which he graciously answered that simple but desperate prayer.

My purpose in this book is not to get enmeshed in the church's debate between psychology and theology. I have

a different goal in mind. I want to show you that there are
biblical solutions for your struggles with depression, anxiety, panic, addictions, and guilt, and that these solutions
lie in your understanding certain basic developmental
tasks—tasks that you may have failed to complete when
you were growing up and tasks that bring changes that
heal. These tasks involve growing up and into the "likeness" of the one who created you. Let me explain.

The Bible says that we were created "in the image of God"
(Gen. 1:27). We were created "like" God. Theologians have
filled libraries with books about the attributes, or characteristics, of God. They distinguish between God's incommunicable attributes—he is immutable (changeless), omnipotent
(all-powerful), infinite (without limitations), omniscient (all-
knowing), omnipresent (everywhere)—and his communica-
ble attributes—he is just, righteous, holy, loving, and faithful.
Obviously, we can't reflect God's incommunicable attributes:
we can never be all-powerful or all-knowing. But we can
become more loving and more holy. The more we become
like him in these attributes, the less we will struggle with
emotional problems.

The apostle Paul writes that God calls us to be "pre-
destined to be conformed to the likeness of his Son"
(Rom. 8:29). What he means is that our goal is to
become more like him. Our destiny is to pursue this family resemblance to God. The problem we face is figuring
out *how* to become more Christlike. How do we work on
becoming "holy" when we feel so powerless to control
our eating habits? How can we be "loving" when we're
burned out by all the requests for our time and energy?

Since becoming like God doesn't seem practical, we try
to solve our day-to-day problems by splitting them into
two different categories. We ask, "Is this an emotional
problem or a spiritual problem?" If we are struggling with
an emotional problem, the Christian psychologist is

called in; if it's a spiritual problem, the pastor gets the call. We assume that our depression, panic, guilt, or addictions have little or nothing to do with our spirituality; they are two separate issues.

But separating our problems into "emotional" problems and "spiritual" problems is part of the problem. All of our problems stem from our failure to reflect the image of God. Because of Adam and Eve's fall into sin in the Garden of Eden, we have not developed the "likeness" of God in the vital areas of our person, and we are not functioning as we were created to function. Thus, we are in pain.

In the course of my own spiritual and professional journey, I have identified four aspects of the personality of God that, if we would cultivate them, would greatly improve our day-to-day functioning. God is able to do four things that we, his children, have difficulty doing:

1. Bond with others.
2. Separate from others.
3. Sort out issues of good and bad
4. Take charge as an adult

Without the ability to perform these basic God-like functions, we can literally remain stuck for years, and growth and change can elude our grasp. In this book I will explain these four developmental tasks, the barriers that get in the way of our achieving them, and the skills we need for completing them.

Because we live in a fallen world, we all have deficits in all four areas. Transforming the effects of the fall and growing in the image of God is not an easy task. But God has promised that the "good work" he began in us, he will carry "on to completion until the day of Christ Jesus" (Phil. 1:6).

But before we set about this task of growing into the

likeness of God, of changing in him, we need to take a brief look at two major qualities of God's character—qualities that, if properly understood, will help us undertake our journey with vigor.

Part I
Three Ingredients of Growth

Chapter

❧ 1

Grace and Truth

ONCE UPON A TIME IN A FARAWAY GALAXY, there was a highly advanced people. They had everything they could ever desire: technology to solve every problem, and more leisure than we get in a lifetime. But they were bored. Bored to tears. They needed something new—something exciting—to liven up their planet.

A committee was established to look into the matter. They discussed coming up with a new sport. Or developing a new amusement park. Finally, an alien named Beezy proposed the winning idea.

"How about creating a god?" he suggested.

Everyone agreed it was a wonderful idea. "It will give our people something to do on Sunday," one said. "And it will be great for conversations," said another.

So they tried to invent a god. But to no avail. Beezy, who had been placed in charge of the research and development of a new god, called all the committee members together.

"Look, this just isn't working," he said. "What good is a god we can invent ourselves? We're smart enough to know *that's* not a real god. Why don't we *find* us a god instead—like that God the earthlings worship?"

The committee agreed, and soon afterward Beezy took a business trip to the Planet Earth. Under his invisible cloak, he visited dozens and dozens of churches and religious institutions. He took copious notes and spent hours writing up his report.

When he returned, the committee gathered, eager to hear of his findings. "Fellow aliens," he greeted them. "I have returned not with one god, but with two."

A gasp of astonishment rippled through the room.

"The name of the first god, or should I say goddess, is Grace. A very attractive goddess she is. She talked about love often. 'Get along, be friends, be nice,' she'd say. 'And if you can't be good, I'll forgive you anyway.'" Beezy looked perplexed. "The only thing is, I'm not sure what she would forgive, since they didn't seem to have any rules to break."

Beezy went on. "I especially liked the things the followers of Grace did, like feeding poor people and visiting prisoners in jail. However"—he shook his head—"these followers of Grace seemed so *lost*. They kept doing the same bad things over and over, and they never seemed to know where they were going.

"Then there's the other god." Beezy took a deep breath. "This god is definitely a man, and his name is Truth. Truth is just as mean as Grace is nice. He kept telling the people all sorts of things about them that made them feel very bad, and his followers did the same thing. But there's a good side to Truth," Beezy reassured the committee. "He campaigns against some very nasty

enemies, such as lying, cheating, adultery, abortion, and
drunkenness. He's like a big religious street sweeper,
sweeping away all his enemies. The only trouble is, he
not only sweeps away bad things; he also sweeps away the
people who do the bad things. As for the smiles you see
on the followers of Grace—forget it. All Truth's followers do is scowl and scream."

Needless to say, after hearing Beezy's report, the committee were ready to opt for the new amusement park
because they didn't like either god. But Beezy had one
last suggestion.

"We have all this wonderful technology for mixing
repelling elements, like oil and water," he said. "How
about if we try mixing Grace and Truth?"

Grace and Truth Divided

Our God is a God "full of grace and truth" (John 1:14).
We often hear the phrase "full of grace and truth," but
we rarely stop and realize its implications for our struggles
here on earth. What *are* grace and truth? Why are they so
important?

Let's take grace first. *Grace is the unmerited favor of God
toward people*. Grace is something we have not earned and
do not deserve. As Frederick Buechner says, "Grace is
something you can never get but only be given. There's
no way to earn it or deserve it or bring it about any more
than you can deserve the taste of raspberries and cream or
earn good looks or bring about your own birth."[1]

To put it another way, grace is unconditional love and
acceptance. Such love is the foundation upon which all
healing of the human spirit rests. It is also the essence of
God. "God is love," writes the apostle John (1 John 4:8).
And God loves us freely, without condition.

The Bible itself does not clearly distinguish between grace and love. As the *International Standard Bible Encyclopedia* comments, "Love stresses God's personal disposition toward unworthy creatures, while grace stresses his freedom from obligation in saving them. But the distinction is not clearly nor consistently made. Both love and grace come to us through Christ (Rom. 5:8; Gal. 1:6). And both are unique in that they are undeserved."

Grace is the *first* ingredient necessary for growing up in the image of God. Grace is unbroken, uninterrupted, unearned, accepting *relationship*. It is the kind of relationship humanity had with God in the Garden of Eden. Adam and Eve were loved and provided for. They knew God's truth, and they had perfect freedom to do God's will. In short, they were secure; they had no shame and anxiety. They could be who they truly were.

Perhaps you have experienced this kind of love and grace with someone. You can be exactly who you are. You do not need to hide your thoughts or feelings; you do not need to perform; you do not need to do anything to be loved. Someone knows the real you, and loves you anyway.

Grace, then, is the relational aspect of God's character. It shows itself in his unconditional connection to us. The first "god" Beezy discovered had this characteristic: Grace was a goddess of compassion and relationship. Her followers did all sorts of loving things for one another; they gave of themselves freely. They tried to connect with people who were in pain and to help them out of their pain. They lived in togetherness.

Those who worshiped Grace had only one problem: they heard little truth spoken. As a result, they continued to fall into bad situations that required more and more grace. It's not that the goddess Grace minded giving more. Grace's grace had no limit. However, Grace's followers needed direction to keep them from falling into the same old patterns over and over again. They needed guidance to steer them away from trouble.

This is where Truth comes in. The second god that Beezy found was very good at setting limits on bad behavior. He gave his followers lots of direction; he told them exactly what they could do and what they could not do. They knew clearly the difference between what was right and what was wrong, what was good and what was not good. They had firm boundaries about where they could play and where they could not.

Truth is the *second* ingredient necessary for growing up in the image of God. Truth is what is real; it describes how things really are. Just as grace is the *relational* aspect of God's character, truth is the *structural* aspect of his character. Truth is the skeleton life hangs upon; it adds shape to everything in the universe. God's truth leads us to what is real, to what is accurate. Just as our DNA contains the form that our physical life will take, God's truth contains the form that our soul and spirit should take.

All of this sounds wonderful, but as was the case with Grace, Truth had his own problems. He was mean. He didn't seem to care about the people who were violating his standards. All he cared about was wiping out the bad. He had none of the compassion Grace demonstrated; at times he seemed downright uncaring. In short, he had no relational aspects: he lacked forgiveness, favor, mercy, compassion—all of the attributes that flowed freely from Grace. If people failed, he just threw them out, or yelled at them.

As Grace left Beezy wanting structure, Truth left Beezy wanting love.

*   *   *

All of us, to some degree, have experienced these two gods—the loving one for whom anything goes and the hard one who lets nothing slide. As you have probably already realized, these two gods are aspects of the one true God's nature, aspects that different churches emphasize. What you may not realize is that these different "gods" are really symbols of the human condition after the fall, when sin ripped grace and truth apart.

Truth without Grace

When Adam and Eve were in the Garden of Eden, they had both grace and truth united in one God. When they sinned, they drove a wedge between themselves and God; they lost their grace-filled and truthful relationship with God.

Without grace, Adam and Eve felt shame: when they heard God walking in the garden in the cool of the day, they hid from him. When God calls out, "Where are you?" Adam explains that he was hiding because he was afraid (Gen. 3:8–10). Shame and guilt had entered the world; human beings were no longer safe.

After Adam and Eve cut themselves off from a relationship with God, they also severed their connection to grace and truth, for those come through relationship with God. However, God did not let them stay isolated for long. Seeing Adam and Eve in their lost state, he decided to give them direction; he gave them truth in the form of the law. The law is a blueprint, or a structure, for people to live by. It offers them guidance, and it sets limits for them.

There was only one problem: God gave them truth without grace. Adam and Eve had to try to live up to God's standards. They soon learned that they could never measure up. No matter how hard they tried to perform, they would always come up short. *Truth without grace is judgment.* It sends you straight to hell, literally and experientially.

Paul writes to the Romans about truth without grace—the law—and the things it does to us:

> Now we know that whatever the law says, it says to those who are under the law, so that every mouth may be silenced, and the whole world held accountable to God. Therefore no one will be declared righteous in his sight by observing the law; rather, through the law we become conscious of sin. (3:19–20)

> Law brings wrath. (4:15)

> The law was added so that the trespass might increase. (5:20)

> For when we were controlled by the sinful nature, the sinful passions aroused by the law were at work in our bodies, so that we bore fruit for death. (7:5)

> Once I was alive apart from the law; but when the commandment came, sin sprang to life and I died. I found that the very commandment that was intended to bring life actually brought death. (7:9–10)

And to the Galatians Paul writes:

> All who rely on observing the law are under a curse, for it is written: "Cursed is everyone who does not continue to do everything written in the Book of the Law." (3:10)

We were held prisoners by the law. (3:23)

You who are trying to be justified by law have been
alienated from Christ; you have fallen away from
grace. (5:4)

And James gives us this discouraging bit of news:

For whoever keeps the whole law and yet stumbles
at just one point is guilty of breaking all of it.
(2:10)

When we look at what the Scripture says about the
law, about truth without grace, we see that the law
silences us, brings anger, increases sin, arouses sinful passions, brings death, puts us under a curse, holds us prisoner, alienates us from Christ, and judges us harshly. No
wonder Beezy did not like Truth!

The law without grace destroys us. No one ever grows
when they are under the law, for the law put us into a
strictly legal relationship with God: *"I'll love you only if you
do what is true or right."* Getting truth before grace, or truth
before relationship, brings guilt, anxiety, anger, and a host
of other painful emotions, as this story of Ruth shows.

Ruth's missionary father had insisted that his twenty-
two-year-old daughter come to see me. Ruth, a college
student, was suffering from depression. She had no
appetite and had trouble sleeping and studying. Her
father accompanied her to the appointment.

"What's the problem?" I asked Ruth, after we had chat-
ted for a few minutes. But it was her father who responded.

"Well, it's pretty obvious," he said, folding his arms
across his chest. "She's not living like she should."

"What do you mean?" I asked.

"She's doing drugs and sleeping around," he said with disgust. "Plus she's flunking out of college, and she has no idea what she wants to do with her life." Before I could ask another question, he continued, "If she read her Bible and went to church, she wouldn't be so depressed. But all she wants to do is hang around those reprobate friends of hers."

"What would happen if she began to do all of the things you think she should?" I asked.

"Well, then she would be happy like her mother and I, and the Lord would bless her."

I could see that I was not going to get very far with Ruth's father, so I thanked him for his information and asked if I could talk with Ruth alone.

When her father had left, Ruth was still hesitant to talk. She refused to answer any of my questions with more than a yes or no. Finally I said, "Ruth, I think if I had to live with your father, I'd take drugs too. Does his attitude have anything to do with your discouragement?"

Ruth nodded. Her eyes filled with tears.

"You are an adult and this is an adults' hospital," I said. "I don't see that you are in any danger to yourself or anyone else, so you are free to go. But before you leave, let me tell you what I think is going on.

"I don't know all of the story, but I can tell that you're very depressed, and I *don't* think it is because you aren't doing the things your father thinks you should do. I think there are other reasons, very good, logical reasons, that he doesn't understand. If you would like to stay, I think we can help you to feel better. If you do stay, though, it will have to be your choice, not his. If he's upset about something, he can get help for himself."

Ruth sat stiffly in her chair, staring at me through her tears. "I'll leave you alone a few minutes to think about it," I said.

Ruth did decide to check in, and what I had suspected was true. Ruth had had many years of "truth without grace." As a result, she was experiencing the things the Bible says the law produces: bad feelings and failure. Everywhere she turned, she ran into some "should," and very little acceptance. The law of sin and death had taken its toll on her, and it was a painful struggle for her to break free of its grip.

As I watched her struggle, I could not help thinking back to what the Bible says about truth without grace: it silences us, brings anger, increases sin, arouses sinful passions, brings death, puts us under a curse, holds us prisoner, alienates us from Christ, and judges us harshly.

Grace without Truth

Truth without grace is deadly, but as Beezy discovered, grace without truth leads to less than successful living as well. In Grace's church, Beezy saw people who were loving, but directionless. In actuality, Grace was not this goddess's real name. In the same way that Truth (without grace) can be called Judgment, Grace (without truth) can be named License. The Scriptures write about her also:

> You, my brothers, were called to be free. But do not use your freedom to indulge the sinful nature. (Gal. 5:13)

> The acts of sinful nature are obvious: sexual immorality, impurity and debauchery; idolatry and witchcraft; hatred, discord, jealousy, fits of rage, selfish ambition, dissensions, factions and envy; drunkenness, orgies, and the like. I warn you, as I

did before, that those who live like this will not inherit the kingdom of God. (Gal. 5:19–21)

What then? Shall we sin because we are not under law but under grace? By no means! Don't you know that when you offer yourselves to someone to obey him as slaves, you are slaves to the one whom you obey—whether you are slaves to sin, which leads to death, or to obedience, which leads to righteousness? (Rom. 6:15–16)

Put to death, therefore, whatever belongs to your earthly nature: sexual immorality, impurity, lust, evil desires and greed, which is idolatry. (Col. 3:5)

For you have spent enough time in the past doing what pagans choose to do—living in debauchery, lust, drunkenness, carousing, and detestable idolatry. (1 Peter 4:3)

He who ignores discipline comes to poverty and shame, but whoever heeds correction is honored. (Prov. 13:18)

In the same way that Ruth's home—one of truth without grace—had led to negative consequences, a home of "grace without truth" can also have devastating results.

Sam was admitted into our hospital program after an accidental drug overdose. He had neglected to keep track of how much cocaine he was snorting. Although Sam was twenty-eight, he dressed like a teenager—torn jeans, a faded Hard Rock Cafe T-shirt, and high-top tennis shoes with the laces untied.

In the first few sessions we discovered that, although Sam had a genius IQ, he had flunked out of two colleges and had never been able to hold down a job. His relational life was equally troubled. He would totally lose himself in a relationship and recklessly abandon the rest of his responsibilities. In the process, he would smother whomever he was dating and scare her away. At the time he was admitted, his latest girlfriend had just left him.

When we asked Sam about his family, he told us that his father had died when Sam was four. Depressed and withdrawn for many years, his mother had never remarried. In an attempt to make up for the loss of their father, she had tried to be as nice to her children as possible. To hear Sam tell it, he had lived "the life of Riley." He had had few responsibilities and plenty of money. His mother had rarely disciplined him when he got into trouble. In fact, several times she had bailed him out of jail when he had been arrested for shoplifting, disorderly conduct, and drug possession.

At first, Sam's lifelong patterns continued at the hospital unit: he would sleep late, miss activities, forget assignments, and fail to groom himself properly. The lack of limits in his life—the lack of truth and discipline—had led to a chaotic lifestyle.

The hospital staff, however, refused to protect Sam from the consequences of his actions as his mother had. Sam learned, after some strong guidance and painful confrontations, to fulfill his responsibilities. And, to his surprise, he discovered that he felt much better about life when he was pulling his own weight.

The Bible doesn't commend either one of Beezy's gods: Truth apart from Grace, nor Grace apart from Truth. Beezy's final suggestion was a good one: how about mixing Grace and Truth together? He wasn't the first to think of this: "The Word became flesh and made his dwelling among us. We have seen his glory, the glory of the One and Only, who came from the Father, *full of grace and truth*. From the fullness of his grace we have all received one blessing after another. For the law was given through Moses; *grace and truth came through Jesus Christ*" (John 1:14, 16–17, italics mine).

This passage shows both how people fail and how they are redeemed. Failure comes through the law, and redemption through Jesus. It is only through him that we can realize two ingredients of growth: grace and truth. It is through him that we can come back into the same relationship Adam had: an unbroken connection (grace) to the One who is reality (truth).

We have seen the destruction that occurs when grace and truth are divided. Let's look at what happens when grace and truth get together.

Grace and Truth Together

Grace and truth together reverse the effects of the fall, which were separation from God and others. Grace and truth together invite us out of isolation and into relationship. Grace, when it is combined with truth, invites *the true self*, the "me" as I really am, warts and all, into *relationship*. It is one thing to have safety in relationship; it is quite another to be truly known and accepted in this relationship.

With grace alone, we are safe from condemnation, but we cannot experience true intimacy. When the one who offers grace also offers truth (truth about who we are, truth about who he or she is, and truth about the world around us), and we respond with our true self, then real intimacy is possible. Real intimacy always comes in the company of truth.

Jesus' treatment of the adulterous woman in John 8:3–11 provides a wonderful example of safety and intimacy:

Jesus had gone to the temple at dawn to teach the people. He had just sat down when the teachers of the law and the Pharisees brought in an adulterous woman and made her stand before the group.

"Teacher, this woman was caught in the act of adultery," they said. "In the Law Moses commanded us to stone such women. Now what do you say?" The Pharisees were trying to trap Jesus. The Romans did not allow the Jews to carry out the death sentence, so if Jesus said, "Stone her," he would be in conflict with the Romans. If he said, "Don't stone her," he could be accused of undermining Jewish law.

But Jesus refused to fall into their trap. He bent down, and started to write on the ground with his finger. When they kept on questioning him, he stood up and said to them, "If any one of you is without sin, let him be the first to throw a stone at her."

When they heard his answer, they began to slink away, one by one. Soon Jesus was left alone with the woman. He asked her, "Woman, where are they? Has no one condemned you?"

"No one, sir," she said.

"Then neither do I condemn you," Jesus declared. "Go now and leave your life of sin."

In this one encounter, Jesus shows what it means to know grace and truth in him. He offered this woman grace in the form of forgiveness and acceptance. He said, in effect, that she did not have to die for her sin. She was accepted and did not have to be separated from him. He also showed the power of grace as an agent to end separation from her fellow human beings as well. The Pharisees were no different from her: she was a sinner, and they were sinners. Jesus even invited the Pharisees to commune with her as a member of the human race, an invitation they declined. Grace has the power to bring us together with God and with others, if others will accept it.

But Jesus did not stop with just acceptance. He accepted her *with full realization* of who she was: an adulteress. He accepted her true self, a woman with sinful desires and actions. He then gives her direction for the future: "Go now and leave your life of sin." These two ingredients together— acceptance and direction—serve to bring the real self into relationship, the only way that healing ever takes place.

Jesus said it in another way in John 4:23–24: "Yet a time is coming and has now come when the true worshipers will worship the Father in *spirit and truth*, for they are the kind of worshipers the Father seeks. God is spirit and his worshipers must worship *in spirit and in truth*" (italics mine). We must worship God in *relationship and in honesty*, or we do not worship him at all. The sad thing is that many of us come to Christ because we are sinners, and then spend the rest of our lives trying to prove that we are not! We try to hide who we really are.

The Real Self Versus the False Self

When the real self comes into relationship with God and others, an incredible dynamic is set into motion: we grow as God created us to grow. It is only when you are connected to the Head (Jesus Christ) and connected to others (the Body) that "the whole body, supported and held together by its ligaments and sinews, grows as God causes it to grow" (Col. 2:19). A coming together of grace and truth in Jesus Christ is our only hope, and indeed it is a hope that does not disappoint.

Jake, a friend of mine and a recovering alcoholic, put it this way:

"When I was in church or with my Christian friends, they would just tell me that drinking was wrong and that I should repent. They didn't know how many times I had tried quitting, how many times I had tried to be a good Christian.

"When I got into Alcoholics Anonymous, I found that I could be honest about my failures, but more important, I could be honest about my helplessness. When I found out that God and others accepted me in both my drinking *and* my helplessness to control it, I began to have hope. I could come forth with who I really was and find help.

"As much as the church preached grace, I never really found acceptance there for my real state. They always expected me to change. In my AA group, not only did they not expect me to change, they told me that, by myself, I could not change! They told me that all I could do was confess who I truly was, an alcoholic, and that God could change me along with their daily support. Finally, I could be honest, and I could find friends. That was totally different, and it changed my life."

Jake found that when he could be himself in relationship with God and others, healing was possible. Problems occur when the real self, the one God created, is hiding from God and others.

If the true self is in hiding, the false self takes over. The false self is the self that is conformed to this world (Rom. 12:2). The false self is the self we present to others, the false front, if you will, that we put up for others to see. Paul speaks of the false self this way:

> You, however, did not come to know Christ that way. Surely you heard of him and were taught in him in accordance with the truth that is in Jesus. You were taught, with regard to your former way of

life, to put off your old self, which is being corrupted by its deceitful desires; to be made new in
the attitude of your minds; and to put on the new
self, created to be like God in true righteousness
and holiness.

Therefore each of you must put off falsehood
and speak truthfully to his neighbor, for we are all
members of one body. (Eph. 4:20–25)

As long as the lying, false self is the one relating to
God, others, and ourselves, then grace and truth cannot
heal us. The false self tries to "heal" us by its own methods; it always finds false solutions, and the real self that
God created to grow into his likeness stays hidden and
unexposed to grace and truth.

The Guilt Barrier

Grace and truth are a healing combination because they
deal with one of the main barriers to all growth: guilt.
We have emotional difficulties because we have been
injured (someone has sinned against us) or we have
rebelled (we have sinned) or some combination of the
two. As a result of this lack of love or lack of obedience,
we are hidden in a world of guilt. We saw earlier that
Adam and Eve had to hide themselves because of the
guilt and shame of their sin, and also because of what
they had become (less than perfect).

Guilt and shame too often sends us into hiding. If we
have to hide, we cannot get help for our needs and brokenness; we cannot become "poor in Spirit," and therefore be blessed. When grace comes along and says that
we are not condemned for who we truly are, then guilt
can begin to be resolved, and we can begin to heal.

Sometimes the church reinforces our inclination to hide. My friend Jake found an end to his hiding only after he joined an AA group. When he came into a culture where he did not have to be ashamed of his failures and was forgiven for his sins, then truth and grace began to have their effect in his life.

It is interesting to compare a legalistic church with a good AA group. In this kind of church, it is culturally unacceptable to have problems; that is called being sinful. In the AA group it is culturally unacceptable to be perfect; that is called denial. In the former setting, people look better but get worse, and in the latter, they look worse but get better. Certainly there are good churches and poor AA groups, but because of a lack of grace and truth in some churches, Christians have had to go elsewhere to find healing.

It is clear why the aliens in Beezy's world decided against worshiping a god. This religious stuff was for the birds. On the one hand, there was acceptance without direction, and that was not good; on the other hand, there was direction without relationship, and that stung! It is only in a combination of grace and truth that the real Jesus is present. It is only when the real Jesus is present that we can begin to grow into the likeness of our Creator. And we really can be healed, if we have one more ingredient. . . .

Chapter
🙢 2

Time

"A MAN HAD A FIG TREE, PLANTED IN HIS VINE-yard, and he went to look for fruit on it, but did not find any. So he said to the man who took care of the vine-yard, 'For three years now I've been coming to look for fruit on this fig tree and haven't found any. Cut it down! Why should it use up the soil?'

"'Sir,' the man replied, 'leave it alone for one more year, and I'll dig around it and fertilize it. If it bears fruit next year, fine! If not, then cut it down'" (Luke 13:6–9).

In this parable of Jesus, the owner of the tree expected fruit from his tree. When the tree bore no fruit for three years in a row, the owner was not only disappointed, he was furious. "Cut it down!" he ordered.

This is often what we do when we examine our own failures, our "fruitlessness" in light of reality. We look at ourselves (the tree), and we expect to be able to keep our marriages together, to raise perfect children, to make loyal friends, and to perform our work without error (the fruit). When we fail and then become depressed, fearful, or anxious (bad fruit), we cut ourselves down by saying, "I should be able to do that." "I shouldn't get so angry." "I should be able to get close to people." "I should be able to accomplish more." "I should be able to be like so and so." At this point, we are like a house divided against itself. Like the tree owner, we want growth, but we judge ourselves quickly and harshly without taking the time to figure out the problem. We operate with truth and no grace as Ruth's missionary father did, with disastrous results.

Sometimes we operate with grace and no truth. We say things like, "It doesn't matter." "That's really the best I could do." "I can't help it that he reacted that way." "I couldn't help myself." Dead wood (fruitlessness) takes up space in our lives (our vineyard). Either we allow our inability to relate to others or to control our anger or to discipline our children to go on as it has been, continually rotting our lives and robbing us of the delicious fruit God has in store for us, or we deny that we have a problem, with even more disastrous results. Recall the havoc grace without truth caused in Sam's life.

To some degree, we all do both: sometimes we yell, "Cut it down," and at other times we ignore it. But one thing is for sure: when we either ignore our failure to bear fruit in the image of God, or we judge its absence with an angry "Cut it down," we end up either in grace *or* truth, and we do not grow.

In the last chapter and in this parable we see another option: graft grace to truth to stimulate growth. Grace and truth in this parable are symbolized by the actions of "digging around" and "fertilizing." Using the trowel of God's truth, we must dig out the weeds and encumbrances of falsehood, sin, and hurt that keep the soil of our souls cluttered. In addition, we must add the fertilizer of love and relationship to "enrich the soil." Grace and truth give us the ingredients to head in the right direction and to provide the fuel we need to keep on growing and changing.

But the Bible tells us that in order for grace and truth to produce fruit, we need a third key element: time.

Look again at verses 8 and 9: "Sir,' the man replied, 'leave it alone for one more year, and I'll dig around it and fertilize it. If it bears fruit next year, fine! If not, then cut it down.'" The gardener, who certainly symbolizes our Lord, the "author and perfecter" of our faith, realized that his work and the fertilizer need *time* to take effect. In short, *it takes time to grow*. And time alone will not do it. *Time must be joined by grace and truth*. When we respond responsibly to these three elements, we will not only heal, but also bear fruit.

Time is not just an act of God's grace to us, "giving us some space." God is much too loving to allow us to continue in sin for one moment longer than necessary. Time is not a luxury, but a necessity.

Redemptive Time

The first couple existed in eternity with God in the Garden of Eden. There was no such thing as evil, or at least Adam and Eve did not know what evil was. Things were all good.

The Bible tells us that God "made all kinds of trees grow out of the ground—trees that were pleasing to the eye and good for food." But in the middle of the garden were two significant trees: the tree of life and the tree of the knowledge of good and evil. God told Adam he was free to eat from any tree in the garden except the tree of knowledge of good and evil.

But Adam and Eve did not listen. They ate fruit from the tree of the knowledge of good and evil, and something terrible happened. For the first time, things were no longer "all good." Humankind "knew" both good and evil. The Hebrew word for *know* here is the same word that Scripture uses when it says that Adam "knew" Eve in the sexual sense (Gen. 4:1 KJV). It refers to the total experience of knowing. This experience of knowing evil—and therefore pain—is what God had tried to protect people from. He knew that it would hurt.

Nevertheless, Eve was deceived by Satan. Satan held out the apple of omniscience and wisdom (Gen. 3:6), and the first couple received evil and pain.

Imagine, for a moment, the situation. God had created a perfect place with perfect creatures to live in eternity. And, suddenly, evil arrived on the scene. What did God do?

God said, "'The man has now become like one of us, knowing good and evil. He must not be allowed to reach out his hand and take also from the tree of life and eat, and live forever.' So the Lord God banished him from the Garden of Eden to work the ground from which he had been taken. After he drove the man out, he placed on the east side of the Garden of Eden cherubim and a flaming sword flashing back and forth to guard the way to the tree of life" (Gen. 3:23–24).

God moved immediately to protect humankind from being in a state of eternal isolation, experiencing pain for a very long time. To protect Adam and Eve from eternal pain, he drove them out of eternity, guarded eternity with a cherubim, and sent them to a new place called *redemptive time*, where we live now. Here God could fix the problem; he could undo the effects of the fall. He could redeem his creation, and then bring humankind back into eternity after it was again holy and blameless.

What an awesome plan! He even gives a clue in Genesis 3:15 about how he would accomplish this: The woman's offspring would eventually crush the serpent's head, a promise fulfilled in Christ's victory over Satan. No wonder the writer of Hebrews calls it "so great a salvation." God not only kept us from eating from the tree that would have thrust us into eternal pain, he drove us into a place where he would have the time to fix us and bring us back into relationship with him!

Philosophers and physicists have for centuries debated the nature of time, but for our purpose, let's define *redemptive time* as "an incubator that exists for the purpose of redemption." It is a place where God can lovingly fix what is wrong. It is a place where evil temporarily exists while God does his work.

Think of it another way. God has a sick creation. He needs to do surgery. Thus, he places us in the operating room of redemptive time. Into our veins he pumps the life-giving blood of grace and truth. During surgery, he excises evil and brings the renewed patient back into eternity in a holy state. We don't know how long this surgery will last. We only know that we are expected to participate actively in our own surgery, and we don't get any anesthesia for the procedure. That's why growing up into the image of God often hurts so much.

Redemptive time, an essential ingredient to growth, will not last forever. Paul says that we need to make the best possible use of time, for we don't have much: "Be very careful, then, how you live—not as unwise, but as wise, making the most of every opportunity, because the days are evil" (Eph. 5:15–16). Scripture tells us that God will at some point put an end to this redemptive time and usher in the return of eternity.

But Why Does It Take So Long?

Psalm 1, which compares us to trees planted by streams of water, suggests that our growth has different "seasons." Some seasons are for planting (spring), some for nourishing (summer), some for harvesting (fall), and some for dying (winter).

Some Christians want every day to be harvest time. Therapists are often asked, "Why does it take so long for someone to get better?" The ultimate answer to this question is that time is God's way of bringing about the wholeness lost in Eden. It takes time to work the soil with his ingredients of grace and truth, and to allow them to take effect. These Christians sound like the impatient owner in the parable. "Cut it down," they yell, and often put people under an ungodly yoke of slavery.

The Teacher in Ecclesiastes understands that there is a time for everything:

> a time to be born and a time to die,
> a time to plant and a time to uproot,
> a time to kill and a time to heal,
> a time to tear down and a time to build,
> a time to weep and a time to laugh,
> a time to mourn and a time to dance,
> a time to scatter stones and a time to gather them,
> a time to embrace and a time to refrain,
> a time to search and a time to give up,
> a time to keep and a time to throw away,
> a time to tear and a time to mend,
> a time to be silent and a time to speak,
> a time to love and a time to hate,
> a time for war and a time for peace. (3:2–8)

Everything happens in its own good time. Paul acknowledges this when writing to the Corinthians: "Brothers, I could not address you as spiritual but as worldly—mere infants in Christ. I gave you milk, not solid food, for you were not yet ready for it. Indeed, you are still not ready" (1 Cor. 3:1–2).

We will encounter problems if we do not realize that a Christian goes through different stages of growth. We must mature in one stage before we can go on to the next. To progress to that next stage, we must have time along with grace and truth. An infant, for example, cannot handle solid food until her digestive system has had time to develop. A six-month-old child cannot pick up his own toys and put them away until he's able to walk to the toy box. The concrete foundation of a house needs time to harden before the frame can be added. An apple tree needs time to mature before its limbs can carry the weight of a ripe fruit. God understands such a developmental process; he invented it. He uses time.

But people often wish to rush things. When Jesus' brothers were trying to persuade him to leave Galilee and go to Judea "so that your disciples may see the miracles you do," Jesus said, "'The right time for me has not yet come; for you any time is right'" (John 7:3, 6). Jesus was following a bigger plan—the saving plan of his Father. He was purposely staying away from Judea because the Jews there were planning to take his life.

Later when Jesus began to teach his disciples that he "must suffer many things and be rejected by the elders, chief priests and teachers of the law and that he must be killed and after three days rise again, Peter tried to interrupt the process in this plan. Jesus uses strong language to rebuke Peter: 'Get behind me, Satan,' he said. 'You do not have in mind the things of God, but *the things of men*'" (Mark 8:33, italics mine).

Jesus knew that he had to go through a process that would take some time and suffering. Although Jesus was the eternal Son of God, "he learned obedience from what he suffered and, once made perfect, he became the source of eternal salvation for all who obey him" (Heb. 5:8–9). Our model for growth is our Savior. We also must go through a process, through a desert journey that takes time. People have always wanted instant, quick fixes.

Think of how the devil tempted Jesus (Luke 4). He offered Jesus instant relief from his hunger, instant glory, and instant safety. Three times Jesus said no. Jesus knew that to gain these good things, he was going to have to go through the process planned by God.

We have always been enticed by shortcuts. But shortcuts often spell failure, and this is Satan's goal. Satan tempts with quick riches and money-making schemes; God offers the blessings of long-time faithfulness: "A faithful man will be richly blessed, but one eager to get rich will not go unpunished" (Prov. 28:20). Satan tempts with instant intimacy through sexual passion, but God offers the faithful building of a loving relationship. Diet fads tempt with quick weight loss, but such diets do not develop the long-term discipline needed to maintain weight loss. Drugs and alcohol hold out immediate relief from suffering, but do not build character that can endure.

In the parable of the sower, Jesus warns us against fast growth that has no depth. The seed sowed on rocky places, "sprang up quickly, because the soil was shallow. But when the sun came up, the plants were scorched, and they withered because they had no root" (Matt. 13:5–6). Quick growth with no firm root will always be superficial and short-lived. Deep growth is always slower. Developmental psychologists worry about children who show drastic, non-age-appropriate behaviors; it usually means that they are growing up too quickly. God's way always takes time.

I am reminded of this truth frequently when people are referred to me for help with a deeply rooted problem. After doing an initial evaluation, I often estimate the amount of time it will take for them to work through the problem. The "quick-fix" type will say, "Oh, that's way too long. I can't wait that long. Can you refer me to a faster therapist?" I usually try to explain why short-term therapy won't ultimately work, but, after they refuse my explanation, I refer them to someone who works this way. Then, in about a year or two, they will call me again and say, "I went to counseling for a little while, and I started feeling better, but now my depression has come back again, and I need some more help."

Unfortunately, these people think they have failed; they should be better by now. In reality, they opted for *guaranteed* failure: growth without time. I am not decrying short-term therapy; it can offer a lot of help in sorting out both the issues to work on and the direction in which to go. But real growth always takes time.

I love the old proverb that says "the longest distance between any two points is the shortcut." By trying to take the short route, we sometimes end up taking longer than we would have had we taken the long route in the first place. Whenever people want something "now," they will often pay later.

Spiritual and emotional growth takes time. And often a transformation happens over time without the person knowing quite how it happened.

Stan came into therapy seeking help for his uncontrollable outbursts of rage. He had tried for years to get his anger under control. He repented often, prayed even more, and studied biblical passages on anger. But Stan was focusing on the symptom of his problem.

Only after he changed his focus and did some "digging around" to find the causes of his anger did things begin to change.

To explore the underlying causes of his anger, Stan joined a therapy group. He found that the other group members were happy to accept him; they had all struggled with similar problems. Their acceptance slowly enabled him to face the truth about himself: he had some very lonely places inside, places that felt bad and unloved. Because he felt so unloved, Stan tried to get people to love him by doing things for them. He felt that he had to do anything a family member, a friend, or even a stranger asked him to do. Soon he resented saying yes all the time. He felt powerless to say no.

As he felt loved and accepted by others, Stan began to feel strong enough to say no. As his sense of power increased, he felt less resentment. He began to relax more.

One day Stan came into group with a big grin on his face. "My wife came at me today with all of these things to do," he said, "and something strange happened. I laughed at how big her list was. I didn't get mad at all. Pretty soon she was laughing with me. I don't know how that happened, but it did."

Stan grew because he experienced grace and truth working over time. The grace of the group members provided a safe place for him to look at himself truthfully. As a result, he was as surprised as a farmer sometimes is on that spring day when the first blossom appears. It seems to appear out of nowhere. This is how fruit grows—over time with the proper ingredients, and much of the process is out of our control.

When Stan said he did not know how it happened, I was reminded of Jesus' description of the kingdom of God:

"A man scatters seed on the ground. Night and day, whether he sleeps or gets up, the seed sprouts up and grows, *though he does not know how*. All by itself the soil produces grain—first the stalk, then the head, then the full kernel in the head." (Mark 4:26–29, italics mine)

This passage illustrates an important truth about the growth process. *It cannot be willed.* It can only be enhanced by adding grace, truth, and time, and then God produces the growth. If we are depressed, for example, it does no good to try to be "undepressed." It does help, however, to cultivate the soil of our soul with the nutrients of grace, truth, and time. Only then will we gradually be transformed to greater and greater stages of joy.

Good Time and Bad Time

Time is an important ingredient for growth, but sometimes we pass through time and get better; at other times we pass through time and do not get better. Why? That's because of what I call "good time" and "bad time."

From our vantage point, time is present experience. The only time we have is whatever we are experiencing at the present moment. Going forward or back in time is impossible. Right this instant is the only place where we can ever live. When we truly live in time, which is where we are now, we are present with our experience. We are present in the "here and now." We are aware of our experience. If we are not aware of our experience, or are not experiencing some aspect of ourselves, that part is removed from time and is not affected by it.

Change only takes place in "good time." *Good time* is

time in which we and our experiences can be affected by grace and truth. If we have removed some aspect of ourselves from time, grace and truth cannot transform it. Whatever aspect of ourselves that we leave outside of experience, that we leave in "bad time," goes unchanged. Grace and truth cannot affect the part of ourselves we won't bring into experience.

The parable of the talents illustrates the difference between time working for us and time working against us. Before a man went on a trip, he gathered his servants and distributed his goods among them. To one, he gave five talents of money; to another, two talents; and to a third, one talent. After a long time the man returned and discovered that the first servant had made five more talents, the second had gained two more, but the third had buried his money in the ground and had only the one talent to hand over.

The man rewarded the first two, but to the third he said:

> "You wicked and lazy servant! So you knew that I harvest where I have not sown, and gather where I have not scattered seed? Well then, you should have put my money on deposit with the bankers, so that when I returned I would have received it back with interest." (Matt. 25:26–27)

The two successful servants whose talents of money grew had brought their talents *into experience, into time*. They had used them. The third servant took his talent *away from experience, away from where time could affect it*. He hid it in the ground. Therefore, time was not affecting the talent, and time was not making it grow. This is what sometimes happens to us. We take different aspects of our person out of time, that is, out of experience, and they remain exactly as they were when they were buried in "bad time." Katherine is a good example of this.

Katherine, a thirty-one-year-old attorney, was an overachiever. She worked long hours and volunteered for many pro bono cases. She was a dream employee. She would always do whatever her boss asked her to do. Suddenly something snapped. Panic would overwhelm Katherine for seemingly no reason. When this happened, she couldn't keep her luncheon appointments, go to the grocery store, or even go out of the house.

When Katherine came to the hospital, we diagnosed her problem as panic disorder. After a few therapy sessions that uncovered some hidden parts of herself, Katherine began to describe strange feelings. She began to feel like an adolescent. She described wanting to go out and play games and be spontaneous and childlike. She also felt the urge to mock the doctors and nurses in the hospital and to flirt with men.

In therapy, we focused on what happened to Katherine in her adolescence. When Katherine was twelve, her parents divorced, and her mother left the family. Katherine, the oldest daughter, had had to grow up instantly. She was the one who took care of the rest of the family as a mother would have done. She became a little adult, and, in essence, she never *experienced* being a teenager. Her teenage parts went into hiding. It was as though those years were not able to "grow up" with the rest of her. As a result, she never completed many adolescent tasks.

Because she had not completed these tasks, such as learning to relate to boys, she had never been able to relate to men as sexual persons. She had many good male friends at work, but the sexual, flirtatious dynamic, a developmental task of adolescence, never entered in.

As she began to experience the split-off twelve-year-old and accept this part of herself as a valid part of who she was, it began to grow up with the rest of her.

When she was released from the hospital, Katherine found that she was able to play more and enjoy life more. Her sense of overresponsibility for the world was gone; she began dating and having fun. Also, she learned how to say no to her boss and other authority figures, and more options opened up to her. Even her image of God changed: she viewed him as less demanding and more loving. In short, when the twelve-year-old became available to time and experience, time with the experience of grace and truth transformed her. The twelve-year-old Katherine completed her adolescent tasks, left unfinished nearly two decades before. And time was on the adult Katherine's side once again. She was not buried in the ground, away from time, or experience.

In Katherine's case, an aspect of her personality was taken out of time because of trauma. The trauma of losing her mother at a very important developmental time meant that she had no one with whom to work out her adolescent struggles. Therefore, she took the adolescent part of herself out of time, and became an adult at age twelve. An adult who has never completed adolescence is subject to all sorts of deficiencies, particularly in relation to authority issues and sexuality. The same-sex parent is integral to the development of an adolescent, and she did not have a mother. Therefore, her twelve-year-old self had to wait, outside of time.

This is true in varying degrees for all of us. To complete developmental tasks well, we need good parents. When parents are absent or abusive, we take that uncompleted aspect of our personality out of time. It goes underground and does not change until it is called out into good time, into time affected by grace and truth, *when it can go through normal development*. When the true self comes into grace-giving relationships, that self can develop over time. Katherine's real self was stuck at twelve, and her false self was "play acting" at adulthood. When her true self came into the light, she began to integrate as a person and then she could be a "true adult." She was no longer faking it.

Some people can remember the specific time they decided to leave good time. Tom, a pastor, said it this way:

"I remember when my big brothers and the other kids would make fun of me because I couldn't do the things they could do. I was not as strong, and I was very afraid. They would call me names, and the hurt was so unbearable I remember saying to myself, 'I will never try to have friends. It hurts too much.' I must have been about eight or nine at the time. From that point on I became a loner."

By the time Tom became an adult, the loneliness had become overwhelming. He had missed out on some important developmental tasks. As a result his work was failing, and his marriage was shallow. Through hard work in therapy, Tom began to regain the trust and vulnerability he took out of time at age eight. His life began to change. His God-given personality began to develop, and trust caught up with the rest of his talents.

Others cannot specifically remember making a decision, but nevertheless, as a result of pain and injury, they were forced underground. They were pushed outside of time, and into a place where they could not experience certain years with their true self.

When an aspect of a person does not enter into time, this person's emotional maturity will stagnate at this level. One woman who had not been able to separate from her family had difficulty separating from everyone else as well. Whenever someone expected something from her, she felt as if she had to do it. Because she had skipped the stage where the "choice muscle" develops in relation to one's family, she had hidden that function of her personality in the ground. As a result, that talent had not multiplied itself and developed in a way that could exercise the choices needed with others. Stuck at an early level of development, this woman could not get on with life until she learned to say no to her parents. After she brought that aspect of herself into experience, she began to handle all of her relationships more maturely.

Another woman was very detached and angry as an adolescent because of an abusive father. He was so terrible to the family that she would not even come out of her room. In late adolescence, this woman became a Christian, and she thought she had to be nice. The angry adolescent went underground.

Years later, in therapy, this angry adolescent surfaced. She described a "time warp" as she began to experience the world of the sixties in the late eighties. As she began to bring this aspect of herself back into time, she discovered all sorts of wonderful "adolescent" things about herself. She was able to play more, be creative, and separate from her controlling mother.

Stagnation is seen often in people who abuse substances such as drugs and alcohol. Their emotional development likely stopped at the age they began to escape life through substance abuse. *One cannot grow when one no longer participates in life*.

The Bible contrasts good time and bad time: "But everything exposed by the light becomes visible, for it is light that makes everything visible. This is why it is said:

"Wake up, O sleeper,
rise from the dead,
and Christ will shine on you."
(Eph. 5:13–14)

God calls us out of the darkness into the light of experience with Jesus and his body. Then time can be good time; it can transform us and develop us as we need to be developed. If we hide, time is bad time, for it is not being redemptive.

It is literally never too late to open up to those who love us and care about our development. Because the aspect of ourselves that goes outside of time in childhood gets stored in its chronological state, it is still that same age when it returns. God can use our current relationships to provide the nurturing we didn't receive as children, the mentoring we missed as school-age kids, or the companionship we needed as teenagers. God has promised that he will take care of us:

> A father of the fatherless, a defender of widows, is
>   God in his holy dwelling.
> God sets the lonely in families,
>   he leads forth the prisoners with singing;
>   but the rebellious live in a sun-scorched land.
> (Ps. 68:5–6)

God can and does redeem the time for us. He provides the experiences we need to develop different aspects of ourselves through his body of believers, the church.

A Second Chance

There is nothing sacred about "the first time around." Because time is experience, we can influence any "past" aspect of ourselves in the present. In the present we can reach the hurting, lonely child of our past. The lonely child, the hurting child, the untrained child, and whoever else we "were," is still alive; he or she is eternal and lives within us.

Look at how you react to different situations. You respond to some situations like a rejected or hurt child. Often this child has not been reached by God's grace and truth because he or she is outside of time. He or she is not brought into experience and is not allowed to grow up. People will tell someone to "stop acting like a child," truth without grace, but never give that person what he or she needs.

When God says that he can redeem the time, he can actually make our past different. If someone missed out on important developmental aspects, just because that stage is past chronologically doesn't mean that it cannot be grown up and transformed. We can all work through the trust issues of infancy, the boundary-setting issues of toddlerhood, the forgiveness issues of young childhood, the role issues of later childhood, and the separation issues of adolescence in our present adulthood. We can all grow up again.

These aspects of the "likeness of God," our personalities, are still there in their pristine form if because of injury they have been separated from time. Through bringing them into the light of experience in grace-giving relationships with our true selves, they can be matured and redeemed in God's masterful process.

Grace, Truth, and Time Together

We have seen what happens when there is grace without truth, truth without grace, and time without either. When they all come together, we can for the first time have the true self loved and accepted, and through practice and experience, grow in the likeness of God.

Grace, truth, and time working together can develop the kind of endurance James talks about: "My brothers and sisters, whenever you face trials of any kind, consider it nothing but joy, because you know that the testing of your faith produces endurance; and let endurance have its full effect, so that you may be mature and complete, lacking in nothing" (James 1:2–4 NRSV).

Just as there is good time and bad time, there is good endurance and bad endurance. When we suffer, is the true self growing or is the false self just enduring pain? If we are on God's surgery table in grace-giving relationships with our real self, time spent suffering will produce completeness; we will grow up, and we will experience changes that heal.

Jesus interacted with Peter in the present, predicted his failure in the future, but also saw his maturity in the more distant future: " 'Simon, Simon, Satan has asked to sift you as wheat. But I have prayed for you, Simon, that your faith may not fail. And when you have turned back, strengthen your brothers.'

"But he replied, 'Lord, I am ready to go with you to prison and to death.'

"Jesus answered, "I tell you, Peter, before the rooster crows today, you will deny three times that you know me' " (Luke 22:31–34).

Jesus, who transcends time, could see the present state of Peter, how he would fail in the future, and how, after his failure, he would mature to help others like himself. And, in all of it, he totally accepted Peter.

The Lord accepts us fully, knowing that we will need time and experience to work out our imperfections. Our failures do not surprise him. If they surprise us, it is only because we have too high an opinion of ourselves. We have a standing in grace that gives us freedom to achieve truth over time.

The truth we need to achieve has many aspects. It includes the developmental needs of the real self, the grace of relationship, and the external truth of the precepts of God. And it takes time for all of these to work.

Part II

Responding to Others

Part II
Bonding to Others

Chapter ✂ 3

What Is Bonding?

I STOOD IN THE FOYER OF THE EMERGENCY room waiting for the ambulance. The police call had not given much information about the suicide attempt—only the age and sex of the patient. Yet that was enough information to make me speculate.

Why would a thirty-five-year-old woman try to kill herself? I wondered. Is it that she doesn't know the Lord? Or her husband left her? Or she lost a child? What would make her think that death was the only answer?

The ambulance arrived, red lights flashing. As they wheeled the woman to the emergency room, I caught a glimpse of tousled blond hair and a flash of defiant eyes. She was fighting—but not for her life. She was fighting for her right to die.

"Get away from me!" she screamed, shoving the nurses away. "You have no right not to let me die! It's my life,

and I can do as I please. You can't do this to me! Don't
do this to me! You can't. . . ." Her eyes dulled, and she
slipped into unconsciousness.

The next morning I visited the woman to give her a
psychological evaluation. She looked pale and tired, but
I could see that she was beautiful.

"How are you feeling?" I asked.

"Horrible, thanks to you people." She folded her arms
against her chest and glared at me.

"Did someone here hurt you last night?"

"You kept me alive. That's hurt enough," she said.
"All I wanted to do was die, and now I can't even do
that."

In the weeks of counseling that followed, I found out
more about Joan's life. And one by one, my speculations
about her problem toppled. She did know the Lord. In
fact, she was a committed leader in her church. She had
a loving husband who was also a well-respected pastor.
She had four beautiful children, and scores of supportive
friends. Yet she desperately wanted to end her life.

Joan's internal world was far different from her external one. While everything outside seemed rosy, inside
she felt only blackness. Her days began with a blackness
inside so deep she could see it. Each day she pulled herself from bed, her chest aching with depression. All was
vanity. Husband, children, friends—they meant nothing
to her. In fact, people terrified her. Underneath their
nice words she detected poisonous hatred.

The long hard days dragged into interminable
evenings. She found comfort only in the thought of
sleep. But in the last few months even sleep fled her. She
would awaken a few hours after falling asleep and stare at
the ceiling. Going into another room, she would open
her Bible, try to read and pray, but nothing helped. God,
too, seemed to have abandoned her.

What was wrong? How could she outwardly have it all, and inwardly feel so desolate that she would try to kill herself? During her weeks in the hospital, the reason became evident. Despite the many people in her life, she was alone—isolated. Cut off from divine and human contact, Joan lived in an earthly hell.

Joan was suffering from a depression so deep that she did not want to live. But depression was not Joan's real problem. Something in the last thirty-five years had prevented Joan from being able to connect with God and with other people. Somehow Joan did not accomplish one of the basic tasks of growing up. She failed to learn what some infants in the right environment catch naturally. She failed to do what she was created to do. She failed to learn how to bond.

What Is Bonding?

Bonding is the ability to establish an emotional attachment to another person. It's the ability to relate to another on the deepest level. When two people have a bond with each other, they share their deepest thoughts, dreams, and feelings with each other with no fear that they will be rejected by the other person.

Robbie, a twenty-seven-year-old account executive with a small corporation, came to see me because he was suffering from a depression so dark that he couldn't eat and he couldn't sleep. Some days he couldn't even drag himself into work. He was desperate.

"Do you have any close friends?" I asked Robbie in our first session together.

"I have lots of friends," replied Robbie. "I work with a lot of people and do a lot of things in my church. I have a lot of people in my life."

"Who could I call who could tell me how you've been feeling in the last few weeks?" I asked.

"What do you mean?"

"When I think of close friends, I think of people who really know me, who know when I'm hurting and know how to help me."

"Are you nuts?" Robbie said. "No one wants to know about my depression! I can't tell anyone. They would think something's wrong with me."

"There is," I said. "You're so depressed you can't function. Yet not one other human being knows how you're really feeling. How do you expect to get better in a vacuum?"

Robbie looked puzzled. "I don't understand what you're talking about."

What I was talking about was bonding. Bonding is one of the most basic and foundational ideas in life and the universe. It is a basic human need. God created us with a hunger for relationship—for relationship with him and with our fellow people. At our very core we are relational beings.

Without a solid, bonded relationship, the human soul will become mired in psychological and emotional problems. The soul cannot prosper without being connected to others. No matter what characteristics we possess, or what accomplishments we amass, without solid emotional connectedness, without bonding to God and other humans, we, like Joan and Robbie, will suffer sickness of the soul.

Nothing grows anywhere in God's universe apart from a source of strength and nutrition. The Bible frequently pictures growth using plants. Think about how plants grow. They must be connected to something outside themselves. The stalk is connected to the roots, which in turn are buried in the soil where they draw moisture and nutrients up into the stalk; the stalk is also connected to the branches, which are connected to the leaves, which catch the sunlight and transform its radiant energy into a chemical energy that feeds the plant.

Probably the most well-known passage using this plant imagery is John 15 where Jesus says, "I am the vine, you are the branches. Those who abide in me and I in them bear much fruit, because apart from me you can do nothing. Whoever does not abide in me is thrown away like a branch and withers" (vv. 5–6 NRSV). In verse 12, Jesus points out the importance of our staying in relationship to one another: "This is my commandment, that you love one another as I have loved you."

Without such connectedness to God and others, we will slowly wither and die, just as a branch cut off from its vine. It was this lack of emotional connectedness that led Joan and Robbie into depressions so bottomless that they both cried out for help.

The Biblical Basis

Why is our need to bond so strong, and why is our failure to bond so disastrous for our well-being?

God is a relational being, and he created a relational universe. At the foundation of every living thing is the idea of *relationship*. Everything that is alive relates to something else.

God Is Not Alone

But to whom can God relate? There is only one God. The answer is that God does not exist alone. He exists— and has always existed—in relationship. He is three persons in one. He is God the Father, God the Son, and God the Holy Spirit. He is part of the Trinity.

This triune relationship is hinted at already in the first chapter of Genesis when God says, "Let *us* make man in our image, in our likeness." And Jesus suggests the quality and timelessness of the relationship when he says to his Father in John 14:24: "You loved me before the creation of the world." Before creation, God was in a bonded, attached relationship with his Son.

Listen to Jesus talk about this connection with his Father:

> I pray for those who will believe in me through their message, that all of them may be one, Father, just as you are in me and I am in you. I have given them the glory that you gave me, that they may be one as we are one: I in them and you in me. May they be brought to complete unity to let the world know that you sent me and have loved them even as you have loved me. (John 17:20–23)

Repeating words like *in* and *one* in this passage, Jesus emphasizes the idea of relationship—his relationship with the Father and our relationship with him. Close connection is a fundamental truth of existence, the very foundation of the likeness of God.

God Is Love

When we search the Scriptures to discover the nature of God, we find out something else. "God is love," writes the apostle John. "Whoever lives in love lives in God, and God in him" (1 John 4:16). In his essential nature and in all his actions, God is loving. And insofar as we are created in his image, love is foundational to being a person and to being a Christian. "Dear friends," says

John. "Let us love one another, for love comes from God. Everyone who loves has been born of God and knows God" (1 John 4:7). Love is the basic identity of God; it is therefore basic to our identity also.

Even truth is held captive by love. When asked what is the greatest commandment, Jesus said, " 'Love the Lord your God with all your heart and with all your soul and with all your mind.' This is the first and greatest commandment. And the second is like it: 'Love your neighbor as yourself.' All the Law and the Prophets hang on these two commandments" (Matt. 22:37–40).

When we understand that the foundation of existence lies in relationship, for it is the way God exists, it begins to make sense why love is the highest ethic. The law is a structure, or a blueprint, for loving. The law is the way that love is to be lived out.

Relationship, or bonding, then, is at the foundation of God's nature. Since we are created in his likeness, relationship is our most fundamental need, the very foundation of who we are. Without relationship, without attachment to God and others, we can't be our true selves. We can't be truly human.

Look again at the plant we discussed earlier. If we were to cut off its roots, the plant would topple over, unable to support itself. If we were to put it under a bushel basket, cut off from sunlight, the plant would grow sick and puny. If we were to stop watering it, the plant would wither. In other words, if we hindered its connection with the rest of creation, the plant would not thrive.

If we are to grow and thrive, we need to be "rooted and grounded in love." We are literally to draw from the love of God and others to fuel our transformation and fruit bearing. We cannot imagine putting a plant in a cardboard box in the garage and expecting it to blossom. The plant would not make it for very long. To grow, it must have sunlight, water, and nutrients,

We sometimes think, however, that we can supply all of our needs without other people. We think that, in a state of emotional and spiritual isolation, we can still grow. This grave violation of the basic nature of the universe can cause serious problems.

When Relationship Was Broken

Adam and Eve were created in relationship to God and each other. From the very beginning of time God placed a basic value on human relationship. He looked at the man he had made and said: "It is not good for the man to be alone." So he set about making "a helper suitable for him."

Adam and Eve had unbroken relationship with God, with each other, and with themselves. They were fully themselves and not in conflict, not "divided against themselves." All their needs were perfectly met. They existed in perfect connection.

Then Adam and Eve disobeyed God. They ate fruit from the wrong tree. For the first time, they became cut off, alienated from God. They were separated. They no longer had the fundamental relationship they needed. This thrust them into a state of isolation—from God and from each other. They became people in pain.

From this point on, alienation has been our primary problem. Where perfect love had been, isolation and hatred came.

The fact that broken relationship is our primary problem is reflected in the way the Bible speaks of redemption. The Bible calls it *reconciliation:* "For God was pleased to have all his fullness dwell in him, and through him to *reconcile* to himself all things. Once you were alienated from God and were enemies in your minds because of your evil behavior. But now he has *reconciled* you by Christ's physical body through death to present you holy in his sight" (Col. 1:19–22, italics mine).

The message of the gospel is one of restoration of relationship, and that is what bonding is all about. Bonding is connecting with God, others, and ourselves.

Because we live in a fallen world, we are not born into connection. It has to be gained, and it is an arduous, developmental process. Without going through that process of bonding, we are doomed to alienation and isolation. Not only do we not grow, we deteriorate.

Physicists have a graphic way of describing this situation. They call it the law of entropy. According to this law, in a closed system such as our universe, the available energy is gradually being used up. As available energy decreases, disorder increases. Without energy from the outside, our universe will become more and more chaotic over time. Physicists speak of the universe "running down" because of this law. The sun, and many other stars that fill the universe, will eventually, one after the other, cool down to dark masses, their energy scattered throughout space, no longer available. They will have reached what physicists call "maximum entropy."

In the psychological and spiritual spheres, this law operates dramatically. If a person is left alone, her world will become more and more chaotic. She will reach maximum entropy.

Susan, a twenty-eight-year-old graphic designer, came to see me for depression. She said that she had been depressed "for as long as I can remember."

When she graduated from college, the depression began to get worse. She told me that in the last few years she sometimes became so confused that she trembled. Other times her moods became so black that she couldn't think straight. Occasionally she would hear voices inside her head.

In the weeks that followed I found out that Susan grew up on a farm, the middle child in a family of five children. She had two older sisters and two younger brothers. Her mother provided for her physical needs, but was often exhausted from both the demands of a large family and from taking care of her sickly brother, who was born less than twelve months after she was. Her father worked eighty-hour weeks and left the child rearing to his wife.

Left alone to wonder about herself and the world she lived in, Susan developed a host of fears. She was afraid of strangers and of situations in which she would be expected to talk to them. She wondered if she were really saved, if God hated her for her dark thoughts, and if she were headed for hell.

Susan never developed a real emotional bond to anyone. Like all disconnected people, she had what psychologists call "paranoid" fears: she feared that others hated her and would hurt her.

Gradually, after months of individual therapy, Susan joined a small group. As she began to trust the members of the group, she felt safe enough to reach out to people in her church. She began to feel a sense of connection, a sense of belonging. Her paranoia subsided, and eventually, she even made a few close friends.

As a result of reaching out to other people, Susan's depression slowly lifted. She would still feel "blue" on occasion, but she did not feel the terror and blackness she had felt before. In addition, she began thinking more clearly. In short, she reversed the law of entropy in her life. As she started to bond with other people and ceased to be a "closed" system, she gained new energy to move forward and take control of her life.

A Developmental Perspective

If everything goes right, we begin to bond naturally as infants. When we are born, we move from a warm, wet, dark, soothing environment into a cold, dry, bright, harsh one. We move from our mother's womb where all our needs are automatically met, to a world where we need to depend upon fallible people to take care of us. For those few moments after we slip from the birth canal into the light, we are in shock, in emotional isolation.

One look at the face of a newborn gives you a good picture of this total isolation. Then the mother takes the child and begins to hold him closely and talk softly to him. Suddenly he goes through a transformation. He stops screaming, and his muscles relax. He turns toward his mother for warmth, for food, and for love. Emotional bonding to his mother has begun.

Over time, the child gradually internalizes his mother's care. He begins storing up memories of being comforted by her. In a sense, the child takes his mother in and stores her inside his memory. This internalization gives him a greater and greater sense of security. He has a storehouse of loving memories upon which to draw in his mother's absence.

A "self-soothing" system is being formed in which the child can literally have a relationship with the one who loves him in her absence. He could not do this immediately because he did not have enough loving experiences. Through thousands of moments of connection the memory traces must be built up.

As this relationship gets stronger and stronger, the child reaches another milestone: he achieves "emotional object constancy." What this means is that the child is able to experience himself as loved constantly, even in the absence of the loved one. And he also is able to love the absent one, whom he has internalized.

If you have ever experienced warm feelings as you think of a loved one, then you know the riches of this treasured ability. If, when you are afraid or in pain, you have thought of those who love you and gained a sense of courage and hope, you have emotional object constancy. This phenomenon is what allows a three-year-old to play in the backyard by himself without panic and a corporate executive to work in his office without his wife by his side. Both sense that they are emotionally secure, even though they are alone.

Spiritually, this is what Jesus was praying for when he prayed for the Father to be in us, and for his love to abide in us. God is consistent in the way that he deals with us. In the same way that a child develops "emotional object constancy," we develop "spiritual object constancy." When we are born again spiritually speaking, we begin internalizing memories of God.

It is refreshing to hear the writers of the Bible continually reminding the people to "remember" when God did such and such, when he led them from here to there, or when he delivered them from such and such an enemy. God calls on our memory of spiritual experiences to give us courage to go further with him. We build a sense of "spiritual object constancy" with God over the years as we log memories of trusting him.

A child's emotional bond with his mother begins all sorts of physiological, psychological, and neurological processes within the child. He begins to develop physically and emotionally as he is nurtured. God has ordained the mothering process to literally "call the infant to life." The connection of their spirits woos the child into the land of humanness, and the child develops a sense of belonging to the human race.

Although mothers throughout the ages have intuitively known the importance of bonding with infants, only in this century have scientists begun to study this phenomenon. One study in 1945 looked at infants in institutions. The physical needs of all of the babies in these homes were met. They were fed when they were hungry, and their diapers were changed when they were wet. However, because of the shortage of caretakers, only some of the babies were held and talked to. The ones who were not held showed drastically higher rates of illness and even death. In addition, their psychological development was either slowed or stopped. This study, and others like it, graphically demonstrate that a baby can get sick and die, or her growth can be stunted, because of a lack of emotional bonding.

If an infant bonds well in her first year of life, in the second year, she begins to learn some independence. In this independent stage, however, the bonding process is just as important. She needs to have the emotional security to try out her newfound independence. Within the security of a bonded relationship, she learns to distinguish good and bad and how to deal with failure.

This security propels her out into the playground to establish bonds of friendship that help her feel confident as a member of a group. After she feels good about being one of the gang, then she can develop further emotional ties, first with same-sex friends and then with boys in a dating relationship.

A few years later, she will need this emotional attachment with friends and family to feel secure enough to separate from home and get a job or go to college to prepare for a career. There she will develop friendships that will help her enter the world of adulthood where she will form emotional attachments that will fuel her and support her for the rest of her life.

The Importance of Bonding

More and more recent research has shown that lack of bonding can affect one's ability to recover from an entire range of physical illness, including cancer, heart attack, and stroke. One study of patients recovering from a heart attack showed that the patients who were given a pet to care for recovered faster than those in a control group without a pet.

Recent evidence in the field of cardiology has shown that the nature of a patient's emotional ties drastically affects whether or not this patient will get heart disease. Experiments have shown that a patient's blood chemistry changes when that patient has a bitter thought. Doctors are now including, in their treatment of heart patients, training in becoming more loving and trusting. A person's ability to love and connect with others lays the foundation for both psychological and physical health.

This research illustrates that *when we are in a loving relationship, a bonded relationship, we are alive and growing.* When we are isolated, we are slowly dying.

The Bible says much about how the status of our "heart" affects the rest of our life:

> Above all else, guard your heart,
>   for it is the wellspring of life. (Prov. 4:23)

> A heart at peace gives life to the body. (Prov. 14:30)

> A happy heart makes the face cheerful,
>   but heartache crushes the spirit. (Prov. 15:13)

> All the days of the oppressed are wretched, but the
>   cheerful heart has a continual feast. (Prov. 15:15)

A cheerful heart is good medicine, but a crushed
spirit dries up the bones. (Prov. 17:22)

A man's spirit sustains him in sickness, but a
crushed spirit who can bear? (Prov. 18:14)

Our emotional and psychological well-being depends
on the status of our heart, and the status of our heart
depends on the depth of our bonds with others and God.
The Bible said it long ago, and science is proving it
today.

If we come into the world learning to attach to others
and to trust them, we begin to develop emotionally,
physically, and psychologically. We proceed along certain prescribed plans outlined by our Creator. If, however, we do not learn to attach to others, then our
growth is stunted, and we may experience problems like
Terry's.

Terry was a twenty-seven-year-old enormously successful Realtor. He started his own company and had opened
numerous real estate offices in the town where he lived.
He was married and had a daughter and two sons. He
came into therapy complaining of increasing tension and
anxiety. The more successful he became, the more his
tension increased. He thought his problems were directly
related to his work.

"It doesn't do any good to pray or read my Bible," he
confessed. "It's not relieving my tension one bit."

As we began to look at his life, we discovered a
startling fact: his work was not creating the tension;
the tension was driving him to work. Whenever he felt
tension and panic, he went to work. Work was protecting him from his pain. At work he was in control. At
work he could perform. But, the older he got and the
more he kept meeting the goals he set for himself, the

less satisfaction he got from his job, and the less protection it was providing him from his pain.

We refocused our attention on Terry's home life. Terry
said he had married his wife for her "beauty, personality,
innocence, and her brains." He was so insecure that he
couldn't stand to have her out of his sight. Whenever he
was away from her, he went into a prolonged depression.
When he was very depressed, he even forgot what his
wife looked like and needed to look at photos of her to
remember that she loved him. But, ironically, when he
was with his wife, he did not feel close to her.

One day we were exploring Terry's latest depression,
which was so deep it seemed bottomless. Suddenly Terry
cried out in terror, "I need my mother inside of me! She's
supposed to live on the inside where she can't get away!"
Terry had never read a book on "object constancy," but
he knew in his soul what he was lacking.

Terry began to attend a small support group sponsored
by his church. He opened up to a few trusted men in this
group. As he shared his problems and concerns and listened to theirs, he slowly began to make connections.
These attachments to others began to provide him comfort. Over time this comfort came to live inside him. He
discovered that he could be loved wherever he was.

His ability to bond with close friends carried over into
his home life. For the first time, he began to empathize
with his wife's concerns about their sons' behavior problems and to listen more closely to his daughter's com-
plaints about boys and homework. Their relationships
grew close. He had always roughhoused and played foot-
ball with his boys, but in time his relationship with them
also became more closely knit: they began to express
their feelings more openly, and their behavior problems
began to clear up.

In one of our last sessions together, Terry observed, "I

didn't know how God works. He had to take me through experiences of emotional connection with others to get me out of pain. But I still wish he had done it an easier way."

Beware of False Teachers

If you did not learn how to bond in your original family, there often is "no easier way." Unfortunately, some spiritual leaders make it even harder.

Many more times than I care to count I have seen hurt, isolated people begin to realize, with the help of a Christian counselor, their emotional need for other people. They begin to open up to other people in the body of Christ, seeing for the first time the meaning of Galatians 6:2: "Carry each other's burdens, and in this way you will fulfill the law of Christ."

Then their "spiritual leader" will tell them that such "relational" teaching from their counselor is "humanistic" and that they should be "depending on the Lord." Such advice can have disastrous results for hurting people.

How can these leaders say that emphasizing relationship is wrong, when the Bible teaches, above everything else, that we need love and attachment? Christ himself taught that the entire law could be summed up in two commandments: Love God, and love others as yourself.

I think Christ was speaking of these spiritual teachers when he said, "They tie up heavy loads and put them on men's shoulders, but they themselves are not willing to lift a finger to move them" (Matt. 23:4). They do not allow people to seek help from those who understand their pain, yet they do nothing to alleviate this pain.

These teachers miss the relational aspect of sanctification, or becoming holy. Sanctification rests on the working out of our relationships with God, others, and ourselves. If any one of these three connections break, we are in trouble. Anti-relationship teaching is not from God. As the apostle John says, "We know that we have passed from death to life, because we love our brothers. Anyone who does not love remains in death" (1 John 3:14). The teaching that we can love God without loving others is heresy. "For anyone who does not love his brother, whom he has seen, cannot love God, whom he has not seen" (1 John 4:20).

These teachers are more concerned with the "rightness" of their theology and rules than they are with people's hurts. Jesus speaks to this when he says, "But if you had known what this means, 'I desire compassion, and not a sacrifice,' you would not have condemned the innocent" (Matt. 12:7 NASB). All over Christendom, innocent, hurting people who need love and compassion are being commanded away from relationship and into self-sacrifice to gain wholeness. There is nothing further away from the heart of God than a theology divorced from love and compassion.

Jesus' quotation—"I desire compassion, and not a sacrifice"—comes from Hosea 6:6. According to the *Ryrie Study Bible*, the Hebrew word for "compassion" in that passage is *hesed*, a word that means "a belonging love" or a "faithful, loyal love" that emphasizes the "belonging together of those involved in the love relationship."

When we begin to see people's need for emotional bonds, we can understand why many people struggle so desperately and why any isolated view of spiritual maturity is unbiblical. Someone like Terry can struggle for a long time with anxiety and tension until his heart is "rooted and grounded in love."

The Benefits of Attachment

Attachment has many benefits, but three jump to mind: people who are attached, or bonded, to God and others have a good basis for morality. They also have an increased ability to handle stress and their accomplishments have meaning. Let me explain.

A Basis for Morality

The Bible talks of a morality based on love, not on principles or rules. If God has created us with a need for connection to himself and to others, then when we wander away, we experience loss and pain.

A good mother doesn't hold her child because she thinks she "ought" to. She picks up her child because she feels his discomfort. She loves him. A friend does not visit her sick friend because she "should," but because she feels for the friend's infirmity. Only compassion drives us to real sacrificial love.

Many times in the Gospels we read that Jesus "had compassion" on the people. The Greek word for "compassion" has a root close to the word *bowels*. It means a deep feeling from a deep attachment and empathy. The Bible does not say that Jesus gave because he should, or thought it was the right thing to do. He did not give to get points with his conscience. He gave out of a deep empathy for others, a deep sharing of others' feelings that comes only from attachment.

Sometimes I ask groups that I am leading this question: "If I handed you a baseball bat and gave you permission to bash my face in, would you do it?" Usually, the members of the group say no.

"Why not?" I ask.

"Because it's wrong to hit someone. It's not right," someone says.

"Because it would hurt you, and I don't want to hurt you," another person says.

"Which person would you trust with the bat?" I ask the group.

The group quickly concludes that the person who doesn't want to hurt me is much less likely to hit me. This person has the ability to empathize with how I would feel if I got clobbered.

Since we often do what we know is wrong, rules rarely keep us in line. Love does a much better job of keeping us moral. We think of how we might hurt the one we love, more often than we think of some code we must keep.

An Ability to Handle Stress

When people have good friends to support them, they can handle stressful situations more easily.

This statement was graphically brought home to me not long ago when I was seeing two very wealthy men. Both were very accomplished and respected in their fields. Both were very active in their communities and their churches. Both reported that they had many, many friends. Then, in the same week, both men went bankrupt. In the weeks and months that followed, their wives left them, and their kids went to live with their mothers. Here's where the similarities ended.

The first man became suicidally depressed. He locked himself in his house for a month and would not return friends' phone calls. Unable to handle his depression, he started taking drugs. When this failed to bring relief, he left town.

The second man also become depressed, but he called a meeting of a few close friends. At this meeting he told his friends he was really going to need their support in the coming months. He asked each of them to promise to buy him lunch on different days so that he would have their support as he tried for a comeback. He called a counselor to help him with his depression and grief over his failed marriage and the loss of his kids. In one year, he had restored his fortune and was on the way to rebuilding his personal life.

These men differed not only in the way they handled their crises. The nature of their attachments was radically different. The first man had never let himself need anyone; he had no deep attachments. He was alone when catastrophe hit, and because he had no deep abiding bonds with others, he did not even know how to ask for help.

The second man was a recovering alcoholic. He had been deeply involved in a support group for years. He had learned the importance of deep attachments with others. He knew that they, along with his relationship with God, would sustain him. He had a soul that was full apart from his riches and accomplishments, for he had the love of others within. As a result, he could reach out to his friends and draw on their strength in his time of need. His bonds of love with others and God brought him through.

Meaning for Accomplishments

Bonded people are able to tolerate, and to use constructively, time alone. Being alone does not mean they are isolated. As we saw earlier when we talked about emotional object constancy, bonded people have the love inside of them for whomever they are attached to. They have it stored up in their emotional tank, and it multiplies itself through a lifetime. Because they are not afraid of being alone, they can accomplish many things.

They also know the real reason for work. They do not work to pile up possessions. They do not work to run from pain. They work for the family of humanity.

One man I knew in real estate complained that his profession was meaningless. He was just "making money." He was emotionally detached, and his sense of accomplishment was totally task-oriented. Another very relational, loving man reported this about his job in real estate: "I love my work. I can exercise my talents and create good communities families can raise their kids in. I love the feeling of building developments that will provide jobs, offices, and safety for others." Here were two men doing the same work with a startling contrast in how they viewed that work.

Bonding gives meaning to one's accomplishments. In addition, it fuels the rest of our development. Learning how to bond creates more ability to attach to others and enables us to develop in all the ways God designed.

But how do we "learn how to bond"? Before we talk about learning how to get what we missed out on while growing up, let's take a closer look at the disastrous results of our failure to bond.

Chapter 4

When We Fail to Bond

PEOPLE WHO CAN'T MAKE EMOTIONAL ATTACH-
ments live in a state of perpetual hunger. They have a
crying need that's not being met. These people generally
go through three stages of isolation.

Because people have a natural need for relationship,
the first stage they go through when they fail to bond
with God and others is *protest*. They protest their lack of
relationship. They feel sad and angry. If you doubt this,
look at a lonely child, or an abandoned lover.

The pain that lonely, isolated people feel is a good
thing, for it points to a vital need. "Blessed are those who
hunger and thirst for righteousness," said Jesus in the
Sermon on the Mount, "for they will be filled" (Matt.
5:6). If our lives were perfect, we wouldn't seek after
God. If we didn't feel hungry, we wouldn't eat, and we
might all starve to death.

If isolation continues too long without relief, the protesting person moves into the second stage of *depression and despair*. The hope that needs will be met begins to wilt, like a plant without water. Depressed people look hopeless: their eyes don't sparkle, their shoulders slump, their faces are drawn and tired. They long for something they are not getting.

In reality, this is still a good stage, because depressed people are at least in touch with what they want; they just feel that they will never get it. "Hope deferred makes the heart sick" says the Teacher in Proverbs 13:12. Depressed people's hearts are sick because of their unanswered need for relationship, but they still feel the need.

If depression and despair continue long enough without anyone intervening to relieve the loneliness, the third stage of *detachment* sets in. People who reach this stage are detached both from their own need for others and from the outside world. They are out of touch with themselves at a very rudimentary level; at times they no longer even feel alive.

One woman client of mine felt impelled to cut herself. She described her detachment this way, "If I can't feel my pain, I start to feel dead inside. That's why I have to cut myself, in order to know that I can still feel something." This self-destruction may sound extreme, but it is really a move toward staying alive. She wanted to know that she was at least physically alive, because emotionally, she felt dead. She was detached.

A more acceptable way in our society to be detached is demonstrated by the successful businesspeople who drive themselves to achieve. They get awards and large salaries, but their spouses and children often tell a different story.

Symptoms of Failure to Bond

Below are some of the more common symptoms of isolation, or the failure to bond. Isolation masks itself in many ways. Often problems with one thing cover up the real problem of lack of relationship.

Depression

Joan, whom you met at the beginning of the previous chapter, suffered from depression. She described it as a "blackness inside so deep she could see it."

Depression is a psychiatric disorder marked by sadness, inactivity, difficulty with thinking and concentration, a significant increase or decrease in appetite and time spent sleeping, feelings of dejection and hopelessness, and sometimes suicidal thoughts or an attempt to commit suicide.[1] Depression can, in part, be caused by a person trying to repress his or her feelings of sadness and anger—the two ingredients of the God-given protest against lack of love.

Depression sometimes manifests itself more subtly than in the deep blackness Joan described. It masks itself as a grayness in outlook. Depressed people lose their range of emotional functioning; they lose the color in their life. Their entire world begins to look gray. Many depressed people prefer gloomy weather because it matches the way they feel inside. Sometimes a sunny day can make them more depressed because sunshine contrasts starkly with how they feel inside.

Depressed people lose interest in doing things and in being with people because simple social activity does not get to the root of the need. They feel so distant emotionally in social situations where others are in more "up" moods. Therefore, they often withdraw from social activities and relationships, which only furthers their isolation.

Feelings of Meaninglessness

Another frequent symptom of failure to bond is a feeling of meaninglessness. People who are isolated emotionally feel that life has no meaning. Because they often confuse this feeling of meaninglessness with not having purpose, they desperately try to find meaning in some activity or ministry. These attempts, however, only push them further into isolation. They are lacking the true meaning of life, which is love. One single man put it this way: "I work hard to make a lot of money and be successful, but it doesn't mean much. I don't have anyone to share it with. I feel empty."

These feelings of meaninglessness often come upon people after they have lost a relationship and have not yet replaced it. In the depression following the loss, they not only grieve, but go into isolation. They cut themselves off from other people. Their envisioning a life without meaning and hope can drive them to suicidal thoughts. They do not realize that lack of bonding is often at the root.

Feelings of Badness and Guilt

To understand this symptom, we have to recognize a basic fact of the emotional world: an isolated self is a bad self. In reality, isolated people who fail to bond aren't bad; they just think they are bad. An alone self seems to be an unloved self, and that translates to a "bad self."

Lonely people feel bad, or guilty, because they feel unloved. Their legalistic brain translates this feeling into something like this: *I feel lonely; therefore, I am not loved. If I am not loved, it must be because I am unlovable. I am bad, or someone would love me.*

We derive our self-worth to a large extent from other people. The baby who feels "good" is the baby who is fed, dry, and held; the baby who feels "bad" is the baby who goes hungry, wet, and uncomforted. These feelings are internalized into a description of the self. We all retain images in our emotional brain of this very early, bodily way of thinking. When we're feeling "crummy," as we do when we're lonely, we feel as if we were bad.

This creates a problem for many people because they feel as though they have done something wrong to cause their feeling of badness. They feel guilty and try all sorts of ways to assuage the guilt. They confess and confess and confess, they read their Bible, they attend adult Sunday school, they volunteer at the local homeless shelter. Yet they still can't seem to feel forgiven. They can't feel forgiven because the root of this kind of guilt is not sin; it's loneliness and isolation.

Addiction

An addiction is a compulsive physiological need for something; in other words, something that someone needs to survive. People are usually addicted to a specific substance, such as alcohol, cocaine, speed, or food. But people can also feel addicted to activities, such as sex, gambling, work, destructive relationships, religiosity, achievement, and materialism. These substances and activities never satisfy, however, because they don't deal with the real problem. We don't really need alcohol, street drugs, or sex. We can live very well without these things.

However, we really do need relationship, and we cannot live very well without it. We have already seen what happens when it's absent. Remember what God said in the Garden of Eden: "It is not good for the man to be alone."

With addiction, as with other symptoms, a real need is getting a false solution based on deceitful desires, as Paul tells us in Ephesians 4:

[Gentiles] are darkened in their understanding and
separated from the life of God because of the igno-
rance that is in them due to the hardening of their
hearts. Having lost all *sensitivity*, they have given
themselves over to sensuality so as to indulge in
every kind of impurity, with a continual lust for
more.

You, however, did not come to know Christ
that way. Surely you heard of him and were taught
in him in accordance with the truth that is in
Jesus. You were taught, with regard to your former
way of life, to put off your old self, which is being
corrupted by its *deceitful desires*; to be made new in
the attitude of your minds; and to put on the new
self, created to be like God in true righteousness
and holiness. (vv. 18–24, italics mine)

Curing addictions requires a return to sensitivity and
humility. Addicted people must admit their powerlessness and their need for God and others, as well as soften
their heart toward those they have injured and realize
their deceitful desires. Addictions are not real desires.
They are substitutes for some other need of the real self.
An essential step in the healing of addictions is finding
out the real need being masked by the deceitful desire.
One of these real needs is attachment and bonding to
others.

Emotionally isolated people can't get relationship, so
they go for something else. Satan convinces them that
they really want the food, the sex, or the crack, and they
order their whole life around it. But they really need
their emptiness to be filled up with loving feelings and
connections with other humans and with God.

When the inner hunger for relationship is filled with
love, then the driving force behind many addictions goes

away. Not all addictions, as we shall see, come from isolation, but many do. If someone cannot bond with another person, they will bond with a prostitute's body, a bottle, or a half-gallon of ice cream, all the while going relationally hungry inside.

One woman struggling with food addiction put it this way. "I remember the first time I chose to call someone instead of eat. I could feel the strong pull toward the refrigerator, but I interpreted that as a pull toward love. So I called someone in the group. After going over to her house and feeling some real affection, some warmth, I wasn't hungry anymore. Since that time, I've learned to do that more and more. I'm finding out it's not really food I want at those times. It's love."

Distorted Thinking

Remember that the law of entropy holds that any system left to itself becomes more and more disordered over time. This is what happens in emotional isolation. As people are shut off from others, their anger, sadness, and depression begin to interfere with their thinking processes. Their circuits overload, and their thought processes become distorted.

Paranoia, a mental disorder characterized by excessive or irrational suspicion and distrust of others, is one form of distorted thinking. People's inner isolation becomes so great that they feel attacked by the pain and project it outward. They fear that others are trying to hurt them and can't be trusted. Therefore, they avoid other people and isolate themselves even more.

Paranoid people don't get better on their own. You can't just tell them to "change their thinking." This is an isolated assignment, and isolation is the problem!

Isolated people come up with all sorts of delusions and obsessions to explain their internal pain. They have to make sense of their pain somehow, and the only way that they have is to imagine that the world must really be the way that they feel inside. When their internal world begins to change, their perception of the outside world begins to change also.

Hurt always interferes with clear thinking. David said it well in Psalm 73. "When my heart was grieved, and my spirit embittered, I was senseless and ignorant; I was a brute beast before you" (vv. 21–22). When David was hurting, he called himself "senseless and ignorant" and "as stupid as a beast."

Emptiness

People who are disconnected from God and others feel very empty. Emptiness is one of the most painful emotions a human can feel. Empty people can't feel their own need for love, and they can't feel others' love for them.

Although some people feel that someone else is going to "fill them up," this is impossible. Someone can love them perfectly, but unless they feel the need for love and respond to this love, they will still feel empty. It is only when they feel the need for love and respond to others' love that the love inside them begins to grow.

Paul illustrates how being connected to others can give great comfort:

> For even when we came into Macedonia our flesh had no rest, but we were afflicted on every side; conflicts without, fears within. But God, who comforts the depressed, comforted us by the coming of Titus; and not only by his coming, but also by the comfort with which he was comforted in you, as he reported to us your longing, your mourning, your zeal for me; so that I rejoiced even more. (2 Cor. 7:5–7 NASB)

Paul shows the incarnational way God loves us and works for us. Paul had a need; he was depressed. God comforted him by sending Titus. God was touching Paul through human relationships. God was comforting Paul, and Titus was his arms.

Compare God's way to the way of some people. These people tell those who hurt that they don't need others; they should just pray and study Scripture! This is like cutting off the hand of God, who wants to comfort the empty by sending his body to minister! James reminds us that people have more than just spiritual needs: "Suppose a brother or sister is without clothes and daily food. If one of you says to him, 'Go, I wish you well; keep warm and well fed,' but does nothing about his physical needs, what good is it?" (James 2:15–16). Many times people have emotional, not just physical needs. They need the presence of another, as Paul did, and this is the way that God wants to love them.

But a hurting person must respond to people's expression of love. Only when a person owns his or her need and responds to another's love will this bond begin to fill the emptiness inside. The person's experience of the bond to the other person "fills" him or her up.

Over and over the Bible talks of being filled. Paul puts it this way in Ephesians 3:17–18: "And I pray that you, being rooted and established in love, may have power, together with all the saints, to grasp how wide and long and high and deep is the love of Christ, and to know this love that surpasses knowledge—that you may be *filled* to the measure of all the fullness of God" (italics mine). We come into the world empty, and God's love fills us up.

Sadness

A lack of bonding not only results in a lack of joy, but produces a feeling of deep sadness. Joy comes through connection and relationship with God and others. "Our

fellowship is with the Father and with his Son, Jesus
Christ," writes John, "We write this to make our joy
complete" (1 John 1:3–4). When we are isolated from
God and others, it is impossible to feel joy.

Fears of Intimacy

We naturally fear what we do not know. People who
have never had close relationships with other people will
fear intimacy and avoid closeness with others.

Feelings of Unreality

Some people get so detached that they literally feel disconnected from the world around them. They can see and
hear others and their environment, but they can't feel them.
Therefore, the world and the people in it seem unreal.

Because God has created a relational world, people
can know their true selves only in relationship. The true
self is a relational self. If people haven't bonded to other
people or to God, they can't experience what is true; this
gives them a feeling that things are false, or unreal. They
ask themselves, "Am I really here?" and they answer by
cutting or pinching themselves to confirm that they
really are alive. Feelings of unreality are very common,
but if one doesn't understand them, they can be very
scary. It is frightening to live in an unreal existence.

Panic

Panic is a sudden, overpowering fright. Many panic
attacks have lack of bonding at the root. The human soul
must be connected to others and filled with love. Some
people's emptiness is so great that, if they do not connect
with others, they can literally feel like they are falling
into a "black hole." When people get close to utter isolation, they panic. It is the most terrifying experience
known to humans.

Rage

Rage, or furious, uncontrolled anger, is often a symptom of isolation. Remember the earlier example of Stan who came to therapy for his uncontrollable outbursts of anger. Only when he faced the truth that he had some very lonely places inside and only when he felt loved and accepted did his rage diminish. Another clear example of this is the infant who is left alone and expresses pure, unadulterated rage. As we grow older, most of us hide this rage, and it comes out in other, more socially acceptable ways such as cynicism or bodily illness. Anger, a natural protest against isolation, is there nevertheless.

Excessive Caretaking

The only way some people can feel close to others is to take care of them. We don't think of a "caretaker," someone who is always putting other people's needs first, as someone who needs to be taken care of. Caretakers seem so strong. However, underneath many a caretaker's mask is a desperate need for relationship.

One can only feel full when he or she brings the real self into relationship. Part of the real self is the needy self; if we are always giving and never receiving, we are denying part of who we truly are. So excessive caretaking may be a symptom of an inability to bond with others.

Fantasy

Fantasy is the process of creating unrealistic or improbable mental images in response to a psychological need.[2] The psychological need here is attachment. People who are unable to make real friends, for example, create imaginary ones as did the orphan Anne Shirley in the Green Gables saga.

A deep sense of isolation often leads to excessive idealism and romanticism. Isolated people do not experience the real, so they escape into the ideal. One can have a safe relationship with an ideal fantasy, but it never fulfills; only a real relationship can do that. Idealism furthers isolation. Real connection cures it.

Barriers to Bonding

A popular song in the 1970s included this line: "People who need people are the luckiest people in the world." Ironically, *neediness* is the highest stance for humankind, for that's where God and others can meet us. Only from a humble place of need can we receive and be filled. "Blessed are the poor in spirit, for theirs is the kingdom of heaven" (Matt. 5:3).

But, if bonding to others is the cure for so many awful maladies, why don't we just do it? Oh, if it were that easy! Because of the fall, a whole host of problems render us isolated and unable to attach to others. Let's look at some of those barriers.

Past Injury

When I was in graduate school, some members of our class found a four-month-old German shepherd puppy wandering in the road. Suffering from dehydration and malnutrition, the puppy also had bruises all over its body. We took it home to care for it. The puppy avoided us for the first month. Whenever we came near, it would shrink and tremble. When we tried to reach out our hands to pet it, it would cower in the corner. It had learned to expect abuse from the hands of humans. It feared the world it had come to know.

It is the same way with children. When we come into the world, we are totally dependent on our parents or caretakers. They are the ones who feed us when we are hungry, change us when we are wet, and comfort us when we are frightened. We develop our perception of the world and how trustworthy it is by how our first caretakers cared for us. We love because our parents first loved us; we love because God first loved us (1 John 4:19).

If we are blessed with loving caretakers who meet our needs, we develop our "trust muscle." We begin to perceive the world as a trustworthy place. In developmental terms, this is called "basic trust."

But if our needs are not met, if we are neglected, abandoned, beaten, abused, criticized, hated, or resented for existing, then our very ability to trust and be vulnerable is injured. And our ability to bond is based on our ability to be vulnerable and needy. We are in trouble if this ability is damaged. It is our key to life.

If, on the one hand, we find the world trustworthy, we learn that being vulnerable is a wonderful thing because it gets us lots of goodies, like love. When this happens, we get more and more because we trust and depend more and more. The rich get richer; loving people find more love.

If, on the other hand, we find the world untrustworthy, we learn that it would be dumb to trust and be vulnerable. We accurately believe that our survival depends on our not being vulnerable. We rightly get into the "I don't need anybody" stance, a smart thing to do in an untrustworthy environment.

God wired us with a memory so that we could learn what satisfies and remember it in order to get it again. This is where hope comes from——remembering that good things have come our way in the past and therefore they are likely to come again. This memory works the same way when things are bad. We draw a mental map of the world, and then we order our journey around it. This is not something we really sit down and think about. It is much more natural and automatic than that. If we touch a hot stove, our pain centers warn us not do that again. If a puppy is hit, its brain warns it to shrink from a raised human hand.

We learn how the world is and adapt to it. We construct a map of relationship, and how it works. The problem is that we may construct our map in a hurtful setting, and then, when we are older and out of that setting, we forget to update it. Our twenty-year-old map then becomes a barrier to living fully, to relating to others.

Distorted Thinking

Some of our convictions about the world are like outdated maps. Although they may have been accurate at one time, they are no longer. However, since we don't have the knowledge or the experience to update them, we still use them to try to find our way.

Our View of Ourselves

"I am bad."

We talked earlier about how a lonely self feels like a bad self and how many guilt feelings have their roots in lack of bonding. If isolated people are alone, they feel bad; and if they feel bad, they stay away from others. This perpetuates the loneliness that caused the "badness" in the first place. It's a vicious cycle.

"I am unlovable."

This person is aware of the need for love, but at the same time feels unworthy of it. The truth is that this person feels "unloved" and translates that into "I am unlovable." Some of the most lovable people in the world feel unlovable, simply because they have not been loved; the result is isolation.

"Something about me scares people away."

Many people have a conviction that something "in" them is faulty and that it "causes" others to move away from them. This may go deep into their history, when as an unwanted baby, their mere existence "drove" their overwhelmed mother away. Something about the world's response got internalized as a conviction about the self.

"My sins are worse than other people's sins."

Many people finally open up and are vulnerable in a therapy group only after finding out that they were not the only people in the world who felt like throwing their children against the wall, or throwing up after eating three chocolate cream pies, or masturbating all the time. They find out that this conviction about themselves—that "no one is as irresponsible, or as big of a drinker, or as sexually addicted as me"—is not true. Feeling different from or worse than anyone else can be a strong isolator.

"I don't deserve love."

We often feel that we get what we deserve. The basic law, "the wages of sin is death," is operating. We think that if we are not loved, it must be because we did not earn it. The truth is, we can't earn love. It is just something that someone decides to feel toward us. We can earn approval, but not love. We don't deserve it; we don't not deserve it. Deserving and love are unrelated.

"My neediness will overwhelm anyone."

People who feel that their needs are evil are in real trouble, because it is our needs that save us. "Blessed are the poor in spirit." When people have the conviction that their needs will ruin a relationship, they often stay in isolation instead of letting those needs be made known to their partner. In fact, it is usually the opposite; people want to see our needs so they can get a chance to love us in return.

"My need for others is not valid."

Many feel that their need for connection is not something that someone should feel. They think that this need is not biblical, or "macho," or healthy. *I should be able to make it on my own*, they think.

"My feelings will overwhelm anyone."

This is a common conviction of people whose feelings were denied by people in their past. If they show certain kinds of emotion, they think it will cause a problem in the relationship. They fear their anger, sadness, and fear.

Our View of Others

"No one is trustworthy."

If we have trusted our real self to others in the past and they have betrayed this trust, we believe that no one is trustworthy. We don't give our vulnerable heart to anyone, for we think they will misuse it.

"People will always leave me."

If we have been abandoned, we fear that others will abandon us also. The map we have for relationship is this: it always ends as soon as we trust. This conviction is heartfelt because it has already been experienced.

"People are mean and critical."

If people have been abusive or have criticized us for our neediness, we are not likely to share our needs again. We are not likely to open ourselves up to this sort of abuse again.

"People will disapprove of me."

Some people feel that others will disapprove of their needs. As a result, the real self cannot bond with another, for it fears judgment. It must stay in hiding, outside of the relationship. Isolated people often hide their most needy parts. Their needs having been resented in the past, they feel like no one could ever accept them now. This keeps them isolated. Remember the earlier example of Robbie. He hadn't even entertained the notion that others might *like* to nurture him. To him, it was a "nutty" idea.

Others feel that parts of them are not desirable enough to bond with. It may be their angry parts, their sad parts, their sexual parts. These are different for different people.

"People will control me."

Many isolated people have been impinged upon and controlled in relationship; therefore, they learn that loneliness is the only place they can really have freedom. They do not believe in freedom within relationship, because they have never experienced it. Their choices were never honored within a relationship, so they gave up bonding in favor of freedom.

"People are faking their care."

Individuals who grow up in a home with "duty-bound" parents, parents who feel obligated to "love" them, come to see others as insincere in their love because that has been their experience. They begin to doubt everyone.

Our View of God

"He really doesn't love me."

Rarely do isolated people feel as if God loves them. People who feel unloved in their human relationships feel unloved by God. Since one of the ways God loves us is through his body of believers, those who are cut off from that body can't feel his love. Isolated people usually do not have a lot of warm, loving experiences of any kind to draw on.

"God doesn't care about the way I feel. He just wants me to be good."

Often the inner life of people has been so neglected by others that they assume that others are not interested in their feelings. They picture the "other" as more concerned with performance. And they transfer this image of other people to God.

"He wants just 'good Christians.' "

Isolated people believe that people who seem close to God or who are obedient are somehow better than they are. Because they feel unable to change, they think they are doomed to a life of being left out.

"He gets angry at me."

Many isolated people have been driven into emotional isolation by angry attacks from others. They learn that these attackers are always angry, or will get angry soon. They expect God to be angry with them also, and this expectation keeps them from trusting him.

"He doesn't hear me."

God shows us his love by being with us, even if he doesn't intervene in our lives supernaturally. But people who feel isolated can't sense God's presence. And since they can't see him doing anything, they infer that he must not be listening.

"He doesn't answer prayer."

God knows that emotional isolation is at the root of

unbonded people's problems. He answers their prayers by offering opportunities for connection with others. But since this answer is not immediate and not what these people were expecting, it seems that no answer is coming.

"He will control me and take away my freedom."

People fear God's control as well as other people's control.

"He won't forgive me for . . ."

Isolated people often believe that God has deserted them and doomed them to hell. They think they have committed some "unpardonable sin." This is really their attempt to get their theology to match their experience, for they feel like they are already in hell. Since they are unconnected, they don't feel a lot of grace or forgiveness. Even when they know intellectually that there's no sin God will not forgive (except the rejection of Jesus), they need human connection to begin to feel it emotionally.

Sometimes people are told just to "change their thinking." But this is no easy task because we're talking about something deeper than thinking. We're talking about convictions, which are held in the heart. We form our view of relationships long before we have the capacity to reason with our minds. They are carved into our hearts, our very "bosom," as the Old Testament puts it. *No real and deep change occurs outside of relationship and trust, for that is the place where the heart lives.* People often say, "I know that in my head, not in my heart." For the heart to know it, the heart must return to the vulnerable place where the rules were first written on it. Through this sort of vulnerability, it can learn new rules.

It is imperative for us to be in a safe relationship to recognize our distorted thinking and to change it. It

would be silly for the puppy, for example, to open up
to abusers. But if God has given us opportunity for
good relationships, then we must face our distortions
of the truth and bring our real self into attachment
with others.

If we can humble ourselves and be vulnerable, God
promises to help us with this task. "Grieve, mourn and
wail. Change your laughter to mourning and your joy to
gloom. Humble yourselves before the Lord, and he will
lift you up" (James 4:9–10). We must humble ourselves
before his hand and allow him to rework our distortions
with his Spirit and his body. Listen to the way David
prays for himself: "Search me, O God, and know my
heart; test me and know my anxious thoughts. See if
there is any offensive way in me, and lead me in the way
everlasting" (Ps. 139:23–24).

Defense Mechanisms

Not only do we struggle with injuries to our "trust
muscle" and with distortions of God, ourselves, and others, we also have built up a wall of defense mechanisms
against relationship. In the beginning, it may have made
sense to have these, for we may have been surrounded by
hurtful relationships.

It makes sense to put on a warm coat to protect yourself against the bitter cold in winter, but when summer
comes, it also makes sense to take the coat off and enjoy
the warm sunshine. We often wear psychological coats to
protect us from injury. But when God transports us to a
warm land with possibilities of warm relationships, a
heavy coat will cause problems instead of solving them.
We don't need it anymore.

God promises to give us new relationships in his family, but we have to work at taking off our coats in order
to enjoy the newfound warmth. Different people have

different types of "coats" to protect them against bonding. Here are some of the more common ones.

Denial

Denial is the psychological defense mechanism in which people avoid confronting a personal problem or reality by denying its existence. Denial of one's need for others is the most common type of defense against bonding. If people come from a situation, whether growing up or later in life, where good, safe relationships were not available to them, they learn to deny that they even want them. Why want what you can't have? They slowly get rid of their awareness of the need.

Notice that I said get rid of their *awareness* of the need, not the need itself. As long as they are alive, the need is present because they were created in the image of God. But these people can turn a deaf ear to the need's cry.

I'll never forget the attorney who was admitted to our hospital program for depression and angry outbursts. The second day he was there he said, "What's all this stuff about needs? I don't need anyone." Slowly, however, as the weeks went by, we noticed that anytime his group would talk about loneliness, he would go and demand a tranquilizer! Much later, he began to realize that these discussions were difficult for him because they got him closer to experiencing his long-forgotten needs for others. As he slowly gave up denying his need for relationship, he began to connect with others. He discovered that "macho needs love too!"

Devaluation

Devaluing available love is a defense used by most people who struggle with emotional isolation. It works like this: Love will present itself, but, instead of responding to it, these people will devalue it, or lessen its importance. Sometimes they will change it from something positive to something negative: "You don't really care," they will say. This is a horrible defense, because people are pushing away what they most need.

In the Gospels, blaspheming the Holy Spirit was the only unforgivable sin against God. The Holy Spirit, the Spirit of grace, was trying to reach into the first-century world and draw people to Jesus by proving who he was. But instead of responding to the Spirit's grace, they turned the good into bad and stayed away from Love. The sin was unforgivable because it kept them away from grace.

It isn't unforgivable to reject human love, but it has the same devastating effects. Blasphemy, or rejection, of the human spirit would be devaluing love when it comes to us. It would be staying in isolation when love is plainly staring us in the face. It would be like starving to death, someone giving us a steak, and our saying, "It's probably poisoned." Because of our devaluation, we remain in a starving state, never able to get food. We remain in isolation because the risks of love are so great.

Projection

Projection is the attributing of one's own ideas, feelings, or attitudes to other people. We will sometimes project our needs onto others instead of owning them ourselves. The Bible says that we are to "comfort those in any trouble with the comfort we ourselves have received from God" (1 Cor. 1:4). This presupposes that we have owned our own needs and know what it is like to "be there."

Caretakers sometimes vicariously meet their needs by projecting them onto others instead of owning them themselves. These caregivers give not out of the fullness they have received, but out of need. We must be careful to own our own needs and not project them outward, where we cannot get them met.

Reaction Formation

Reaction formation is a defense mechanism in which people express a feeling or trait that's the exact opposite of a feeling or impulse that they are (often unconsciously) suppressing. In simple terms, it means to do the opposite of what you really want to do. For example, people who are feeling lonely may try to become overly independent. They appear extremely strong and will often preach against dependency and neediness. These people may construct an entire theology around the denial of the need for relationship, going in the opposite direction of what they unconsciously need.

Mania

Mania is an excitement of psychotic proportions which shows itself in mental and physical hyperactivity, disorganization of behavior, and elevation of mood.[3] If people stay busy enough, then they can deny their need for others. If they are able to do all of the things they do, they must not have any needs. Some workaholics tend to be manic.

Idealization

Idealization is the act of thinking of something as ideal or perfect, or as more nearly perfect than is true. This defense mechanism is very similar to the symptom of fantasy we discussed earlier. People who have trouble falling or staying in love sometimes suffer from idealization. They search for an ideal partner, who will fulfill all of their needs. This "fantasy" makes up for their being without. A very lonely person can get lost in fantasy, but the idealizer is really looking for his or her "ideal" other.

Substitution

Substitution is simply the substituting of one person or thing for another. When people can't get real relationship, they will find something to take its place. As we saw above, addictions are substitutes for some other need of the real self. Drugs, food, or sex may be substituted for love. People use these substitutes to defend against their real need for other people and God.

Telling someone to repent and stop a certain behavior is a good idea, but unless the person has the need met, the behavior will return (Luke 11:24–26). This person needs to fill his or her soul with the love of God and others.

Learning God's Ways

Past injuries, distorted thinking, and defense mechanisms are direct results of the fall; everyone has them to differing degrees. The Bible directly addresses all three.

Injuries to our sense of bonding can be devastating both to the one who has been injured and to the people around them. On the one hand, people who have been injured say, "Why can't I just be close to people and stay that way?" or "Why do I still run from people after all this time?" On the other hand, those around them say, "Why can't they just understand they are loved and get on with it?" or "I think they are being selfish and lazy."

Early developmental injuries take time to heal, and it takes time to grow. We are talking about the most vulnerable aspect of our hearts; it takes time for that to be strengthened. Paul understood this when he said, "And we urge you, brothers, warn those who are idle, encourage the timid, help the weak, be patient with everyone" (1 Thess. 5:14).

Injury to the heart is like any other injury. First, the person will feel pain and go into shock. If the person has support, his or her heart will thaw out, and the pain will return. (There is truth to the old adage, "It has to get worse before it gets better.") As the pained heart comes back into relationship, it is strengthened and grows, but this process is like exercising a very sore limb or muscle. People with sore muscles, or sore hearts, must learn to be patient while rehabilitating.

We inherit distorted thinking from the system of relational rules operating in the family in which we were raised. The family was set up by God to be a spiritual system, to impart to children the spiritual laws of the universe. The family is where we were supposed to learn God's ways of loving attachment, freedom of choice, forgiveness, and growing in skills and talents. However, we do not live in perfect families, and many families' rules are much different than God's.

Sometimes I ask group members to each write out the ten relational commandments of their family. Jesus tells us that sometimes we live according to the "traditions of our elders" or "the rules taught by men" instead of the ways of God (Matt. 15:1–9). People living according to family rules may be in direct contradiction with God's rules.

Here is an example of someone's list:

1. Thou shalt not let anyone get emotionally close to you. Keep your distance.

2. Thou shalt not tell the truth about how you are feeling. If you are hurt, keep it a secret.

3. Thou shalt always lie, if it will keep the peace.

4. Thou shalt try and look good on the outside. It is more important anyway.

5. Thou shalt achieve highly and bring honor to the family name.

6. Thou shalt never leave and cleave, for that would make the rest of the family very sad.

7. Thou shalt not talk about any family matter outside the home, or any hurt that you sustain here. Breaking loyalty is an abomination.

8. Children are to interfere in the parents' conflicts. They are to take the focus off the struggles the parents are having. This is a loving and acceptable sacrifice.

9. Tender feelings are an abomination.

10. Thou shalt be emotionally independent from birth.

This list is far from God's list. However, many Christians do not turn away from the "tradition of their elders." They live according to a false religion, the spiritual system of their family. In order to grow, they must renounce the theology of their dysfunctional family and adopt the spiritual principles of God's family.

When this shift happens, they can open up to a family of connection:

Then Jesus' mother and brothers arrived. Standing outside, they sent someone to call him. A crowd was sitting around him, and they told him, "Your mother and brothers are outside looking for you."

"Who are my mother and my brothers?" he asked. Then he looked at those seated in a circle around him and said, "Here are my mother and my brothers! Whoever does God's will is my brother and sister and mother." (Mark 3:31–35)

Jesus' reply was not meant to reject his natural family, but to emphasize the higher priority of his spiritual relationship to those who believed in him. Jesus continually taught that we have been transferred from one kingdom to another (Col. 1:13–14). A vital part of this transfer is to realize who our "family" is to be. In a real sense, God is saying that we need to get our family support from the ones who do his will. We have to renounce the rules of relationship we learned in the first spiritual system and learn God's ways of connection.

When we start to make this shift, we may enter into conflict with many friends, spiritual leaders, and even family members. The Bible speaks to that conflict in many places and asks us to make the shift. Jesus says that when we begin to value love, if our "loved ones" do not hold to God's values, conflict may come:

"Do not suppose that I have come to bring peace to the earth. I did not come to bring peace, but a sword. For I have come to turn

'a man against his father,
a daughter against her mother,
a daughter-in-law against her mother-in-law—
a man's enemies will be the members of his own
household.'

"Anyone who loves his father or mother more than me is not worthy of me; anyone who loves his son or daughter more than me is not worthy of me." (Matt. 10:34–37)

Those are tough words. But Jesus does not mean that we are to turn against friends or relatives who do not believe in God's ways of love. We are to love our enemies and to pray for those who persecute us (Matt. 5:44). However, we must see those who do not believe in the importance of love as enemies of our souls; those who reject love reject God's ways.

We must seek out people who can lead us toward the likeness of God, not away from it. As David pledged to God in Psalm 101:

> My eyes will be on the faithful in the land,
>   that they may dwell with me;
> he whose walk is blameless
>   will minister to me. (v. 6)

In addition, we need to stay away from hurtful people:

> No one who practices deceit
>   will dwell in my house;
> no one who speaks falsely
>   will stand in my presence. (v. 7)

We need to examine our relationships to see if they are helping us grow in the image of God. Saying no to bad relationships and yes to good is difficult if someone is tied to the bad. The psalmist states that when someone has been oppressed from youth, "furrows" are created in his back. Every emotionally abused person knows what those feel like. But the psalmist assures us that God has cut us free from the cords of the wicked (Ps. 129:1–4). Then we can "open wide" our hearts to those who walk in the ways of the Lord.

Chapter

❦ 5

Learning to Bond

HAVING GOOD EMOTIONAL CONNECTIONS IS as natural as a plant taking in water. But we are not plants living in the Garden of Eden. Therefore, we require some serious gardening in order to bear fruit. The fig tree gardener planned to "dig around and fertilize" the tree that wasn't bearing any fruit for a year to help it bear fruit.

Learning to bond when you missed out the first time around won't happen overnight either. As you'll see at the end of this chapter, it took Joan, the depressed woman who tried to commit suicide, months of hard work to make human connections. Susan, the twenty-eight-year-old graphic designer, couldn't just join a graphic artists guild or a church study group to develop emotional bonds. She wrestled with her problem in both

93

individual therapy and group therapy before she was ready to reach out in the "real world."

Making human connections when you grew up without them takes a good dose of grace, truth, and time. Here are some skills that will start you on the long road to making changes that heal.

Skills for Bonding

Realize the Need

Many of you do not realize that your problems stem from a lack of bonding and attachment. You may have grown up in a family where closeness was not valued, or you may have been injured to the point where you have forgotten how to bond. Thus, the first thing you need to do is to realize how much you need attachment.

A careful reading of the Bible will show the value God places on connection. Paul uses the image of the body to make this point: "Now you are the body of Christ, and each one of you is a part of it" (1 Cor. 12:27). You are part of a body, and you cannot be emotionally amputated from the blood flow and expect to thrive. "The eye cannot say to the hand, 'I don't need you!' If one part suffers, every part suffers with it" (1 Cor. 12:21, 26).

Move Toward Others

It is wonderful when others move toward you and seek out your heart, for that is what God does. Often, though, others cannot see what you need and how emotionally isolated you really are. Therefore, to the best of your ability, actively reach out for help and support. Earlier, we saw how alien this idea was to Robbie. He could not imagine how someone would be interested in connecting with him at a deeper level.

Be Vulnerable

You can move toward others, get socially involved, and have relationships, but still be isolated. Your isolation may stem from your inability to be open, your inability to show your real selves to others. Learn to be vulnerable. The word *vulnerable* literally means "open to criticism or attack." You need to be so open with your needs that you are open to attack.

Realization of need is the beginning of growth. Humility and vulnerability are absolutely necessary for bonding to take place at a deep level.

Being vulnerable at a social level may be too threatening at first. Maybe you need to start with a pastor, counselor, or support group. But vulnerability is a skill that opens up the heart for love to take root. When you can admit that you need support and help, and can reveal your hurt and isolation, a dynamic is set into motion that can literally transform your personality and life.

Challenge Distorted Thinking

Distorted thinking blocks you from relating to others. This essentially causes you to repeat what happened in the past. Challenge the distortions that keep you in bondage. To the extent that you continue to see the world through your childhood eyeglasses, your past will be your future.

If you don't, for example, challenge the belief that "all people will leave me," you will never form an abiding attachment, and you will recreate the isolation of your past. The Lord has promised to reveal the truth to you. Ask him to show you your particular distortions.

But distorted thinking was learned in the context of relationship, and that is the only place where it can be unlearned. You need new relationship to undo the learning of the past; there your real self can be connected in grace and truth and thereby be transformed.

Take Risks

To learn new relational skills and the way of attachment, take risks. Listen to Jesus' invitation: "'Here I am! I stand at the door and knock. If anyone hears my voice and opens the door, I will come in and eat with him, and he with me'" (Rev. 3:20). You have a responsibility to hear the voice and open the door. People and God will call to you, but if your distorted thinking and your resistance to risk get in the way, you will keep the door closed so that attachment cannot happen. Allow yourself to risk valuing someone emotionally. Risk getting hurt again. This is difficult, but essential.

Allow Dependent Feelings

Whenever you begin to allow someone to matter to your isolated heart, uncomfortable needy and dependent feelings will surface. These are the beginnings of a softening heart. Though uncomfortable, these feelings are a key to attachment. Many times you think you need to "keep a stiff upper lip," but allowing your tender, needy sides to show to the ones you need will cement the attachment and allow it to grow.

Recognize Defenses

Recognize your own particular defenses against attachment. As soon as you can spot the old familiar patterns, you can begin to notice them in operation and take responsibility for them. You may need to say something like this, "Oh, there I go again, devaluing someone who is trying to love me. I'll try and let them matter this time."

Remember, you are responsible for your own growth. Challenge your old ways of acting and allow the Holy Spirit to empower you to resist your defenses.

Become Comfortable With Anger

Often people will avoid attachment because they fear their anger at the one whom they need and love. As a result, anger leads them into isolation to protect the loved one. It is natural to feel angry toward people you need. The more you can feel comfortable with angry feelings toward "good" people, the more you can integrate those feelings into the relationship and not spoil it. We will look at this process more closely in Part 4, but it has many implications for attachment. The angry self is an aspect of personhood that many people prefer to leave "unbonded." They believe that it is the unlovable aspect of who they are.

Pray and Meditate

In Psalm 139:23–24, David asked God to reveal who he was at a deep level:

Search me, O God, and know my heart;
    test me and know my anxious thoughts.
See if there is any offensive way in me,
    and lead me in the way everlasting.

Pray David's prayer along with him, and God will reveal the true state of being in your heart. Ask God to unravel the problems in your ability to attach. Abiding is God's highest value for you so you can be assured of his desire to help you reach this goal. As David says in Psalm 51:6, "Surely you desire truth in the inner parts; you teach me wisdom in the inmost place."

Be Empathic

Empathy is the ability to share in another's emotions, thoughts, or feelings. Empathizing with others' needs, identifying with their hurt, softens your own heart. Many hardened people have melted by getting close to the hurts of others. I'm not implying a "give-to-get" or a "get-your-mind-off-yourself" strategy. I'm talking about identifying with the struggler in order to get in touch with your own hurt and loneliness.

Rely on the Holy Spirit

The Holy Spirit empowers you to change and to come out from the bondage of your old ways of being. Ask him to free you from the death grip your defenses have on you and to give you the courage to take the first steps to attach to others.

Every time you find yourself at this crossroad, at the place where you can either respond defensively in an old pattern or risk the new, ask for help. You can't do it alone. When you come face to face with your inability to bond, you must confess this inability and ask the Spirit to help you. You can't change on your own. Rely on him to help you make changes that heal.

Say Yes to Life

The task of bonding to others and God is one of saying yes to life. It is saying yes to God's and others' invitation to connect with them. People who struggle with isolation say no to relationship in many ways.

When you hide behind defense mechanisms, you are saying no. When you avoid intimacy, you are saying no. When you make excuses, you are saying no. Connection requires that you begin to say yes to love when it presents itself. This may mean accepting invitations to be with people instead of always withdrawing. It may mean giving a different answer in safe contexts when you are asked, "How are you doing?" It may mean empathizing with another's hurt. Whatever the opportunity, it means saying "yes" to relationship.

Joan

This section of the book began with Joan. Isolated among an army of friends, filled with a black depression, she had tried to end her life.

Joan's first weeks at the hospital were tumultuous. Daily she fought off the staff's attempts to get to know her. She hid herself in her room, and even when she came out, she would not talk about her problems.

But as she began to observe the pain in other patients' lives, she slowly began to allow some people to get close to her. At first, she only revealed the surface things that she had built her life on—her wit, her charm, her attractive personality, her intelligence. Later, however, she began to open up to a few trusted people and tell her story.

Raised in a strong Christian environment, Joan had been instilled with a strong sense of right and wrong. However, she had never attached to her parents on a deep emotional level. "I never loved my mother," she confessed. "She was too passive. And my father—well, all he was interested in was whether I was 'being good.'" As a result, Joan had grown up with her act together, following all the rules and toeing the line, but on the inside she felt only emptiness.

Joan said, "When I met Dave, he was a bright, promising seminary student. We married young, and he meant the world to me—at first. Then I found out how much of a perfectionist he was. He was a hard driver, and we built a successful ministry together. But I always felt so alone, even when I was with him."

Joan never admitted her need for other people, not even for her husband, Dave. From her first family, she had learned to ignore her needs, to suppress them and cover them up. And she maintained that same pattern in her marriage and in her friendships.

At the hospital, Joan began to open up for the first time in her life. She shared her pain. She cried. And she was amazed when people loved her even when she showed them her weaknesses.

As she began to sense the limits of her own independence, she slowly allowed others to matter to her. She reached out to her fellow residents, realizing that even though she was "needy," her strength did not disappear. And she invited old friends to visit her, marveling when they did not reject her in her vulnerable state.

In addition, Joan examined her marriage, sensing in that area another lack of vulnerability. Together she and her husband worked hard to establish the intimacy they had missed because of their individual backgrounds and fears. After much time and work, they were able to establish a new and more intimate relationship, one based on mutual sharing and vulnerability.

Over time, Joan's depression began to lift. She began to see reasons to live. For the first time, she saw that meaning and hope arise from relationships. And for the first time, she actually experienced the love of God, husband, family, and friends. She continued to work hard on establishing intimacy and bondedness. Now, years after her long hospital stay, she is doing very well.

Joan's battle was not an easy one. Like a terminally ill patient, she literally had to fight for her life. One day, however, she can face her Savior and be proud that she "fought the good fight," the one of love, and regained the lost "likeness of God" caused by the fall and her family background. Until then, she and her family will enjoy being rooted and grounded in love.

Joan no longer lives in an earthly hell of isolation. Instead, she lives in the "heaven on earth" of intimate, loving relationships—the one Jesus promised we could know.

Part III
Separating from Others

Chapter
✂ 6

What Are Boundaries?

FIFTEEN YEARS AGO, STEPHEN BEGAN HIS ministry enthusiastic about serving God and others. His wife shared his vision. Together, he felt, they would have a wonderful marriage and ministry.

But his life hadn't turned out as he had planned. He had burned out. Sitting in my office, he described symptoms of fatigue, mild depression, low motivation, anxiety, and fantasies of "tossing it all" and running away.

"I've had trouble in my work before this," Stephen admitted to me, "and I've always wondered why."

As we continued to talk, I saw before me a loving and compassionate person, someone who was very good with people. In fact, he was almost too good. Having a soft heart, he could not bear to let a suffering person go without help. Whenever anyone called, he would drop whatever he was doing to help the person in crisis.

As a result, however, the rest of his ministry suffered. He missed deadlines on budgets and reports, he showed up late for meetings, and he forgot appointments he had made. In addition, he had taken on too much work. Every minute of his time was jammed with activity, yet he didn't seem to have any time for the things he enjoyed doing. He began to resent the church for demanding so much of him without giving him the recognition he deserved.

The church, in turn, had its own doubts about Stephen. They were tired of late reports and bungled meetings. They began to wonder whether Stephen's good qualities outweighed his irresponsibility.

More disturbing than Stephen's failing ministry was his faltering marriage. His wife continually nagged him to complete tasks he had promised to do. For weeks he would neglect the yard. Often they received notices from the bank that some payment was late or that their credit rating was suffering.

Stephen felt like he was always giving in to his wife. Whenever they went somewhere or did something, he "gladly" agreed to do what pleased her. He resented her wishes, yet he felt selfish when he disagreed with her. He seemed to think he should do whatever she or the church requested because to deny their wishes made him suffer terrible guilt.

When he finished explaining his situation, Stephen shrugged apologetically. "I didn't want to come here," he said. "I should be a people helper, not a counseling patient." He sighed. "I had such good intentions. So why did I end up in such a mess?"

Stephen had no limits on others' control of him, no sense of personal boundaries and space, and very little of what the Bible calls "will."

Boundaries, in a broad sense, are lines or things that mark a limit, bound, or border. In a psychological sense, boundaries are the realization of our own person apart from others. This sense of separateness forms the basis of personal identity. It says what we are and what we are not, what we will choose and what we will not choose, what we will endure and what we will not, what we feel and what we will not feel, what we like and what we do not like, and what we want and what we do not want. Boundaries, in short, define us. In the same way that a physical boundary defines where a property line begins and ends, a psychological and spiritual boundary defines who we are and who we are not.

Stephen encountered many problems because of his lack of boundaries. He could not choose what he wanted to do apart from what others wanted him to do. Because he felt obliged and compelled to serve others, he couldn't say no. And because he was overresponsible for others, he couldn't take responsibility for his life. His lack of limits led him to chaos, resentment, panic, and depression. He was out of control.

Stephen is not alone. Many people struggle to discover, set, and guard their personal boundaries. They truly cannot tell where they end and someone else begins, and thus they suffer from lack of purpose, powerlessness, panic, identity loss, eating disorders, depression, irresponsibility, and a whole host of other problems, all of which lead to a lack of real intimacy with others.

Probably the most destructive result of lack of boundaries is physical and emotional abuse. People who are unable to set boundaries allow themselves to be repeatedly controlled and even injured by others. Stories of brutal spouse abuse abound because of the victim's inability to limit the evils inflicted upon her or him. Few things are more heartbreaking than to see some loving person continually abused because of badly built boundaries.

If you can identify with these symptoms, you may have a problem in establishing and keeping boundaries. As with bonding, God created you in His image to have boundaries, and God has specific ways you can repair badly broken boundaries or build new ones. In this part of the book we will look at how boundaries are destroyed and how they can be rebuilt. Rest assured that God can restore your damaged boundaries and your will.

No Boundaries

"Why don't you just tell your mother that you don't want to come home for Thanksgiving? You're thirty years old. That's old enough to choose to spend a holiday with your friends," I said.

"But that would make her very angry," Sandy replied. "I could never do that. It's mean."

"How can you 'make' her angry? Why do you think you have that much power?" I asked.

"If I didn't go home for the holidays, that would make her mad. It's as simple as that."

"Then I guess you think you have the power to make her happy as well. Is that right?" I wondered aloud.

"Well, of course," Sandy replied. "If I do what she wants, I can make her happy."

"You're a very powerful woman," I said. "It must be frightening to have that much power. But, if you are that powerful, why don't you have the power to make yourself feel good?"

"I don't know the answer to that. That's why I came to see you. So you could make me feel better."

"Oh, I see. Making your mother feel good makes you feel

bad. Then, you come to see me, and I'll make you feel good. What am I supposed to do if that makes me feel bad?" I asked. "Maybe I could call your mother, and she could make *me* feel better."

"You're crazy," she said. "How's she gonna make you feel better?"

"I don't know," I answered. "But as long as everyone is responsible for everyone else's feelings, I'm sure she would try to find a way."

Imagine what it must feel like to live a life of being responsible for someone else's feelings and out of control of your own. If we look at Sandy's situation more closely, we see a basic problem: she did not know where her responsibility ended and her mother's began. In short, she did have a life apart from her mother's. This is the essence of boundaries: where do I end and where does someone else begin?

Biblical Basis for Boundaries

In the last part of this book we saw that one of the most important things in life is to be attached to others and to say yes to connection. But, how do we establish an attachment and still remain an individual? How do we determine what is actually ourselves versus someone else? How do we set a course for ourselves within an attachment and know that it is a personal choice? What happens when we do not agree with the one to whom we are connected? Or we want to do something different from the one to whom we are connected? Or we don't want the loved one to hurt us anymore? Or we want some time apart from our friend or spouse? Sounds complicated, doesn't it? It is.

But, lest we begin to feel that relationship is too difficult and confining, let's look at the second developmental task of growing up in the "likeness of God": establishing boundaries and a sense of separateness.

God is a bonded person. The Father, Son, and Holy Spirit are always connected; they have an eternal "oneness." However, just as unity is the most basic quality God possesses, he has diversity within this unity. The Father, Son, and Holy Spirit are distinct, separate persons. They are not "fused" in a way that they lose their individual identity. They have boundaries between them. They each have their own talents, responsibilities, wills, and personalities. They can be in different places at the same time, and they can be doing different things without losing relationship.

In addition, God is separate from his creation. He knows what is him and not him. He is not the god of pantheism, which fuses God with creation. He is a separate person from us. He can have relationship with us, but he is not us, and we are not him. Boundaries exist between our identities, wills, and responsibilities. He knows where he ends and we begin.

Because his will is separate from ours and we are two distinct people with separate identities, real relationship is possible.

Likewise, on the human level, as we are created in his likeness, we are separate from one another. We have distinct personalities, wills, talents, and responsibilities. There is diversity in our unity also. Separateness is an important aspect of human identity. We are to be connected to others without losing our own identity and individuality. We are to be "like him" in this respect. We are to master the art of "being me without losing you."

But on the human level, just as our connection was marred in the fall, so is our sense of separateness, boundaries, and responsibility. We are all confused as to where we end and someone else begins. We have difficulty having a will of our own, without getting it entangled with someone else's. Often we don't know who we really are as opposed to who someone says we are. Sometimes we don't know what we think or feel unless the culture feels it first. The boundaries between us and the world get blurred. In this section we will look at these conflicts of separateness and boundaries from a biblical perspective to rediscover our own boundaries within our relationship to the ones we love.

When we think of relationship, we think of love. When we think of boundaries, we think of limits. Boundaries give us a sense of what is part of us and what is not part of us, what we will allow and what we won't, what we will choose to do and what we will choose not to do.

We see God doing this over and over again in the Bible. He is continually defining himself by saying who and what he is and what he is not, what he loves and what he hates. Here he defines himself by saying who he is:

"I am your shield." (Gen. 15:1)

"I am God Almighty." (Gen. 17:1)

"I am the Lord." (Ex. 6:6)

"I, the Lord your God, am a jealous God." (Ex. 20:5)

"I am compassionate." (Ex. 22:27)

"I am holy." (Lev. 11:44)

"I am the first and I am the last." (Isa. 48:12)

"I, the Lord, am your Savior." (Isa. 60:16)

"I am merciful." (Jer. 3:12)

Here he defines himself by saying what he feels and thinks:

"My heart pounds within me, I cannot keep
  silent." (Jer. 4:19)
"I am tired of relenting." (Jer. 15:6 NASB)
"I, the Lord, love justice." (Isa. 61:8)
"I have been grieved by their adulterous hearts."
  (Ezek. 6:9)

And here he defines himself by what he chooses to do:

"Let there be light." (Gen. 1:3)
"But I will establish my covenant with you."
  (Gen. 6:18)
"I will make you into a great nation and I will
  bless you." (Gen. 12:2)
"I will give you a new heart and put a new spirit
  in you." (Ezek. 36:26)

Numerous times his attributes, feelings, and thoughts
are defined in the third person:

"The Lord works righteousness and justice for all the
oppressed. He made known his ways to Moses, his deeds to
the people of Israel: The Lord is compassionate and gracious, slow to anger, abounding in love" (Ps. 103:6–8).

God's attributes, talents, feelings, thoughts, behaviors,
and will determine who he is. They form his identity.
Just as positive affirmations define who he is, so do negative affirmations. He says what he is not by saying what
he hates:

"There are six things the Lord hates, seven that are
detestable to him: haughty eyes, a lying tongue, hands
that shed innocent blood, a heart that devises wicked
schemes, feet that are quick to rush into evil, a false witness who pours out lies, and a man who stirs up dissen-
sion among brothers" (Prov. 6:16–19).

Biblical writers name things that the Lord loves and hates so that we can understand who he is. What he chooses and what he wills, what he wants and what he does not want, what he thinks about things and what he does—all of these things define the boundaries of who he is. We define ourselves by much the same functions.

Our Physical Appearance

Physical appearance is a part of identity. Our body has physical boundaries that define who we are. The skin is the clearest picture of a boundary that exists for a person. Our skin clearly defines where we begin and end. It has color and texture. It has shape.

Skin keeps the good in and the bad out. It keeps our blood and organs inside our body, where they can work for us. If we puncture our skin, we lose blood; if the wound is big enough, we may lose something worse. At the same time, our skin keeps poison from entering our body and contaminating us. It keeps germs on the outside so we are not infected. If we come into contact with some infectious liquid, but do not have a cut, our skin protects us. If, however, we have a cut, then germs can get inside and we can be infected.

On the one hand, we have the ability to physically open ourselves up to good things from the outside. If we open our mouths, we can let in a nourishing glass of milk. We can choose to let our skin boundary down. (We let our emotional boundaries down when we say yes to love.) We can open our eyes to see something beautiful. Or we can allow music to come into our ears or spring air into our noses. We have the ability to govern what gets into our bodies.

On the other hand, we can choose to keep bad things out when they try to enter through an opening. We can vomit spoiled food, sneeze when the air is dusty, shut our eyes when the light is too bright, or cover our ears to keep out loud sounds.

Skin naturally protects our bodies, but we also have choice about what goes into our bodies. We have responsibility for taking care of our bodies. We know best what our bodies need. We feel hungry and we eat. We feel tired and we take a nap or go to bed early. We feel sluggish and we go for a walk. We feel pain and we search out the cause of the pain.

Other boundaries work similarly. If I own a house with a yard, I am responsible for what's inside my property line. If I want my leaves raked, I need to rake them or get someone else to do it or they will remain on my lawn. In like fashion, my responsibility ends where my boundaries end. If my neighbor's yard has leaves, I can't be so presumptuous as to climb over the fence that separates our yards and start raking his leaves without his permission. If I want to help, I can ask and he can choose to open the gate and let me cross his boundary line. But, it is his choice.

Our Attitudes

Another aspect of our personhood is our attitudes. Our attitudes are our opinions about or mental positions toward something. We have seen how God defines his attitudes and beliefs toward various things throughout Scripture. By reading the Ten Commandments, we can get a very good idea of where God "puts his foot down" on certain issues. God is not scattered about, trying to figure out what are his attitudes toward life, good, and evil.

We are responsible for our own attitudes, for they exist inside our "property line." They are within our hearts, not someone else's. God repeatedly tells us to examine and take responsibility for the attitudes and beliefs that govern our lives. They form the structure of our personality. In the beginning of life, we "soak up" attitudes; as we mature, we need to take more and more responsibility for making sure our opinions are ours and not someone else's. We choose them.

God tells us that if our attitudes, or beliefs, about things are his, then our way will be prosperous: "Do not let this Book of the Law depart from your mouth; meditate on it day and night, so that you may be careful to do everything written in it. Then you will be prosperous and successful" (Josh. 1:8). Every family or individual dynamic that produces problems in people is a violation of God's attitudes. We can trust God's attitudes because they will get us out of pain. When we take responsibility for our attitudes, we can begin to "get our house in order"; we can make sure that what we have inside our property line is what we want.

In the area of bonding, we saw some hurtful attitudes. Joan's attitude that "all my weakness is bad" caused her great depression (see Chapter 3). When she began to see her responsibility for this attitude, she could begin to get it in line with God's attitudes toward relationship and need. As this changed, she came out of her isolation.

Sandy, however, was taking responsibility for her mother's attitude (something we should never do): "Everyone must do exactly what I want. I should always get my way." When things didn't go her mother's way and her mother got angry, Sandy felt responsible for her mother's anger. This is a gross confusion of boundaries. Sandy's mother's anger was caused by her own attitude, not Sandy's behavior. Her mother's position was outside of Sandy's property line, and therefore outside of both Sandy's control and responsibility. Trying to take responsibility for anger and attitudes not her own put Sandy in a bind. She was trying to control her mother's state of being, trying to "make" her happy. Proverbs 19:19 warns against this.

In taking responsibility for her mother's attitudes, Sandy was not taking responsibility for her own. Sandy's attitude could be stated something like this: "I am responsible for another person's pain. I should always give in to people's demands." Sandy was not working on what she did have the responsibility to change: herself. This is why she could feel so powerful and powerless at the same time. She had taken responsibility for something she could not control (her mother) and ignored something she could control (herself). Our attitudes and beliefs are our responsibility, not someone else's. Other people's attitudes and beliefs are their responsibility, not ours.

Our Feelings

Another aspect of ourselves that lies within our property line is our feelings. Both our physical feelings of pleasure or pain and our emotional feelings are on our property and no one else's. We are responsible for our own feelings.

Feelings signal our state of being. Feelings tell us how we are doing, what matters to us, what needs changing, what is going well, and what is going badly.

To disown our feelings, to ignore responsibility for them, is one of the most destructive things we can do to both ourselves and others. David shows how destructive it is to be out of touch with feelings: "They have closed their unfeeling heart; with their mouth they speak proudly" (Psalm 17:10 NASB).

The writer of Ecclesiastes shows the importance of owning feelings: "The heart of the wise is in the house of mourning" (7:4). People who do not deal with their feelings are not wise; they can "lose touch" with themselves.

Solomon writes in Proverbs of people who do not take responsibility for their anger and hatred, and thus become dishonest flatterers: "Like an earthen vessel overlaid with silver dross are burning lips and a wicked heart. He who hates disguises it with his lips, but he lays up deceit in his heart. When he speaks graciously, do not believe him, for there are seven abominations in his heart. Though his hatred covers itself with guile, his wickedness will be revealed before the assembly" (Prov. 26:23–26 NASB).

Jesus clarified boundaries in the gospels by commanding people to take responsibility for their own feelings. Look, for example, at the story of the workers who were hired at different hours of the day for the same wage (Matt. 20:1–15). Those who were hired at the beginning of the day were angry at the landowner: "These men who were hired last worked only one hour, and you have made them equal to us who have borne the burden of the work and the heat of the day." But Jesus made them own responsibility for their feelings and pointed out that he had the right to do whatever he wanted with his property: "I am not being unfair to you. Didn't you agree to work for a denarius? Take your pay and go. I want to give the man who was hired last the same as I gave you. Don't I have the right to do what I want with my own money? Or are you envious because I am generous?" He is basically saying, "Take responsibility for your anger, and don't blame me. Your anger comes from your envy, and you need to deal with it."

Our feelings can move us to righteousness and compassion. They can connect us to others as we saw in the section on bonding. A feeling such as joy aids our state of physical, mental, and spiritual well-being. At the same time, our feelings can tell us when something is drastically wrong with us and needs changing, just as physical pain can warn us of a dangerous cancer. If we could not feel physical pain, then we might all die every time we got sick, for we might not be able to rectify the problem in time. The same is true emotionally.

Our Behavior

Another aspect of personhood that lies within our responsibility and boundaries is our behavior, or the way we act or conduct ourselves. God takes responsibility for what he does. He requires us to take responsibility for what we do. If we disown responsibility for our behavior, we are out of control, or powerless. We cannot go where we want to go in life if we do not own both what we do and what we don't do.

People out of touch with this truth feel powerless because they have no faith in the basic law of cause and effect. This law is also called the law of reaping and sowing, which governs the entire universe. God has set up an ordered universe: if we behave in a certain way, certain things will happen. It is the basis for our security, for it gives us control of ourselves and our life. Irresponsible people hate this law, and suffer greatly. Responsible people thrive on it. Let's look briefly at how it works.

"Do not be deceived: God cannot be mocked. A man reaps what he sows. The one who sows to please his sinful nature, from that nature will reap destruction; the one who sows to please the Spirit, from the Spirit will reap eternal life" (Gal. 6:7–8). "Make level paths for your feet and take only ways that are firm" (Prov. 4:26). "Lazy hands make a man poor, but diligent hands bring wealth" (Prov. 10:4).

God has set up a dependable system. Like in the laws of physics, for every action, there is an equal reaction. If we do something, something happens; if we do nothing, nothing happens. If we want to stay healthy, then we must eat good food. If we want to have money to pay the mortgage, then we must work. God intended for us to have this feeling of power over our lives. On the one hand, we can cause good things to happen. If we want to build a good relationship with someone, we can smile at her or give her a hug. If we want to be a veterinarian, we can go to school and study and gain animal doctoring skills. This principle of owning our behavior is the basis for having a sense of power as people. It says that we can affect, or influence, our lives and the lives of others.

On the other hand, we can cause bad things to happen. This is the law of natural consequences of behavior. If we don't steer our moving car, we will crash. If we are lazy and don't study, we will flunk out of school and not find a good job. If we don't show up for work, we won't get paid and we won't be able to pay the mortgage and the electric and telephone bills. If we beat up those we love, we'll have little intimacy. To a large degree, our well-being depends on our behavior. Learning the law of sowing and reaping will not only prevent much pain, but also give great satisfaction.

People who obey this law of the universe feel in control of their lives, to the extent that we are able to feel in control. If they have a need, they behave in a way that will get their need met: They pray, they go to work, they ask for help, they exercise, they make friends, they behave in ways that bear fruit in their lives, and they get somewhere.

People who don't obey this law of cause and effect, who don't own their behavior and the consequences for it, feel enormously powerless. They become dependent on others who encourage their irresponsibility to maintain their dependency. They have no confidence in their ability to cause an effect. This is why Paul says in 2 Thessalonians 3:10, "If a man will not work, he shall not eat." He knows that there is dignity and joy in good behavior.

Anyone raised without the law of cause and effect is destined to battle continually with reality and live a life of chaos. To own our behavior, to admit it, to recognize it, to acknowledge it, in short, to take responsibility for it, is an important aspect of knowing our boundaries. Another important aspect is knowing that others are responsible for their behavior. These two principles can clear up many identity problems, as we shall see. We are always better off if we do not follow Adam and Eve's example of saying, "Someone else made me do it!" If we do that, we will stumble again and again in our own lives.

Our Thoughts

Our thoughts are another important aspect of who we are. God has given us all some capacity for thinking and has called us to love him with all our mind (Mark 12:30). To love God with all our mind is to grow in knowledge and in thinking, to take responsibility for our thinking and for the development of our minds. Many people do not think very often about what they think about. They just let their thoughts live inside their head, without observing or questioning them.

God calls us to active thinking and questioning. As Paul says to the Corinthians: "We demolish arguments and every pretension that sets itself up against the knowledge of God, and we take captive every thought to make it obedient to Christ" (2 Cor. 10:5). When we take every thought captive, we take responsibility for and evaluate it. We are not repressing or denying thoughts. We are owning them. We are taking inventory of them and weighing them. We need to see what they say about the status of our minds and our hearts, and develop them in the same way that we develop any other aspect of ourselves. They lie within our boundaries and we must own them.

Challenging distorted thinking is a way of owning or taking responsibility for our thoughts. If I think, for example, that you are going to do me harm, but I have never even met you, I need to take responsibility for the way this thinking affects my life. I need to decide whether there is real danger or whether I am just being paranoid. If I find out that I lack knowledge that I need in some area of life, I can own that lack and seek understanding in that field.

Passing thoughts can sometimes indicate unconscious preoccupations that may need to be examined. If we find ourselves thinking and dreaming about dying, we may need to look more closely at where those thoughts are coming from. Or, if we find ourselves thinking often about how to get revenge upon a certain person, we may need to examine the condition of our heart.

Our assumptions about others can negatively affect our relationship with them. A classic example of this occurred when the boy Jesus remained behind in Jerusalem after the Passover celebration. Mary and Joseph did not immediately discover his absence on their trip home to Nazareth (Luke 2:42–49). When they came back and found him in the temple, his mother Mary confronted him: "Son, why have you treated us like this? Your father and I have been anxiously searching for you." Jesus replied, "Why were you searching for me? Didn't you know that I had to be in my Father's house?"

Mary and Joseph had made a wrong assumption about Jesus' whereabouts. The story says, "Thinking he was in their company, they traveled on for a day" (v. 44). They should have checked where their son was before leaving. Their expectation that Jesus would follow them led to hard feelings.

Many times we assume things without checking them out, and then blame others for the results. We must take responsibility for our faulty thinking and work on correcting it. Paul says, "For who among men knows the thoughts of a man except the man's spirit within him?" (1 Cor. 2:11). No one except God can read our thoughts; God has built this boundary into human existence. Your thoughts are your thoughts, and no one else's.

When we take responsibility for someone else's thoughts, we invade their boundaries; we interfere with their property. If we expect them to take responsibility for ours, we have a similar problem.

This dynamic of "owning" one's own thoughts is very important in establishing identity because what we think is an essential part of who we are. If we cannot separate our own thoughts and opinions from another, we have ceased to be a person in our own right, and have denied something that God will one day hold us responsible for.

A second-grade Sunday school teacher once asked her class, "What's gray, lives in a tree, gathers nuts, and has a bushy tail?" Not one boy or girl raised his or her hand, so she asked again. "Come on, class. What's gray, lives in a tree, gathers nuts, and has a bushy tail?" Again, no one would venture a guess. She asked the question one more time. Finally, one little boy raised his hand. "Okay, Johnny," she said. "What's the answer?" Johnny squirmed a bit and said, "Well, it sure sounds like a squirrel to me, but I'll say Jesus anyway."

Many people, like Johnny, find themselves conditioned to think in a certain way in a certain context. They are hard-pressed to find their own thoughts in the midst of situations where they feel their thoughts don't fit. We are not talking here about whether or not someone will approve of our thoughts. Our concern here is whether or not we even have thoughts apart from others. Thinking our own thoughts is the beginning of freedom and responsibility.

Our Abilities

Another important aspect of our identity is our talents and abilities. God has given each of us certain talents and abilities, and he holds us responsible for developing them. Many times people do not explore their own talents. They accept others' definitions of them, without seeing if these definitions fit. Sometimes they will deny their own gifts and live vicariously through the gifts of others.

Many frustrated people try to live their lives as others have defined them. I remember one extremely artistic and creative teenager whose parents, both physicians, decided that he would continue the medical tradition. He tried to fight this label to little avail; he could not perceive his talents apart from his parents' wishes for him. He tried to be a doctor, but his medical school education was fraught with difficulty because he did not have the talent. He finally finished school, but was in serious trouble in his residency.

It was only after he failed as a resident that he finally became separate enough from his parents to figure out where his real gifts lay. He could own his own talents and forsake the feeling that he "should" have the talents his parents wanted him to have. He carved out a satisfying career in the creative arts. But he had to go through the arduous task of "finding himself" apart from the ones he loved.

We lose our true self when we so conform to others that we lose our own separateness and identity. Paul writes about this kind of fusion of ourselves with others:

Do not conform any longer to the pattern of this world, but be transformed by the renewing of your mind. Then you will be able to test and approve what God's will is—his good, pleasing and perfect will.

For by the grace given me I say to every one of you: Do not think of yourself more highly than you ought, but rather think of yourself with sober judgment, in accordance with the measure of faith God has given you. Just as each of us has one body with many members, and these members do not all have the same function, so in Christ we who are many form one body, and each member belongs to all the others. We have different gifts, according to the grace given us. If a man's gift is prophesying, let him use it in proportion to his faith. If it is serving, let him serve; if it is teaching, let him teach; if it is encouraging, let him encourage; if it is contributing to the needs of others, let him give generously; if it is leadership, let him govern diligently; if it is showing mercy, let him do it cheerfully. (Rom. 12:2–8)

We are separate people with separate identity, and we must not be conformed into someone else's wishes that may conflict with what God has designed for us. We must own what is our true self, and develop it with God's grace and truth.

Peter says it like this, "Each one should use whatever gift he has received to serve others, faithfully administering God's grace in its various forms" (1 Peter 4:10). Jesus stated it like this, "To one he gave five talents of money, to another two talents, and to another one talent, each according to his ability" (Matt. 25:15). God has made each of us different, and we are responsible for discovering our gifts and developing them.

Our Desires

Our desires are an important aspect of what lies within our boundaries and fences. Each person has different wants and desires, wishes and dreams, goals and plans, hungers and thirsts. And, like the other aspects of what we must own as our own, our desires clearly lie within our own yard.

Our desires are a major part of what it means to be created in God's likeness. He has given many desires to us; others we have chosen. Both can be good. But some of our wants and desires are not good. In either case, we must begin to own them to straighten out what is good and bad, as well as to choose between the good and the better.

When we do not acknowledge our desires, we cut ourselves off from who we are, and we limit our future satisfaction, our future service to God and others, our motivation, and our sanctification. God uses our desires to fulfill his purposes, as well as to satisfy himself as a giver. Think of how frustrating it must be for the biggest giver in the universe to not be able to give to one of his children because they do not realize that they desire what he has to give. God would get stuck with his gifts and lose out on the joy of giving.

Only when we admit our desires can God work with us to meet them, delay them, encourage us to give them up, or whatever would be helpful. But we have to own up to them before he can do something with them.

James names some of the consequences of not taking responsibility for our desires: "You want something but don't get it. You kill and covet, but you cannot have what you want. You quarrel and fight. You do not have, because you do not ask God. When you ask, you do not receive, because you ask with wrong motives, that you may spend what you get on your pleasures"

(James 4:2–3). Mixed up in many fights and quarrels, says James, are two kinds of unmet desires: those not asked for and those asked for out of wrong motives.

An example of the first would be people envying others' talents but not asking God to help them go to school to develop their own. They have not because they ask not. An example of the second kind would be people going to school, not to develop their gifts for service, but to get a degree to flaunt. One desire to go to school is good, the other is not. But either way, the desire must be owned and given to God to work with.

On the one hand, God is delighted to give us good things, if they fit who we really are. A longing fufilled can be "sweet to the soul" (Prov. 13:19). Whether we be homemakers, ministers, machine workers, sports figures, or in any other position, we can take pride in ourselves and in our work (Gal. 6:4). On the other hand, God is not delighted to help us inflate our ego. God will grant our desires to further our development and his work. But it takes a real relationship between us and God to determine what is good desire and bad.

Therefore, we need to own our desires and take them to him. This relationship is pictured in many places, but one of my favorites is Philippians 2:12–13: "Work out your salvation with fear and trembling, for it is God who works in you to will and to act according to his good purpose." God is at work in our desires, and we need to bring them into relationship with him.

In the same way, we need to own our desires in our relationships with other people. Most of us have had the frustrating experience of being with people who would not tell us what they really wanted. We know they have wishes and desires, but it is difficult for them to own them. If we ask where they would like to eat or which movie they want to see, for example, they say, "It doesn't matter. Whatever you want is okay." If we ask which of two pieces of pie they would like, they say, "You pick." It is easy to see their discontent when we pick the "wrong" restaurant, movie, or piece of pie, but they will not own their desires. It begins to make us uncomfortable. We fear they may be resenting us for always having our way. For any relationship to thrive, two separate people need to work out their own particular likes and dislikes, giving and receiving accordingly. This give-and-take builds love and intimacy, and a knowledge of the real person we are in relationship with. If a person never "owns" his or her desires, then intimacy and knowledge of that person is limited. Those who do not define themselves remain "non-persons."

Owning our desires also gives us a stronger sense of where we stand on things and with other people. When we are with people who are clear about what they want, we get a sense of being with solid entities. Their person-hood has definition, and their personality has edges. These edges do not have to be rough, or hurtful, but they need to be present nevertheless. If people are not definite about themselves, we have little feeling of having been with them at all.

In addition, owning our desires and wants helps us to reach our goals in life. "The laborer's appetite works for him; his hunger drives him on" (Prov. 16:26). Realizing our desire motivates us toward any goal. People all through the ages have pursued their dreams and followed their desires, and this has led to a better life for all of us. The writer of Ecclesiastes puts it this way: "Follow the ways of your heart and whatever your eyes see, but know that God will bring you to judgment" (11:9). We are called to be aware of our desires, and at the same time to include God in the working out of our plans and goals.

Our Choices

The next aspect of identity we need to be aware of and own as part of our property is our choices. Just because this characteristic is so far down the list doesn't mean it is less important than the others. Nothing could be further from the truth. Choices are the foundation upon which boundaries are built. But *our choices are not true choices unless we are aware of all the aspects of our identity that go into them—our feelings, attitudes, behaviors, wants, and thoughts*. To own and make our own choices, we must be aware of all the aspects of ourselves that go into any decision. In addition, we must be aware that we are making a choice about almost everything we do.

Let's take Sandy, for example. If she wants to celebrate Thanksgiving with her friends, but feels like her mother "is making her" come home, she would not feel responsible for missing Thanksgiving with friends. She would feel like her mother was responsible for making her miss out. In reality, Sandy's mother did not have a gun to her head, "making" her come home. Sandy has chosen to please her mother instead of herself, but because she doesn't realize that she has a choice, she blames and resents her mother for her own choice. Sandy has chosen to give away her freedom; she needs to take responsibility for the feelings her choice has left her with.

Paul is very clear about this dynamic: "Each man should give what he has decided in his heart to give, not reluctantly or under compulsion, for God loves a cheerful giver" (2 Cor. 9:7). Whenever we give anything, whether it be money, time, energy, talents, or possessions, we need to give only what we have decided in our heart to give. We are the ones deciding to give, and we need to think out and own that decision. To say it another way, we need to realize that we have given "on purpose." If we don't, then we are giving out of a feeling of obligation or compulsion, because we feel like "we have to."

Few dynamics in life have more potential for wrecking people than this one. It ranks second only to isolation. If we do not feel like we have a choice, we feel we are out of control of our lives, and we resent the ones we perceive as being in control of us. It is the opposite of freedom and the opposite of love.

Choices have two directions: yes and no. We can choose to do something, or we can choose to not do it. We can choose to give to someone or we can choose to not give. In either case, we are responsible for the consequences. This is the essence of having a sense of limits and the cornerstone of love.

Many people give out of obligation and compulsion, which leads to resentment. They go to lunches they can't say "no" to; they spend weekends they resent spending; they give others time and energy motivated out of guilt instead of love.

These actions can lead to the martyr syndrome, in which people sacrifice their own desires to arouse feelings of pity or guilt in others. Parents sacrifice time and money for their children, then try to make them feel guilty: "Well, if it weren't for your schooling, then we could have traveled more or we could have had a nicer house or car." It makes children feel guilty for their very existence, like they somehow have the power to ruin their parents' lives by accepting the "gift" of school tuition.

I remember one woman whose mother would almost beg to babysit her children and then gripe about the inconvenience for weeks to come. She could not acknowledge that she had chosen to take care of the kids, and her daughter had not "made" her do it.

Further, we negate that we have choices about how we

spend our lives and time. We may complain about how bored we are, but do not accept responsibility for learning a new skill or hobby. We may gripe about our "crummy" pastor, but not take responsibility for writing the pastor a letter, getting on the board, or looking for a new church.

There are certainly things in life over which we have no control, but we always have a choice about how we will respond to these things. Our choices determine our direction in life, but if we do not own this fact, we don't know where we are going, and we resent where we end up as if it were someone else's fault.

In the story about the workers hired at different hours, the angry one tried to deny the choice he had made to work for a certain amount. Jesus answers his complaint: "'Friend, I am not being unfair to you. Didn't you agree to work for a denarius?'" (Matt. 20:13). In other words, "Didn't you choose to work for this wage? That choice is your responsibility. Own it." Complaining and griping without trying to do anything about a situation is the essence of denying choice, and it renders us powerless and resentful.

God wants us to own our choices and thus realize who we are. Joshua said it clearly,

> "But if serving the Lord seems undesirable to you, then choose for yourselves this day whom you will serve, whether the gods your forefathers served beyond the River, or the gods of the Amorites, in whose land you are living. But as for me and my household, we will serve the Lord." (Josh. 24:15)

He then goes on to describe what a significant choice this is and what the consequences of each choice would be. Not making a choice is making a choice. God will hold us accountable for every choice we make, even when we do not think we are making one: "But I tell you that men will have to give account on the day of judgment for every careless word they have spoken" (Matt. 12:36). We may think that some action or word is insignificant, but everything we do has meaning, everything we do or don't do bears fruit. We have a choice: "Make a tree good and its fruit will be good, or make a tree bad and its fruit will be bad, for a tree is recognized by its fruit" (v. 33). Our lives have fruit; we have no choice about that. We do have a choice, however, about the nature of the fruit we bear by choosing to own our "tree," our heart, and allowing God to work on it.

Our Limits

When we examine our boundaries, we discover our limits. Just as our yard has physical boundaries, so our lives—emotional, psychological, and spiritual—have limits also. God has designed us in his likeness with one exception: he is infinite, and we are finite. This truth has serious implications for our idea of boundaries.

We all possess a finite amount of ability, time, money, energy, and so on. The amounts are not static, however. We may get more or less as time goes on, but it is still true that, at any given moment, we have fixed amounts. Our salary limits what we can spend. Our energy level limits how many projects we can take on.

Many people don't take responsibility for their limits and overextend themselves. It takes time to learn our limits in the various areas of life, but they can be learned if we are aware of our feelings, attitudes, and behaviors. If we are feeling overburdened, we must realize where we have overextended our limits and say no. Sometimes, we don't know the limits of our love, and we love past where we should.

Other people have too narrow limits. They "sow sparingly" as Paul says in 2 Corinthians 9:6. They do not extend their boundaries far enough to give what they can give. They too tightly restrict their feelings, attitudes, behaviors, thinking, and choices. They narrow their perception of what they can do. Many Christians do not take advantage of the amount of room God has given them to experience all that is within them. They think, as I heard one man say of his legalistic background, that "any sensation stronger than an itch is sinful." They don't stretch the limits of their feelings, and thus narrow their experience of the "likeness of God."

We can err in either direction. As we saw in the first two chapters, it takes much grace, truth, and practice in time with others to discover our limits and to take responsibility for them. This is the balanced life. We should neither overextend, nor underextend ourselves. If we are going through a season of depression, for example, we must realize that we have limited amounts to give and cut back accordingly. If we are "rich in love" for a season, we have much to give away. It takes responsible assessment before God to determine our limitations.

One important aspect of realizing our boundaries is limiting the effects of others on us. If someone is asking too much of us, we must draw the line as to what we will give and what we will not. If someone is abusive to us, we must set a limit. Family expert Dr. James Dobson in his book *Love Must Be Tough* calls this a "line of respect." It means basically, "I will not allow myself to be treated this way."

If our neighbor dumped trash in our yard, we would confront our neighbor or perhaps call the police. We need to do the same thing if someone is crossing our limits of time and energy.

Negative Assertions

Much of our identity comes from the positive assertions of who we are. We say things like "I love sports" or "I believe Jesus is Lord." We are asserting positive truths about who we are. We are sports-lovers and Christians.

We have also seen how God asserts his identity by saying who he is and who he is not. Just as God describes his boundaries by negative statements, so do we. When I say, "I hate injustice," I am saying what I am against, and that is an important identity statement. If I say "I do not like science," I am making just as important an identity statement as when I say, "I love philosophy."

Many people are not in touch with their "not-me" experiences. The boy who was not medically talented did not assert strongly enough what he was not. He needed to scream at the top of his lungs, "I hate medicine," until someone finally heard him. Negative assertions always come out in one form or another. His came out in his poor performance in school and his failure in residency. Negative assertions are a reality. Just as we need to take responsibility for what lies inside our boundaries, we need to admit to ourselves what lies outside.

A beautiful example of negative assertion is found in the story Jesus told of two sons who worked for their father:

> "There was a man who had two sons. He went to the first and said, "Son, go work today in the vineyard.'
> "'I will not,' he answered, but later he changed his mind and went.
> "Then the father went to the other son and said the same thing. He answered, "I will, sir,' but he did not go.

"Which of the two did what his father wanted?"

"The first," they answered.

Jesus said to them, "I tell you the truth, the tax collectors and the prostitutes are entering the kingdom of God ahead of you." (Matt. 21:28–31)

In effect, the second son did not know who he really was. He didn't want to work in the vineyard, but he couldn't say, "I won't go." Thus, he was out of touch with himself. The first, because he could say no, was in touch enough to later say yes. This kind of person can say no, and then his yes means something. We must be in touch with our no and in control of it, or it will control us. The second son could not own his no, so it owned him. Nos always come out in some form or fashion. In his case it was in his procrastination.

Some negative assertions would be: "No, I don't like to speak before large audiences." "No, I do not like it when you tease me in front of other people." "No, I will not work for that amount." "No, I will not allow swearing in this house." "No, I do not like cocaine." "No, I do not want you to touch me there." "No, I do not agree with your theology." "No, I do not like that movie, or restaurant, or whatever."

By being in touch with our "not-me" experiences, we further define ourselves to others and the world. If we can't say what we are not, we have no hope of holiness, for we cannot hate evil and be separate from it. People with weak boundaries cannot reject what is not them. It would be like skin that doesn't reject foreign bodies; the blood would forever be infected. If we cannot say what is "not us" in terms of all of the above elements—our body, feelings, attitudes, behaviors, thoughts, abilities, choices, desires, and limits—we cannot keep the bad stuff out of our souls. We own things that don't belong within our boundaries—some good things that don't belong there and some bad things that don't belong anywhere. In either case, they are "not me."

For Sandy, a "not-me" statement would be, "Mother, I love you, but I don't want to spend this Thanksgiving at home. I want to be with my friends." If her mother became angry, Sandy could assert, "I am sorry you are angry with me, but that's something you'll have to deal with. You are going to have to make other plans for Thanksgiving. I will not be there."

This may sound mean, but this straightforward assertion may be required with controlling people who won't take responsibility for their own disappointments. In reality, this statement helps Sandy more than her mother. It helps her to realize who is responsible for what. If her mother is so controlling that she blames her daughter for her disappointments, she probably wouldn't hear it anyway.

It is extremely important to be able to make negative assertions. We must be able to say what is "not me" in order to have a "me." What we like has no meaning unless we know what we don't like. Our yes has no meaning if we never say no. My chosen profession has no passion if "just any one would do." Our opinions and thoughts mean very little if there is nothing we disagree with.

Chapter ❦ 7

How We Develop Boundaries

JANE CAME INTO THERAPY BECAUSE OF "PANIC attacks." Her husband's increased drinking was causing problems in the home. She tried to be loving and supportive, but this was doing no good; it was only making matters worse.

She had begun to read some books on setting limits on abusive behavior and how to not be an enabler. She realized that she had to say no to his behavior, and at times this meant leaving him alone when he was on a binge.

However, when she began to put limits on his behavior, she experienced severe panic. She felt as if she were "falling into a hole." She shook and felt terror. She felt as if some awful loneliness was going to "swallow her up."

As she began to understand herself better, she found that she did not have very good bonding inside of her. She was isolated internally; she didn't have the ability to maintain emotional connections with other people in their absence, what we referred to earlier as "emotional object constancy." If she were not in the presence of the one she loved, she felt horribly alone.

If she separated from her husband, she felt panic. But, if she stuck to him, she enabled his abusive behavior. She was in a double bind that many abused people find themselves in. They literally "can't live with him, and they can't live without him." They can't live with him because of the abuse, and they can't live without him because of the isolation.

Jane learned a crucial lesson: *There must be internal bonding for one to be able to establish boundaries*. Without it, boundaries as they were meant to be cannot exist. It is limits without love, and that is hell.

As Jane began to understand why she could not set and keep limits on her husband's behavior, she began to work on her lack of attachment to others. She joined an Al-Anon group and established supportive relationships with others who would reinforce her setting limits on her exposure to her husband's behavior. She found that she could have a sense of separateness without isolation, and that just because she set limits did not mean that she had to go without love. Her support group stood by her in her separateness.

Jane no longer enabled her husband's abusive behavior. Before, because of her lack of bonding with others, he could pretty much do whatever he pleased, and she would have to go along. When she gained outside support, she could stand up to his abuse, and he was forced to deal with himself. He had to realize that his behavior was causing him to be alone, and for the first time, he had to suffer the consequences of his own behavior. Consequences are what change behavior, and Jane was not able to allow him to suffer the consequences before then.

Gradually, he became sober, and they were able to work things out. But, without the intervention of a group to provide her bonding needs, Jane would not have been able to establish separateness with his evil behavior. Bonding must always precede separateness.

Bonding

Bonding is the first and foremost stage to growth. We must be able to have relationships with others to be alive. This is the unity that underlies the relational aspect of the image of God.

If someone cannot attach, then separateness has no meaning. It is a no without a yes. We must be able to be "a part" of someone or something before we can be "apart." Attachment gives us the safety and the strength to separate.

Reconciliation to relationship is the first step in establishing intimacy with God. "I write to you, dear children, because your sins have been forgiven on account of his name" (1 John 2:12). The first step is forgiveness, which brings us into bonding.

As we look at how a person develops, the first year is one of bonding. It is one where there is very little separateness and assertion. This year lays the foundation of being "rooted and grounded in love" (Eph. 3:17 NASB), which will give us the safety and connectedness necessary to venture out in separateness. We can never be truly separate from someone if we have not first been bonded.

Becoming Separate

After a year of bonding and attachment, the process of separateness begins to "kick in." The infant develops wonderful new abilities, called secondary processes because they develop secondarily to the primary processes of feeling and loving.

Secondary processes promote separateness and identity; they are based in mobility, language development, development of thinking and language-based thought, realization of consequences and the law of cause and effect, more ranges of behavior, realization of increasing physical and emotional separateness, and the beginnings of the process of "willing." Since these sound like wonderful things, it's strange that some call this time the "terrible twos!" (I heard a friend of mine call this time the "terrific twos"; she relished her child's budding autonomy and separateness. It was a refreshing comment to hear.)

As these processes unfold, the entire world turns around for the child and the mother. What was formerly pretty much of a unit becomes more of a relationship between two separate people. Think of the wonderful way in which God has designed the process: Trust and relationship is established in an initial bonding period, and from this trust comes the working out of a separateness that is not frightening because of the bond. It is the basis for what God calls bond servanthood in the New Testament. Because of our love for God, he can give us the freedom of our separateness. The relationship keeps us "in check." Love constrains us.

As love is established between an infant and mother, the child begins to slowly work out his sense of separateness from her. He is beginning to realize his boundaries and sense of separateness from mother. He is beginning to realize what is "me" and what is mother. As the infant gains the ability to move around, he begins to walk away from mother. He is learning to have a life of his own, albeit a small one. He is exploring the world "apart" from the one he was once "a part of." The budding faculties we mentioned above all aid in this process. As he gains mobility, he can get further away from his mother on his own. He can venture out, and all separateness for the first time is not caused by her. It is caused by his wishes to move away and explore by himself.

As his capacity for thought grows, he can better negotiate the world he is exploring and can even begin to name things. He begins to order his world. He realizes what things are and how to use them in a goal-oriented way. He can talk about them, ask for them, demand them, scream when he does not get them. He is learning how to think about and talk about a world apart from mother.

At the same time, he is learning increasing separateness from mother in other ways. He learns that when he walks, he sometimes falls down as a result of his actions, not hers. When he takes a tumble or discovers things, he feels the pain of falling or the joy of discovery; as mother shares these experiences with him, he learns to value and own them.

Similarly, he learns that he has certain abilities to do things. This is the beginning of competency and goal-directedness. Along with that, he learns that there are limitations on what he can do and that sometimes he needs help. An important aspect of boundaries is feeling both the elation and accomplishment of his separate behavior as well as its consequences. He needs to learn that there are limits to what will be allowed, and there are consequences to his omnipotence. He is gradually learning to co-operate with the world.

The child learns that he can want some things and get them, either by his own efforts or through someone's help, but he will not get everything he wants. Internal boundaries on desires are being created.

He realizes that he is responsible for his choices. If he chooses to hit his sister, for example, there are consequences. If he chooses to wander into the street, there are consequences. (This is a description of a process of gaining separateness, not of child discipline. Therefore I will not go into specific consequences for behavior at various ages.) If he walks to the window, he experiences the good consequence of seeing a beautiful flower. He discovers the law of cause and effect: "My choices to be mobile can bring me pleasure." At the same time, choices can bring pain. "When I choose to touch the heater, it hurts."

Through every action, feeling, and choice, the child comes to an increasing realization that he, not his mother, is responsible for these things. He also learns that his thoughts and feelings are not always the same as his mother's. He may think it is a great idea to stay in the sandbox longer, but she thinks it is time for a nap. He may not wish to take a bath, but she wants him to. If he is allowed to have his thoughts and wishes without having all of them gratified, he learns how to own what he thinks, feels, and chooses, without being out of control. This is the delicate balance of being allowed to "be all of who he is" and not being able to be "all that there is." This is the balance of being able to have a self without being self-centered.

Failures in development of boundaries occur in both extremes. Some people's boundaries are confused because they are not allowed to own their feelings, thoughts, and behaviors, so they never own who they are. They don't know how to deal with these things later; they have no map. Other people, not limited enough in their feelings, thoughts, and behaviors, think they are the only ones who matter. These two later become the overresponsible and the underresponsible people. (Usually they find each other and get married!)

Increasing Separateness

From the second year of life onward, bonding and separateness must work hand in hand. As children reach age four or five, they increase the separateness to include more and more people in their world. They learn to relate to two people at a time instead of only one. They have playmates and kindergarten friends, as well as more and more experiences. Their world away from their primary attachments is growing, and they can stand to be away from them for more than twenty minutes. They can spend a whole half day at kindergarten and enjoy it, instead of finding it overwhelming.

As abilities, thinking, behaviors, and feelings develop, separateness extends into the world of school. They have more and more responsibility as they own more things within their boundaries. Later, they move out of the house and go to college or get a job. Those who go to college eventually move from the safety of college into the "real world." All along, they learn how to stay in relationship, but increase in the ability to be a separate person from the ones that they are bonded to. This enables them to lead full, productive work lives and to be relational people. Love and work come together through the balancing of bonding and separateness.

When We Fail to Develop Boundaries

Ownership is crucial in creating boundaries. On the one hand, people who are not allowed to own their own thoughts, feelings, attitudes, behaviors, desires, and choices never develop a true sense of responsibility. They continue to have conflicts between bonding and separateness. They do not know how to have a relationship and at the same time be separate. They don't know that each person is responsible for each of the elements that are within their boundaries.

On the other hand, people who own other people's

thoughts, feelings, attitudes, behaviors, desires, and choices extend their boundaries too far, encroaching on other people's property. This is what happened with Sandy and her mother. Sandy's time belongs to her; her mother's time belongs to her mother. However, Sandy had never learned to limit her mother. For years she allowed her mother to think that her mother owned her time as well. Sandy was not free to give time to her mother as she "purposed" in her heart; she was "obligated and compelled" to give to her mother what her mother felt she owned anyway: Sandy's life. The wish to control someone else's life and not allow their separateness is a serious relationship destroyer. It is the source of more parent-child struggles, friendship struggles, marital breakups, work conflicts, and struggles with God than any other dynamic.

In the Fall, our boundaries were destroyed. Since we no longer had grace, we could not tell the truth about who owned what. Adam said it was the woman's fault, not his. She "caused" him to do it. Eve said it was the serpent's fault, not hers, for he "made her do it." They could not admit that their own desires, attitudes, and behaviors led to their choices. They could not take responsibility for themselves. They wanted to eat the fruit and to become godlike. They thought that they should have whatever they wanted and that God really did not know what was good for them. They chose to reach past their allotted boundaries. And God held them responsible for all of those choices.

Since the Fall, we have all had difficulty owning what is ours. We disown what is ours and try to own what belongs to others. Sandy's mother disowned her responsibility to raise a daughter who would grow up and leave her parents, clinging to others in adulthood. She disowned her responsibility for her disappointment in

Sandy's not coming home for Thanksgiving. Just as the two-year-old has to deal with his disappointment of not being able to stay up all night with Mommy, Sandy's mother has to deal with her disappointment in not having Thanksgiving the way she wants it. Sandy's mother also tried to own things that were not hers, like Sandy's time and course of life.

Parents, children, friends, and spouses often have trouble working this out. There are two wills in any relationship, so allowances have to be made if love and responsibility are to be forthcoming. I saw a bumper sticker that read, "If you love something, set it free. If it really loves you, it will return. If it doesn't, HUNT IT DOWN AND KILL IT!" We all feel this way to varying degrees. We may want the people we love to be able to make their own choices, but many of those choices are going to limit us in some way. And when they do, we do not naturally want to deal with those limitations responsibly. We would rather blame.

If Sandy chooses to spend Thanksgiving with her friends, her mother will have to choose to deal with her wishes being limited by Sandy's choices. The healthy thing to do would be to grieve for this wish and carve out some sort of satisfactory holiday apart from her daughter. Instead, she will probably blame Sandy and play the victim, crying out about how her daughter is ruining her holiday.

It is easy to say we love others, but difficult to allow them the freedom inherent in love. When they do not want to do what we want them to, then we "hunt them down and kill them" in various ways. We pout, cry out angrily, send guilt messages, and attempt to control them. These actions kill freedom and will, and eventually, they will kill love. Love cannot exist without freedom, and freedom cannot exist without responsibility.

We must own and take responsibility for what is ours, and that includes our disappointment in not getting everything we want from another person. The disappointment that comes from our loved ones exercising their freedom is our responsibility. We must deal with it. This is the only way to keep love alive.

This is true even when others' freedom leads them to sin against us. The pain we feel is not our fault, but it is our responsibility to deal with. Sandy wasn't sinning against her mother. Her mother was sinning against her, for she was coveting Sandy's life. But, many times people do sin against us when exercising their freedom, and we are responsible for dealing with the injury. If we don't, we will stay stuck in a blame position, powerless against their sin. This "victim" mentality keeps many people stuck in their pain.

Jane's husband was sinning against her, drinking to an extent that was affecting the family. The sin was his responsibility; the pain she was feeling was his fault. But she was responsible for dealing with the pain he was causing her, and she did a wonderful job. In effect, she said, "I cannot control his behavior, but I can take responsibility for dealing with the way that it affects me and this family. I can own the hurt and the pain and use it to motivate me to change how I deal with him. In that way, I can limit the effects of his behavior on me."

She dealt with her hurt and anger. When she felt isolated, she took responsibility for that. As she did that, she was no longer under his power and control; she found happiness in her support group apart from him. Because she had taken responsibility for her pain, she found freedom. And a favorable side effect was her husband's changed behavior.

Many, however, do not take responsibility for their lives. (Again, I'm not saying "fault," I am saying responsibility. It is not my fault if I get hit by a truck, but it is my responsibility to learn to walk again. No one can do that for me, but they can help me. I must own the injured legs and begin to exercise them.) They remain stuck because they want other people to change. They want others to make it better, and often those people will not. As a result, they are in bondage to others. Freedom comes from taking responsibility; bondage comes from giving it away. Many spouses of alcoholics will not do what Jane did, but continue to blame someone else for their misery. This is the essence of powerlessness.

I recall one woman whose husband left her abruptly with four small children. What he did to her was horrible; she had every reason in the world to feel betrayed, angry, abandoned, depressed, and overwhelmed. As long as she expressed those feelings of "look what he's done to me," there was no movement. These are natural feelings to have when one has been sinned against, but they should gradually lead one to a sense of ownership of the situation and a grief of letting go of the loss. This was not happening. She would hear nothing of the suggestion that she was going to have to do some things to get out of the situation he left her in. She would get angry with me for suggesting that she had the power to make some choices to help herself. Instead, all she wanted to own was the right to blame him for the situation. For quite a long time, she continued to blame and eventually left therapy. Much later I heard that she was still blaming— and still miserable.

She was in the same situation others find themselves in, but with much different outcomes. These people go through the appropriate blaming stage as well, for that is needed. Part of the forgiveness process is to call sin, sin. We must confess how we have been sinned against in order to forgive. However, after an appropriate period of blame, we must begin to take responsibility for the mess that someone else's sin has left us in. Our situation is part of our property; we must own it and deal with our feelings, attitudes, and behaviors to get unstuck even if we did not cause it.

Bobbie's husband "left her for his secretary." She was left alone with three small children and without much child support or many marketable skills. He had virtually stolen everything through the divorce. She was truly victimized and mistreated. She went through all the proper attempts to reconcile and to work on the relationship, to no avail.

When it was clear that the marriage was over, she was devastated. Twenty years of marriage had ended overnight, and Bobbie was in distressing circumstances. She had not been to school in two decades and had mostly done volunteer work, with some other minimal employment. Her depression was serious, and her financial needs worse.

But after recognizing the reality of the sin against her and processing her feelings, she began to own her plight. Even though she had not caused it, she was responsible for dealing with it. She got out of the blaming stage and got busy. She arranged to take some courses at night while working during the day. She networked with other single parents at her church to carry each other's load. She did some other creative part-time work that did not take her away from her children.

After quite a while, she finished her classes and was able to get back on her feet financially. She had created a new circle of friendships and had developed several supportive bonds with people. She attended workshops on divorce recovery and working through painful emotions; she learned about the patterns that had led her to choose someone like her husband, and also the ways that she had slowly allowed him to isolate her emotionally and render her powerless.

In short, even though the divorce and abandonment were not her "fault," she took responsibility for her situation. She owned what fell within her property line, within her boundaries. She assumed responsibility for her feelings, attitudes, and behaviors and developed them. In addition, she pursued some desires and wants, and she made responsible choices that led to greater degrees of happiness for herself and her children. Where she found herself alone and isolated, she took responsibility for that and created support and regained her ability to trust people. Through it all, she found God to be faithful to his promises to sustain her.

Chapter

✂ 8

Crossing Over
Boundaries

THE ESSENCE OF BOUNDARIES AND LIMITS IS knowing what we own and what we do not own. This leads to responsibility and love. What happens, however, when we do not own the things we should own? When we do not own ourselves as separate people from the ones we are bonded to, we develop unclear boundaries, and we allow people to cross those boundaries when we should be saying no.

Body

Our most basic boundary is our body. The New American Standard Bible calls our body a "vessel," saying that we are to possess our own bodies "in santification and honor" (1 Thess. 4:4). *Possess* is a beautiful word for owning what is within our boundaries. When we possess our bodies, we know they belong to us. We can feel them, we can own the pleasure they bring us through our senses, and we are in touch with them.

To invade another person's body, to cross over this person's boundaries, is the most basic act of abuse. The first effect of a crossover in body boundaries is that the person whose boundaries are crossed feels more like a thing than a person. Forcibly using a girl's body against her will, for example, does away with that girl's basic feeling of owning her own life. This can happen in several ways.

Sexual abuse is one of the most blatant examples of crossing boundaries, for someone takes what is not theirs. Our sexual functioning was meant to be freely shared with a partner of our choice, not stolen against our will. People who have been sexually abused may disown their bodies. They may feel that their bodies do not belong to them: they belong to their abusers. Anyone whose body has been violated has had his or her personal boundaries horribly injured.

Sexual abuse can occur in marriages where spouses are treated as if they were things, not people. One spouse uses the other's body for his own satisfaction and is not concerned with what feels good or bad to his partner. This is invasion, not respect.

In the single world some people take what is not theirs to have and use somebody's body instead of respecting the individual's ownership of it. Many women feel that they lost their bodies in their teen years or in young adulthood, when they were used physically. They must work hard to regain their bodies again and declare dominion and authority over what is theirs.

In *physical abuse*, the same kind of violation happens.

A husband may cross his wife's body boundary by pushing her down or slapping her across the face. A parent may cross her child's body boundary by hitting him. People who have been physically abused often lose touch with their bodies and are not able to feel them and experience them in meaningful ways. They learn that others can do what they want with them.

In a less serious crossing of boundaries, parents sometimes make their children's bodies an extension of their own narcissism and do not allow their children to express themselves as separate people. They do not allow their children to make decisions about their own bodies, to have a say in what they will wear or eat. Certainly, there are limits, but children need to have some choices about what goes on or into their bodies.

Some people can't experience themselves as sexual persons because of rigid teaching. They have so much guilt about their sexual feelings that they disown that part of their body. Instead of being taught how to own and even delight in sexual feelings, they were taught that those feelings should be repressed.

Some people learn that admitting pain is wrong. They were taught to keep a stiff upper lip when they were in pain; as a result, they lost touch with their ability to sense their bodies. Consequently, both pleasure and pain have little meaning for them.

Problems arise when people do not own their own bodies. Often, to be fully functioning human beings, they must work on reclaiming what they have lost. For example, sexual counseling may be necessary for people to relearn how to feel pleasure; they have to reown what is rightly theirs.

Feelings

Our feelings, whether good or bad, are our property. They fall within our boundaries. Our feelings are our responsibility; others' feelings are their responsibility. If other people feel sad, it is their sadness. This does not mean that they do not need someone else to be with them in their sadness and to empathize with them. It does mean the person who is feeling sad must take responsibility for that feeling.

Sandy was confused about her boundaries because she felt responsible for her mother's feelings. She felt like she had to change her mother's anger to happiness by changing her own behavior, that is, coming home for Thanksgiving. This puts Sandy's mother's anger in control of Sandy's life. One day Sandy will have to give an account of her life. Jesus will say, "Why didn't you go to school where I told you to?" Sandy might reply, "It would have made my mother angry." Jesus might say, "Why didn't you stand up to the abuse that your husband was dishing out to your children?" She might reply, "It would have made him angry." "Why didn't you say 'no' to your kids' demands not to do their homework?" "It would have made them angry." Jesus' response might go something like this: "I will confront your mother about her temper, your husband about his anger, and your kids about their irresponsibility, but I want to know why you didn't take responsibility for your life." And Sandy can only reply, "It would have made them angry."

If we feel responsible for other people's feelings, we can no longer make decisions based on what is right; we will make decisions based on how others feel about our choices. Jesus said, "Woe to you when all men speak well of you" (Luke 6:26). If we are always trying to keep everyone happy, then we cannot make the choices required to live correctly and freely.

We can't determine how successfully we are living the Christian life by who is unhappy with us. If we feel responsible for other people's displeasure, we are being controlled by others, not God. This is a basic boundary disturbance.

If Jesus had tried to make everyone happy, we would all be lost. If self-centered people are angry at you, it means you are learning to say no to evil. If mean people are displeased with you, it means that you are standing up to abuse. If pharisaical Christians judge you, it means that you are becoming like your Savior. If your parents don't like the decisions that you as an adult feel God has led you to make, it means that you are growing up. "Blessed are you when men hate you, when they exclude you and insult you and reject your name as evil, because of the Son of Man. Rejoice in that day and leap for joy, because great is your reward in heaven. For that is how their fathers treated the prophets" (Luke 6:22–23).

Whenever I speak to a Christian group, I can tell how I'm doing by the various reactions. If the hurting people feel understood *and* if the noncompassionate, critical people hate me, I know I have done my job. If the hurting people hate me, I have missed God's heart and must reevaluate. I have failed to be empathetic and give grace and truth. Whenever people hate us for being compassionate and offering forgiveness and truth, we know we are on the right track. If we take responsibility for their feelings, we have sided with evil. God is against proud, arrogant people who do not have compassion for hurting people.

Jesus said that he did not come to bring peace, but a sword, and that families may be divided when someone follows his ways (Matt. 10:34–36). Division in the family does not only happen when one member converts to Christianity; it goes much deeper than that. Following Christ, in all of his ways, may leave other family members with negative feelings. Here are a few examples.

God says that a man should "leave his father and mother and be united to his wife," but how do some parents feel about their son separating and becoming an adult? If the young man takes responsibility for his parents' empty nest, he can't become an adult and follow God's leading.

God says to speak the truth, but how does an alcoholic feel when his wife stops lying to the boss for him? If his wife takes responsibility for his feelings, she can't obey God.

God says that if a person doesn't work, don't let her or him eat. How does an irresponsible twenty-five-year-old feel when her parents cut her off? If her parents take responsibility for the tough time she will have, they are not allowing her to grow up by suffering the natural consequences of her acts.

God says to give as we purpose in our heart instead of from compulsion. How does a controlling wife feel when her husband decides that next weekend he wants to go deer hunting with his pals? If he feels responsible for his wife's anger at being abandoned, he will stay home out of compulsion and be guilty of the sin of resentment.

God says all people should use their talents. How does a controlling husband feel when his wife takes a position that uses her talents but requires much time away from home? If she feels responsible for his immaturity, she can't develop as God has asked her to.

Many controlling people are stuck in the stage of development where they think that they can control others by getting angry or sad. This tactic often works with people who have no boundaries, and it reinforces the controlling person's immaturity. When we take responsibility for our own disappointments, we are setting clear boundaries. When we take responsibility for others' feelings we are crossing over their boundaries.

Some of you may think that this approach is mean and insensitive. Please hear something loud and clear. We should always *be sensitive to* others' feelings about our choices. But we should never *take responsibility for* how they feel. Taking responsibility for someone else's feeling is actually the most insensitive thing we can do because we are crossing into another's territory. Other people need to take responsibility for their own feelings. If they are mature, they will process their own disappointment and own it. If they are not, they will blame us for their disappointment. But dealing with both their disappointment and their blaming is their responsibility. None of us gets everything we want. Take a look at the example of someone who had no boundaries with his wife.

The Case of Jim

Jim came into therapy because of his inability to get things done at home. He said, "I am irresponsible, and my wife is very displeased with me. I can't seem to follow through on anything."

"What sorts of things don't you follow through on?" I asked.

"Well, Jean wants me to rake the yard, plant a flower garden, fix the patio, remodel the kitchen, take the kids to the movies, make more money, plan a family devotion time. . . ."

The list went on and on. "Did you promise to do all those things?" I asked, when Jim paused to take a breath.

"Yes."

"Do you want to do all those things?" I asked.

"Not really, but I have to," he replied.

"What do you mean, 'You have to?'" I asked further.

"Well, if I don't, Jean will get mad and say that I don't love her."

I was beginning to get the picture. "You mean that you promise to do anything Jean wants? How in the world can you make more money, and at the same time spend all of your time working in and around the house?"

"Well, I can't," Jim said. "I really do intend to do it when I promise. But I can't seem to get around to everything."

"Have you ever thought about what might be reasonable to promise her and what isn't?" I asked.

"What do you mean?"

"Well, it seems that for Jean to be happy, she is going to need three or four husbands. You are only one."

When Jim looked confused, I explained that maybe Jean's unhappiness was her problem. Maybe she is unhappy that she has only one husband who has only limited amounts of time. "If I were you, I would give her a choice," I said. "I would say, "Honey, I love you, and I want to work hard for your happiness. I have ten hours this month to do work around the house. How would you like me to spend them?'"

"She would hit the roof if I said that! She would think that ten hours is not enough."

"That is precisely my point," I told him. "She gets angry because she can't have everything she wants, and you feel responsible for her anger. If you don't change your feeling that you are responsible for her anger, you will never accomplish what you promise, because you will never be able to say no honestly."

I explained to him that, in reality, he was already saying no by his behavior. With his mouth he was saying yes, with his actions he was saying no. The problem wasn't that he was irresponsible; the problem was that he was lying. He was saying yes when he really meant no.

Whenever boundaries are crossed, when one person becomes responsible for another's feelings and happiness, this person is unable to be free from the other person, and as a result, is unable to love them. Guilty compliance is never love; it is slavery.

At the heart of many of the problems for which people seek counseling is a crossover in boundaries. The Fall so warped our sense of responsibility that we are all confused as to who is responsible for what. We try to make others responsible for us, and we take responsibility for them. The Bible sends a clear message that we are to be responsible *to* others, not *for* them. This is an important difference.

If Jim were being responsible *to* his wife, he would sit down with her and say something like, "Honey, let's look at our goals as a couple, as a family, and as individuals, and see how we can help each other meet those goals. Let's look at our time and resources and figure out how we are going to spend them." It would become clear that her wants had few limits and that he had very few wants.

If he were to continue to be responsible to her, he would not procrastinate, but would say instead, "I understand you want all of those things right now, but I can't do all that. The kids and I wouldn't get any of the things we want. I'm sorry you are upset, but I want us all to work together."

If she has any awareness about herself, she will be able to see her self-centeredness and realize that she has been controlling the family with her anger. If she doesn't, she may get angrier, and Jim will need to be very firm about letting her be responsible for her own anger. If she pouts, he needs to learn to say things like, "Jean, I love you, but I don't want to be around when you are pouting. Come into the den when you feel better."

In some ways this is like dealing with a two-year-old. People who control others by their anger or sadness or depression are very immature.

The Case of Peter

Peter had taken an overdose of drugs. At twenty-four, he had dropped out of school and was living at home. Since his parents were "good Christians," his behavior was very upsetting to them. It tarnished their image in the church, so they brought him to therapy.

As Peter and I began to explore why he was suicidally depressed, I discovered that his parents were having serious marital problems. They would get into screaming fights and then wouldn't speak to each other for days. They would bring Peter into the conflict. Peter's father would ask Peter to tell his mother something, and vice versa.

At other times, Peter's parents would both confide in him about the other person, instead of confronting each other directly. Peter's mother told him that she could never stand to be left alone with his father. If Peter left home, they would divorce. If that happened, she said, she would commit suicide, implying it would be "Peter's fault."

Peter wanted to move out of his parents' house and get on with his life, but he was afraid that his moving out would cause his parents' divorce and his mother's suicide. He felt he had no choice.

After months of hard work in therapy, Peter learned that he had another option. He learned that he was not responsible for his parents' feelings toward one another, nor was he responsible for his mother's depression if she got divorced.

I will never forget the day in a family session that Peter gathered up his strength to confront his mother:

"Mom, I have been thinking. I think it's time for me to finish school. I want to be able to get a job."

"But the family needs you here. Your father and I are still . . ."

"No, Mom," he interrupted. "What you and Dad do is up to you. I'm twenty-four, and I'm going to get on with my life."

Suddenly she began to cry.

"Mom, you can turn off the tears, 'cause they aren't going to work anymore. Every time I have ever tried to do something for me, you cry, and I change my mind. I am not going to do that anymore. If you are sad about my leaving home and you and Dad are going to fight, that's your problem."

Peter had learned what his mother had never learned: each of us is responsible for our own feelings. Trying to change the way someone else feels is like losing the ability to steer our car. It is like allowing the car in the next lane to steer us by blowing its horn. We are out of control.

The Path to Problem Solving

If we take responsibility for our feelings, we can use them to solve problems. Remember the woman who took responsibility for her depression when her husband abandoned her. She solved her problems and got her life back together again.

If we take responsibility for our feelings, we can use them to make our relationships better. Our anger is often a signal that someone has sinned against us. If we feel that the person who has sinned against us is responsible for our anger, we are in trouble. We will stay angry until the other person decides to make it better, and that could be a very long time.

However, if we realize that our anger is our problem,

we can take responsibility for it. We can use it to begin to solve the problem. Jesus has told us how: "If your brother sins against you, go and show him his fault, just between the two of you. If he listens to you, you have won your brother over" (Matt. 18:15). Or listen to Moses' command: "Do not hate your brother in your heart. Rebuke your neighbor frankly so you will not share in his guilt" (Lev. 19:17).

In these two examples, the responsibility for dealing with the feelings lies with the one having them. Moses points out that we have two choices: either we reprove the one we are angry at, or this anger will turn into bitterness and hatred. When we go to the one who has angered us and work it out, then the anger can get resolved and the relationship can get better, for "iron has sharpened iron." Each person is better for it. But if we do not deal with our feelings after having been sinned against, they can turn into hatred and continue to fester.

The issue of confrontation can be confusing when people who have *not* been sinned against get angry. I can see Jim's wife "confronting" him with her anger toward him for "all he is not doing." She doesn't realize that by not obeying her wishes, he is not sinning against her, and she really has no right to confront. If she did not have those wishes, she would not be angry. When we are truly sinned against, there is a concrete offense by the other apart from our wishes and feelings.

Jesus makes this clear in the story of the boss who pays the workers exactly what he had agreed to. Some workers were angry because they wanted more (Matt. 20:1–15). Jesus cleared up the boundary confusion over who was responsible for the anger. He told the worker who confronted him that he had done him no wrong and that the worker needed to deal with his envious heart. If the boss had not paid the workers what he had agreed to, he would be sinning against them, and they would have a just grievance.

This whole issue of taking responsibility for our feelings and not each other's is a key to responsible living. If we can be angry and then deal with our anger either by (1) confronting the one who has sinned against us and forgiving, or (2) giving up our own expectations that are causing the anger, then we will clearly communicate with others, and we will give up trying to control their lives.

Attitudes

When we look further at crossed boundaries, we see that we often do not own our own attitudes; instead, we take responsibility for the attitudes of others.

People often complain how this person or that person is "putting expectations" on them, as if an expectation were something you could Velcro to someone's brain. While we do internalize our parents' expectations, becoming an adult involves separating from our parents, figuring out how our attitudes and expectations are different from our parents'. When we begin to take responsibility for our own attitudes, we can be free from the expectations others put on us.

Whenever we feel "victimized" by another's expectations, we need to find the attitude that's allowing us to feel pressured by that expectation. In Jim's case, his wife's expectations of what he "should" do were her problem, not his. His problem was his attitude of "I should do what she wants." If his attitude were something like "I should take into consideration what she wants and then choose what I want to give," Jim would be more straightforward with Jean, and for the first time, she could take responsibility for her life. However, as long as he continued to enable her to keep her attitudes by his taking responsibility for them, they stayed stuck.

Jim did change his attitudes, though, and stopped enabling hers. Gradually, Jean began to realize that her attitudes toward what a husband should be were not in accord with reality. She was forced to either change them or be frustrated. This is precisely what reality does for us. It gets us in touch with our confused ways of looking at the world and forces us to deal with them. If someone is protecting us from our attitudes by taking responsibility for them, we never grow. This is the essence of crossed boundaries: owning what is not ours and not owning what is ours.

Whenever we feel pressured by someone to do something, it is our problem and not the problem of the one who is putting the pressure on. In reality, our "feeling pressured" is our tendency to agree with the pressurer's attitude instead of setting forth our own. We must get in touch with how we are getting hooked into saying yes and not put the blame on the other person.

The Case of Donna

Donna was one of the angriest women I have ever seen. She was angry at her family's excessive expectations of her. Her mother expected her to call her every week and to accompany her on shopping trips. Her father expected her to come home for Sunday dinner. Her sisters expected her to buy birthday and Christmas presents for all their children. Her brothers expected her to babysit whenever they didn't plan far enough ahead to book their regular babysitter.

I agreed with Donna that her family's expectations were extreme. But when I suggested that her family was not going to change and that she had to free herself from their expectations by changing her attitude, she got angry at me. She felt that if I did not see her as a victim, I didn't care. I assured her that while she had indeed been victimized growing up, she had to stop allowing herself to be victimized by freeing herself both from her family's expectations and from her expectations of them.

"I don't have any expectations of them," she replied. "They are the ones with the 'shoulds.'"

"On the contrary," I said, "you're just like them. They say that you *should* come over for dinner every Sunday, and you say that they *should* stop pressuring you to come." In other words, her expectation was that they should not have any expectations.

Over the course of many sessions I tried to help her to see that until she took responsibility for her own attitude that her family "should" change, she would never be free. Since I would not agree with her that her family needed to change in order for her to get well (which was out of her control), we hit a stalemate.

She could feel I was on her side if I would agree with her that her misery was their fault and not hers. I *could* agree with her that they had deeply injured her and were the *source* of much of her pain, but they were not the ones who were continuing it in the present. She was now an adult who had control over what she did and what she allowed others to do to her. But, because she felt that I was "on their side," she quit.

When I saw her three years later, she was still stuck, still blaming her family for their attitudes toward and expectations of her.

The Case of Robert

Robert came into therapy because he couldn't keep a job. Enormously talented and intelligent, he had been raised by a doting mother and a harsh, critical father.

Every task his father would require of him, he found too difficult to complete. His mother, wishing to protect him, would do the work for him.

She carried her doting even further, requiring very little of him as he was growing up. Over the years she trained him to think that the world would take care of him because he was "special." She told him that certain jobs were for less gifted people than he; he was entitled to much more. Robert adopted his mother's attitude toward him: "I am special and therefore entitled to special treatment. The world owes me considerations that others don't get."

When he entered the business world, he found that his boss did not share his attitude. The boss's attitude was, "I expect work from someone I pay!" You can guess what Robert's track record was when those attitudes clashed.

The situation was further complicated by Robert's wife. She reinforced his thinking, that is, until the creditors started knocking at the door.

In therapy, Robert needed to realize that it was *his* attitudes that were causing his problems, and not the attitudes of the "jerks" at work. He had to take responsibility for his mistaken views of work and the world. In addition, his wife had to learn that she was enabling him to keep those views.

Slowly, he began to change how he saw things. As a result, he got along with people better and was actually able to keep a job. If he had not first taken responsibility for his attitudes, he could never have changed. He would have continued to jump from job to job. As Jesus says, "First take the plank out of your own eye, and then you will see clearly to remove the speck from your brother's eye" (Matt. 7:5). Robert couldn't see others clearly because he was blaming them for the problems his own attitudes were causing. By taking the log out, he could see them clearly.

Behaviors

Our sense of being able to own our own behavior is critical for having a sense of power and a sense of control over our lives. The law of sowing and reaping is the most trustworthy law of behavior. We can trust it to bring us satisfaction or misery.

However, the law of sowing and reaping is like the law of gravity: it can be suspended. In other words, a buffer can protect us from certain consequences. If I drop a glass, the law of gravity will pull it to the floor and break it. If I tie a rope around the glass and suspend it from the ceiling, I have taken away the consequences of gravity.

The law of sowing and reaping can also be suspended by someone taking responsibility for another's behavior. The law says that if people don't work, they don't eat. But this law can be suspended by someone giving the people a handout. These people have not sowed anything yet they are reaping food. They have lost out on the security of knowing that their actions have consequences. They begin to feel utterly powerless and dependent on the "enabler," or the person covering for them.

An alcoholic home is a classic example of this. The husband drinks and behaves in a way that would have natural consequences, but the enabler, usually the wife, protects him from the consequences of his drinking. She calls in sick for him. She tells the neighbors that their daughter fell playing, instead of that her husband pushed her down while in a drunken stupor. As a result, reality does not force him to change and to grow up. Alcoholism is an irresponsible lifestyle; without someone to act as a buffer, it cannot go on.

Whenever anyone is not allowed to "own" their own behavior, or suffer its consequences, boundaries are being crossed. Someone else must come in and take up the slack to prevent the irresponsible person from suffering. To shield people from the consequences of their behavior is unbiblical. God gave us gravity so that we could learn to walk. He gave us wages so that we could learn to work. If limits and consequences are not placed on our behavior, we are out of control.

Some children are taught that they can do pretty much whatever they please, and someone will rescue them if they get into trouble. They think this will continue in adult life, and they can usually find someone to carry on the tradition, but at the expense of that person and everyone else. This is the classic enabling syndrome: you do the behavior, and I'll pay the price.

The Case of Harold

Harold came to see me to "straighten out" his thirty-five-year-old daughter, Stacey. He told me that Stacey, who refused to come with him for this appointment, was not working and was taking massive amounts of drugs.

"What does she do with her time?" I asked.

"Well, she spends most of it at the club, playing tennis," he said, with irritation. "I can't understand how someone as smart as she is would waste time like that."

"How can she afford it?" I asked. "That's an expensive place. If she doesn't work and spends money on drugs, she must have a supply of money somewhere."

"She is living off a trust fund I set up for her. She has plenty of money. Money's not the problem. It's her wasteful life that bothers me."

"I think money is at least part of the problem."

"How's that?"

"You're a smart man, Harold," I said. "What would your clients do if you didn't deliver?"

"They would go to another firm," he said. "I would be out of business. But what does that have to do with Stacey?"

"Stacey's getting paid pretty well for 'not delivering,'"
I said. "In fact, I wouldn't mind having her job. You're
allowing her to waste her life away. There's no chance for
her until you cut her off."

As we continued to talk, I learned that Harold had
always had a special fondness for his daughter, who was
the daughter of his first wife who had died. He had stayed
very close to Stacey as a way of staying close to his first
wife. He could never bring himself to let her suffer the
consequences of her actions, for fear that she would leave
him. He had been "bailing her out" since college. She
would overspend her budget and wreck her car, only to
get a check in the mail to cover the expenses or to buy a
new car. Never having learned the law of cause and
effect, she was out of control.

"What would she do if I didn't give her money?"
Harold asked. "I would be afraid she'd starve."

"That would be up to her," I replied. "If she decided to
use her very expensive education, she could do quite
well. She would also have to go into drug treatment and
get her act together. But, the way it's set up now, she
doesn't have to do any of those things. She has the best
of both worlds. She can be lazy and have lots of money.
Exactly the deal I've always wanted, haven't you?"

Harold smiled. He saw how ridiculous the whole situation was. He was a very bright man who had made a fortune requiring responsible behavior out of himself and
others. But his love for his daughter and his grief for his
first wife caused him to "cross" his daughter's boundaries.
When he started "owning" her behavior, he became blind
to the truth. The crossed boundaries worked like this:
She loafs, he pays. She snorts, he pays. She sleeps, he
pays. He did not work this way in any other area of life,
yet in the relationship most important to him, he was
enabling irresponsible behavior, much to his daughter's

detriment. Proverbs says that "he who spares the rod hates his son, but he who loves him is careful to discipline him" (13:24). If she had had the discipline of consequences earlier, she probably would not be in the mess she was in. Because he was not dealing with this grief within his boundaries, he crossed her boundaries.

Many times someone's love for another makes it difficult to allow that person to suffer the consequences of her or his behavior. This is most often true in abusive marriages. The abuser should always suffer consequences. The spouse should say, "I will not allow this behavior, and until you are able to control it, I will be staying at my mother's house." But, because people have not set firm boundaries, they often enable the abuser to continue to cross those boundaries for years, with no consequences, and they pay the price. The spouse pays for the behavior with depression, or the children with fear and isolation. The abuser never has to take responsibility for his or her behavior because someone else does. The spouse must refuse to participate in such evil if there will be hope for change.

Thoughts

As with feelings and attitudes, we must own our own thoughts. Our thoughts have much bearing on our emotional growth. Not all emotional disturbance comes from thinking, but it does play a vital part. (In reality, our emotions affect our thinking more than the other way around because feeling is primary, and thinking secondary. But this is not a book on theories of psychology. Let's just say that emotions and thoughts affect each other, and both must be owned.)

Our thinking affects how we respond to people and situations. In the section on bonding, we noticed that we can have thoughts that make us move away from relationship. We may think, *They would never like me anyway, so I won't call.* This is an example of thinking oneself into isolation. We must own all thinking that prevents interpersonal relating. Condemning thoughts about others always hurt us. We must own our critical thinking and confess it, allowing God to change the way we think.

At the same time, we can't be responsible for the thoughts of others. If someone is thinking good or bad about us, we must accept it. We can try to affect it, but we can't control it. We must give people the freedom to think what they will. Ask Jesus. People had some pretty crazy notions about him, which he allowed.

When we choose to follow God, some will think we are wrong. We should always listen to what people are saying and evaluate it. But, if we are convinced in our heart that we are doing what is right, we must allow them the freedom to think whatever they want.

When Harold cut his daughter off from her trust fund, she thought he was mean. When the alcoholic's wife refused to tolerate his drunken behavior, he thought she was a traitor. When the father grounded his teenage daughter, she thought he was an old fuddy-duddy. Whenever we do anything, people will have an opinion about it. We must allow them to own their opinions and not try to cross their boundaries to change them.

When Jim began to set boundaries on how much time he would spend doing chores, his wife, Jean, thought he was selfish because he would no longer try to do everything she wanted. She called him an immature adolescent, running from responsibility. She didn't realize that, for the first time, he was taking responsibility for what he could and couldn't do. He had to allow her to think what she would and not try to change her thoughts, either by talking her out of them, or by changing his behavior. He had to accept it.

If we are afraid of people's condemnation, we are in serious trouble. Many people do not take responsibility for their own lives, and they will think we are bad for not taking care of them. We must allow them to think negatively of us and to take responsibility for their own opinions. Remember what the Jews thought of both John and Jesus. "John came neither eating nor drinking, and they say, 'He has a demon.' The Son of Man came eating and drinking, and they say, 'Here is a glutton and a drunkard, a friend of tax collectors and "sinners" ' "(Matt. 11:18–19). Some people will be critical no matter what we do.

We must not worry about what other people say about us, but we should pay close attention to what we think about ourselves. Self-condemning thoughts are clearly unbiblical. "There is now no condemnation for those who are in Christ Jesus" (Rom. 8:1). We have to take dominion over and responsibility for such thoughts. They have no rightful place on our property.

All distortions, prejudices, and generalizations find no home on our property. Some people teach "the precepts of men" as though they were doctrine (Matt. 15:9 NASB). These teachings bind people's souls. If people have a real need, such as love, freedom, responsibility, and their theology does not allow for it, the theology must be changed. Boundaries get crossed in thinking when people try to put their interpretations onto others, putting them in prison. As Jesus said, "They tie up heavy loads and put them on men's shoulders" (Matt. 23:4). This sort of boundary crossing can wreck someone's spiritual and emotional life. We will discuss this more in the section on taking charge of your life.

Abilities

Earlier we examined accepting and owning our abilities and gave some examples of crossed boundaries. Basically they come in two forms: one, trying to own what is someone else's property; the other, allowing someone else to own what is ours. We should never compare ourselves to others, for God made each of us unique. "We have different gifts, according to the grace given us" (Rom. 12:6).

We must stay within our own boundaries, realizing our own abilities. People who cross boundaries in this area are in danger of feeling either false pride or false guilt. An eye may look at a hand and say, "I can see so much better than that hand! Aren't I great!" or "I can't pick up anything like that hand can! I'm so stupid." Both appraisals are inaccurate.

In addition, we must not allow someone else to cross our boundaries and try to tell us what our abilities are. Parents are often guilty of this kind of boundary crossing. Parents, for example, may want their child to be an intellectual when he is an athlete, or an athlete when he is an intellectual. Enormous pain results from our not being able to be our true self with the ones we love most. If loved ones cannot appreciate and value our real talents, we often conform to their expectations and deny our real abilities.

Choices

Probably no area of crossed boundaries is as significant as this one. The essence of boundaries is taking responsibility, and the hub of responsibility is choice. God has given every human the ability to choose. When choice is taken away, something less than human remains, something less than the "likeness of God."

Boundaries are crossed here whenever we make some-one else's choices for them, or whenever we think they are responsible for making our choices for us.

Making Others' Choices for Them

Nothing strikes at the heart of God quite like our making others' choices for them. The Old Testament is full of situations in which God's people had their freedom stolen. His cry was always, "Let my people go" (Ex. 5:1) or "Is not this the kind of fasting I have chosen: to loose the chains of injustice and untie the cords of the yoke, to set the oppressed free and break every yoke?" (Isa. 58:6). God wants his people to be free to make choices to love him as they will. He is against people who bind them and sin that binds them. He has always been a releaser of the captive.

Whenever we try to "bind" others by taking away their choices, we have reduced them to slavery. We arrogantly say, "My will is the only one that counts here" and we try to force them, either actively or passively, to do what we want them to do. This is a terrible evil.

Guilt Messages

One of the most common ways of taking away peo-ple's choices is through guilt messages. Whenever peo-ple say, "How could you do this to me?" they are trying to make another person feel guilty for a choice they have made. In actuality, the person has not done any-thing to them. The person has simply exercised her free-dom of choice.

Sandy was a good example of this. Suppose she chooses to spend Thanksgiving with her friends. If her mother says, "How can you leave me all alone on Thanksgiving?" she is using guilt to bind Sandy's choices. This is a very good way of producing an indecisive person. If one's choice muscle is bound with vines of guilt, it doesn't work very well.

Burt was the twenty-five-year-old son of Christian parents. From childhood, his parents made most of his spiritual choices for him. He wasn't allowed to question, doubt, or make up his own mind about God. They told him when to go to Sunday school, youth group, and catechism. They told him when to make profession of his faith and when to take Communion. They made other choices for him also, and criticized the ones he made: the way he dressed, the girls he dated, and the friends he brought home.

When Burt left home, he went wild. He started to drink and party to the point of feeling like he was gaining more "control" over his life by "losing control." This is exactly what Paul means when he says the law increases sin.

But his parents did not understand. They were unable to take the stance of the prodigal son's father who said, in effect, "I love you and I disagree with your values; but they are your free choice, and I will set you free to pursue your choices. But, remember this, I love you very much and you are always free to come back. I will never say, 'I told you so.' I will only welcome you and rejoice that you have chosen what is good."

We had a family meeting with Burt's brothers and sisters, parents, and grandparents. I told them that Burt was an adult, and he could make whatever choices he wanted. God had allowed him the freedom to choose evil, and they must also. It was the only way that he would ever be able to freely choose God's ways.

They did not hear what I said. They continued to try to get him to be like them and make him feel guilty when he was not. The cycle continued. He kept moving away from their control to make his own choices. My hunch is that one day he will gain enough distance to experience what the prodigal did. He will learn that the pigsty is not a nice place to sleep, and he will choose God's way. But he probably will not do that until his choice can be his own.

Manipulation

Manipulation is another common way of trying to take away people's power of choice. Look at Jim. Whenever he chose to spend some time not doing work for his wife, she would withdraw love from him. She was trying to use love to manipulate Jim to do what she wanted him to do. She was trying to bind his choices. Intimacy does not thrive where someone is not free to choose separateness without guilt.

Look at Peter's dilemma. If he chose to be an adult and leave home, his mother threatened to commit suicide. That is hardly giving Peter a choice. She had crossed his boundaries in trying to control his choices through manipulation. He had nowhere to go and feel free and loving at the same time.

There are countless other ways that people try to make other people's choices for them. Think about when we say no to someone's request and they give us the silent treatment. We have a choice, but we become unloved. We become "bad."

Or think about the times we have heard, "If you love me, you will do this or that." Jesus is the only one that can say that, and he never uses it as a power move. He uses it descriptively: "If you love me, you will obey what I command" (John 14:15). Obedience naturally follows love. Jesus is not manipulating us; he is just stating a fact.

However, when people say, "If you love me, you will . . ." they are most often crossing boundaries to take away someone's free choice of how they will love. To say "If you love me, you will not go bowling," is an attempt to say, "If you love me, you will do anything I want and not have choices of your own unless I like them." Those sorts of statements should always be confronted with a clearing up of boundaries: "That is not true. I love you, *and* I'll choose how I'll spend this evening. You can't decide whether or not I love you. That's my choice."

This dynamic may be behind Jesus' statement: "Do not put the Lord your God to the test" (Luke 4:12). When someone says, for example, "If God really loved me, he would send me a husband," we are denying God's freedom to be his own person and to love us the way that he wants to love us. To those kinds of challenges, he will reply: "I love you, but I won't send you a husband right now." He can't be manipulated. We are free to make requests of him, but some he will choose to give us, and some he will not. This is a real relationship.

This doesn't mean that we cannot be angry about his choices. It does mean that we must realize that our anger is our problem and not his. Think of the difference it would make to Sandy if her mother said, "I don't like it that you aren't coming home for Thanksgiving. I'm angry about that, not because you are bad, but because I am not getting what I want. I don't want to deny the fact that I am angry, but I don't want to blame it on you either."

This owning of responsibility is the essence of allowing someone to be free to make their own choices. It says, in effect, "I do not want you to go bowling tonight. I get sad and angry at your leaving me, but it really is your choice to make and I don't blame you for it. My feelings are my problem." This allows each person to empathize with the losses that choices bring, and at the same time have their choices. This is how a good relationship works: "Oh, I'm sorry you are not coming for dinner. I will miss you," instead of, "That figures. You always do whatever you want anyway!"

Invariably, people who cross boundaries and try to take away others' choices call those other people "selfish" when they try to take back their power of choice. For instance, Jim's wife, Jean, would say that he was selfish for saying no to doing the yardwork she requested. She doesn't see how selfish it is for her to determine what Jim must do! She called him selfish for doing something for himself, yet she wanted to have control of his life as well as hers. She wanted his life to revolve around hers. This is the true selfishness: self-centeredness.

The Bible never says that doing things for ourselves is bad; it assumes that we need to do some things for ourselves. However, it does speak harshly against making ourselves the center of the universe, living only for ourselves. This self-centeredness is evil. We are to look out for others' interests as well as our own (Phil. 2:4). Sandy's mother, Jim's wife, and the bowler's spouse were well aware of their own interests. There is nothing wrong with that. The evil comes when they don't look out for the interests of the other. This is true selfishness—where no one's wishes matter except our own.

Binding someone's choices by guilt or manipulation is not love; it is slavery. Remember, whenever you tie a chain around another person's ankle, it will invariably end up around your neck.

Making Others Responsible for Our Choices

The second way we cross boundaries is when we make others responsible for our choices.

If Sandy, for example, allowed herself to be manipulated by her mother and went home for the holiday, she would be making a choice. Granted, not one freely given, but a choice nonetheless. She would be giving her time to her mother out of her own free will. Sandy might, however, be tempted to tell her mother, "You made me come." Her mother did act manipulatively, but we can never be manipulated without our permission. Going home for the holidays is Sandy's choice; if she does not like it, that's her problem, not her mother's.

This is invariably the fruit of passive-aggressive people. These people resist demands by indirect tactics. They will not take responsibility for their own choices; instead, they turn around and blame someone else for making them do it. Or they will agree to do things that they don't really want to do, and then gripe about the person behind her back. "I get sick and tired of everything she makes me do!" The reply should be, "Then why don't you please tell her when you don't want to do it?" Some people are so hurt by passive-aggressive "givers" that they are afraid to make requests of anyone for fear of being resented. It becomes very difficult for some to receive after having been given to by people who really resented their giving.

As adults, we can never blame anyone for what we choose to do. If others try to make us feel guilty for a choice we make, we must choose our own attitudes about that. We must realize that we choose the attitudes that make us feel guilty. If someone tries to manipulate me, and I know that manipulation is evil, then I will not feel guilty for saying no. Instead, I will think, My, *aren't they being controlling?* But, if I believe that I should keep them happy, I'll think, *I should do what they want, and I'm guilty if I don't.* The point is, I can choose whether or not I will continue in the attitudes that make me feel guilty. Or I can choose to develop new attitudes that will not allow for guilt manipulation.

If we do not take responsibility for our choices, controlling people can have a field day with us. They can set our course for a day, an evening, a weekend, or even a lifetime. Our giving and our course should be determined by us and God, as we work out our salvation with him. We need to let others have their choices, and we need to take responsibility for ours.

Desires

Basically, desires are like feelings and any other element of what lies within our boundaries. We must own ours, and ours only. They are our responsibility and not someone else's.

Jim's wife, Jean, had a desire for a nice yard. This was her desire, not his; therefore, she is responsible for it. She can certainly ask Jim for help, and he may give it to her. But she is still responsible for obtaining it. If he doesn't give it, and she still wants it, she must take responsibility for getting it. If she doesn't get it, that's her problem also.

If we don't see our desires as our responsibility, we blame others for our deprivation. Remember the woman who was abandoned by her husband and took responsibility for her wants. She got an education and achieved her goals. If she did not see those as her responsibility, she would be blaming life for cheating her. Victims declare, "The world is responsible for me," and never do anything to better their quality of life.

Paul writes, "Each one should carry his own load" (Gal. 6:5). A few verses earlier, he says, "Carry each other's burdens, and in this way you will fulfill the law of Christ" (6:2). Here is where individual and corporate responsibility come together. Both are always present in the Bible. In the Old Testament, people were commanded to leave food for the poor, but the poor were required to pick it up.

Just as we must own our own desires, we must not own other's desires. Jim must not own his wife's desire. He must realize that an immaculate yard is her wish, not his. He can then choose to grant her request, or not, but he is not responsible for it.

He will be able to choose what he wants to give and what he does not want to give if he understands that she is responsible for her wants. He can decide whether doing yardwork is one way that he wants to show love for her. Then he doesn't feel controlled into it and resist it.

Owning our desires breeds responsibility and love. We can lovingly give others their requests, for we know that we don't have to in order for them to love us. We can be motivated to get what we want if we do not expect the world to drop it on our plate. Then we are not bitter for what we do not have; we are curious about how we can achieve it.

It refocuses our attention away from obligation and guilt and on love and sharing. If we do not believe we have to run from obligation, for example, we can approach others and find needs that we want to meet. As long as we have a choice, we are more apt to give. Realizing the freedom God gives us motivates us to give out of freedom and gratitude.

Limits

Crossed boundaries work the same way with limits. We must own our own, and not others'. We decide what limits we will set on ourselves, and let others be responsible for the limits they set on themselves. If we have limitations of time, money, or energy, we must set those. If we extend them too far, it is our fault. At the same time we cannot decide where someone else's limits are.

Setting Limits on Evil Behavior

In the alcoholic home, if a wife chooses not to limit her drinking, this is her responsibility. However, other family members can set limits on how they will be affected by it. If an alcoholic continues to drink, the husband can only limit himself, not her. He can say, "I will limit my exposure to your behavior. If you continue to drink, the children and I will move out until you get sober." He cannot stop her from drinking, but he can stop himself from being affected by it.

It is the same way for abuse. We cannot stop someone from being abusive; but we can stop exposing ourselves or our kids to the abuse. We can call the police, and they will limit our exposure. We can call the church elders, and they will come over when the person gets abusive. We can leave and go to a friend's house or a shelter for battered women. When we begin to draw our own line against evil behavior instead of hoping that someone else will, things can begin to change.

If we can't set limits ourselves, we need to enlist the aid of others. This is still taking responsibility. If we call the police and ask them to help limit our exposure, we are taking responsibility. If we call a friend every time we feel out of control in some area and ask him or her to pray or counsel with us, we are taking responsibility for our own lack of limits. This tactic has worked for people with compulsive behaviors for years. They find themselves without limits, and so they take responsibility for getting help in setting them.

Our limits are our fence around our property line. They define for us what we will allow and what we will not allow into our yard. The fence around our yard has an important function: it keeps good things in and bad things out.

We all must be longsuffering and forgiving in relationships, but, at some a point, longsuffering enables evil behavior to continue, and limits must be set. Every one of us has different limits in different areas, and we must take responsibility for those individually. Here are some acceptable limits to set:

"I will no longer allow myself to be with you when you are drunk. If you choose to drink, I will leave until you stop."

"I will no longer allow you to abuse the children. If you hit them again, we will move out."

"I will no longer be talked to that way. I will go into the other room until you can stop yelling at me and have a mutual conversation."

"I will no longer bail you out of financial difficulty. If you choose to overspend again, you will pay the consequences."

"I will not lend you my ladder again. Every time you have used it, something is broken. Please buy your own."

These examples illustrate ways of establishing one's limits on what one will allow and what one will not. Establishing limits is essential in every relationship and is the basis for mutual respect and love. This does not mean that we will not forgive, or not continue to love and work on conflict. It does mean that we will require responsible behavior on the other's part, for only then can the conflict be worked through.

I am not saying that we require perfection. We should overlook multitudes of things, as the Scripture affirms in many places (1 Peter 4:8). But, limits must be set on dangerous, repetitive patterns of evil. Not liking some trait or habit of a friend or spouse is one thing. But, some things are very destructive, and to allow them to go on does not help the person or the love between us. Evil behavior must be limited.

This is a consistent theme throughout the Bible. We are commanded to set limits on what we will tolerate:

"If your brother sins against you, go and show him his fault, just between the two of you. If he listens to you, you have won your brother over. But if he will not listen, take one or two others along, so that 'every matter may be established by the testimony of two or three witnesses.' If he refuses to listen to them, tell it to the church; and if he refuses to listen even to the church, treat him as you would a pagan or a tax collector. I tell you the truth, whatever you bind on earth will be bound in heaven, and whatever you loose on earth will be loosed in heaven." (Matt. 18:15–18)

In this passage, Jesus tells us to limit evil. We "bind" evil by not allowing it to dominate our homes and relationships. If we are dealing with responsible people, we will "win them." But sometimes we need to set stronger boundaries to bind the evil, especially in dealing with abuse. Allowed to continue, abuse has long-term effects on the family. Many hurting adults have expressed the wish that one of their parents would have put some limits on the abusive parent in the home. Their lives would have been much different. Instead, they watched the abusive behavior dominate for years and years. Unbridled evil not only does not subside on its own, it grows.

Setting Limits on Ourselves

In the same way that we must set limits on what we allow others to do to us, we must set limits on ourselves as well so that we can live responsibly. We must limit our body, feelings, attitudes, behaviors, thoughts, abilities, choices, and desires appropriately.

Because some people have overly strict limits on these things, they never find their true capacities. Others have very few limits, and overextend themselves. Maturity is the process of properly realizing what our real limits are. For example, some people never admit that they are angry, missing out on the message their anger is trying to convey. Others are angry all the time, never finding out what drives it.

We should not limit our desires to the point of misery (Col. 2:20–23). Our limits need to be broad enough to enjoy God's blessings. But if there are no limits, our desires take over life and reality.

Fences, besides keeping good in and bad out, enable the exchange of good and bad. If I owned a farm, I would have a gate in the fence that allowed the delivery truck to bring groceries and supplies in and the garbage truck to take the trash out. On the one hand, flexible spiritual boundaries, or fences with gates, let good things in; they allow others to come into our space and hearts for the sake of love. On the other hand, these kinds of boundaries let bad things out; they allow us to confess our sins and find forgiveness. Spiritual gates permit an exchange of good and bad within the soul.

Leviticus 19:17 speaks of this exchange when it says, "Do not hate your brother in your heart. Rebuke your neighbor frankly so you will not share in his guilt." When we reprove those we love, we are "taking the trash out," not letting it turn into hatred or bitterness.

In the same way, the gate allows us to take some of the good we have on our farm and give it to others. We can load up our wagon and take some milk and vegetables to our neighbor. The gate allows us to open up to the world and share what we have in a loving way. Many people are so closed off with locked gates that there is no way for love to be given or received. They have "love concealed."

* * *

Our limits tell us much about where we end and some-one else begins. With limits, we can know what we want versus what someone else wants, and who is responsible for what. The same is true with the other attributes. We can figure out what we will allow on our property and what we will not, so that evil will not take over our house. In addition, we can bring good in and out, as well as take out the trash in confession. Realizing our spiritual and emotional property line is the key to responsibility, freedom, and love.

Chapter

9

When We Fail to Develop Boundaries

NUMEROUS PROBLEMS ARISE WHEN WE FAIL to set good boundaries and maintain them. If we do not realize what we are responsible for and what we are *not* responsible for, we can suffer from the following symptoms. Symptoms, you recall, point to the existence of an underlying problem. No one has ever come in my office and said, "Dr. Cloud, I have trouble setting boundaries, and I need your help in learning how to set good boundaries." But people do seek help for the following symptoms, when their real problem is often confusion about where and how to set boundaries.

Symptoms of Failure to Set Boundaries

Depression

Many people experience depression because they do not set good boundaries. The lack of boundary setting sets them up for being mistreated, and much pain follows.

185

Others are depressed because they turn inward their anger at people who are controlling them. If they aren't in touch with their choices, they think they have no choices, that other people have control over their choices. They become resentful, perhaps even bitter.

Panic

Panic disorders—attacks of sudden, overpowering fright—most often fall in this category. Many people panic because they think they have no control over what happens to them. They think they must do whatever anyone wants them to do, and they feel out of control. Having others in control of one's life and choices can be very scary. It's a prescription for panic disorder.

Resentment

Many people resent things they are doing because they are doing them "reluctantly or under compulsion" (2 Cor. 9:7). Too often, they comply with others' wishes and do what they really don't want to do, then resent it later. Martyrs—people who assume an attitude of self-sacrifice or suffering in order to arouse feelings of pity or guilt in others—often display this symptom. Their giving is not really giving because it has strings attached.

Passive-Aggressive Behavior

Passive-aggressive behavior is characterized by indirect resistance to demands for adequate performance in social or work settings. For example, if a woman is pressured to serve on the school's cultural arts committee, she may say yes and then resist passively by forgetting appointments, procrastinating on projects, or misplacing important materials. She did not have the courage to set proper boundaries and just say no to the request to be on the committee.

When we do not set limits and let our "yes be yes and our no, no," we may set those limits passively. Many who struggle with uncompleted promises to others are really being passive-aggressive. They express the aggression of saying no in a passive way.

Codependency

Codependency is a learned pattern of attitudes, feelings, and behaviors in which people seriously neglect their own health and well-being for the wishes of others. Codependent people always put the other person first, often to their own detriment. They do not see who is responsible for what and often enable evil. These people are always confused about boundaries. In taking responsibility "for" others, they fail to act responsibly "to" them.

Identity Confusion

Identity comes from owning who we are and realizing all of our attributes. People who are not taking responsibility for what falls within their boundaries, and being separate from others, are unable to tell what is them and what is someone else. We need to know who we are apart from others.

Difficulties with Being Alone

Some people have not established good enough boundaries so that they are able to have a self apart from others. They fear being alone, for they will not be with anyone; there is no one inside. They do not have the internal structure to contain the love they have for and from others. They always have to be with someone to survive.

These people have not failed to bond, but they have failed to develop an internal structure to hold the bonding inside. It is like pouring water into a cup with no bottom. The more love they get, the more they need. They have no ability to hold on to it. They need limits—boundaries—to help them form some internal structure.

Masochism

Masochists are people who get pleasure from suffering physical or psychological pain inflicted by others or by themselves. Masochists are unable to set limits on others' abusive behavior. They get a perverse pleasure out of being subjected to pain or humiliation. The pain causes more and more need, which makes it harder to set limits on the other person. They need someone so much, they can't limit them. Masochists need to establish a support network to learn to set limits on abuse.

Victim Mentality

People who suffer from a victim mentality see themselves as victims of circumstances and other people. They never take responsibility for themselves. They use words like, "I had to" and "I had no choice." Everything happens to them. They deny any sort of responsibility, especially in the areas of choices. They think they have no choices.

Blaming

Blaming is similar to victim thinking; blamers always direct responsibility for pain and change toward someone else. No doubt others cause us pain, but when we get into the "blame game," we make others responsible for dealing with our pain, and that keeps us stuck. People who stay in the blame stage never change, for they take no responsibility for their own attitudes, feelings, or behaviors.

Overresponsibility and Guilt

People who do not have clear boundaries feel responsible for things that they should not feel responsible for, like others' feelings, disappointments, and actions. They feel guilty for not being what others want them to be and for not doing what others want them to do. They feel like they are bad for not carrying through on "their" responsibility: to make others happy.

Underresponsibility

People who feel overresponsible for others often neglect their own backyard. They do not carry their own load (Gal. 6:5), for they are too busy carrying the load of others. In this typical codependent behavior, people feel so responsible for others that they do not deal with their own pain and life.

Feelings of Obligation

Paul mentions in 2 Corinthians 9:7 that people have these feelings when they are not choosing what they will give and what they will not give. They feel compelled to give to others; they are not free and in control of themselves.

Feelings of Being Let Down

Since many are so good at taking care of others, they feel that others are obligated to take care of them. They feel let down when this doesn't happen. They perceive others to be unloving and uncaring if they aren't taking responsibility for them. They feel like they are the "givers" and others are "takers."

Isolation

People who experience boundary confusion, distorted thinking, and a lack of freedom often avoid relationship in order to feel a sense of boundaries. For them, getting close means losing their boundaries and ownership of themselves. It is so frightening and potentially conflictual that they eliminate relationship as an option and choose a world of isolation. Being alone means they won't be invaded or controlled.

Extreme Dependency

People who have never gotten a feeling of owning their own lives believe they can't function responsibly on their own. They will often depend upon someone else to negotiate the world for them, and they tend to fuse their identity with this negotiator. They are very fearful of separateness.

Disorganization and Lack of Direction

People who do not have a clear definition of themselves often lack direction and purpose. They cannot choose their own goals, likes, and dislikes. They get easily sidetracked by whatever anyone says to them, so they are scattered.

Substance Abuse and Eating Disorders

Many people who feel out of control of their lives turn to food, drugs, or alcohol to either dull their pain or to be able to take some control over something. This is especially true with people suffering from anorexia or bulimia. Boundaries are almost always an important issue in these disorders.

More often than not, boundaries are a strong issue in the resolution of addictions. Usually, when boundary conflicts are cleared up, when people with food or substance addictions begin to have a clearer sense of their own person, they begin to exercise self-control. Bulimics especially need to resolve issues of separateness. The ambivalence expressed in food is resolved as the ambivalence of relationship is cleared up through boundary definition. They no longer express the "I want it, I don't want it" feeling by binging and purging.

Procrastination

Procrastination, or putting off unpleasant tasks until some future time, often results from a lack of clear boundaries. Procrastinators do not feel like they are really choosing; their no is not a real no. They say yes when they mean no; then they express their no through not following through. It is a distorted sense of control.

This is the dynamic that was operating in the parable of the two sons (Matt. 21:28–31). The procrastinating son was not honest about his no. Recall that he said yes to working in his father's vineyard, and then he never went. The other son first said no to his father, then changed his mind and went to work. This son could be honest about his no, so he could be honest about his yes also.

Impulsivity

Impulsive people invariably have a boundary problem. They lack internal structure. Whatever they think, they do; they have a limited ability to say no to themselves. As they clear up their boundaries and learn enough self-control to say no, they begin to gain control of their impulses.

Generalized Anxiety

Some people struggle with a vague tension and anxiety that is sometimes related to lack of boundaries. Their internal lack of structure makes them unable to process and contain all the feelings they have, as well as to handle all the external demands. While these people often can't point toward one particular conflict or problem, they still feel anxious. Instead of working on a particular "issue," these people sometimes need to firm up their sense of who they are by creating stronger boundaries. This gives them a greater sense of self-control, a greater ability to process feelings, and, as a result, less anxiety.

Obsessive-Compulsive Behavior

Obsessive people are preoccupied with often unreasonable ideas or feelings; compulsive people have irresistible impulses to perform irrational acts. Obsessive-compulsive people struggle with both persistent preoccupations and irresistible impulses. For example, a man who feels compelled to wash his hands every hour would be displaying obsessive-compulsive behavior. This man is obsessed with the idea of catching a cold and feels compelled to handwashing to prevent it.

Boundary setting is aggressive, or bold, behavior. People who can't set clear boundaries turn this aggression against themselves in the form of painful obsessions, or compulsions that they must perform to be safe. People can often resolve these painful realities by strengthening their ability to set and keep boundaries. Setting boundaries provides the internal structure that can say no to both attacking thoughts and compulsions. They give them back the self-control that the compulsions were trying to provide.

By their very nature, compulsions indicate a lack of freedom. Developing boundaries and the ability to say no to others creates the freedom needed to work through compulsive problems.

Barriers to Creating Boundaries

Injury and distorting thinking can get in the way of our creating boundaries. Following are some examples that illustrate how this happens.

Past Injury

We have all grown up in a world that is severely mixed up about where one person begins and another ends. As a result, we grow up not understanding what we own and what we don't, what we are responsible for and what we are not.

To the degree that we have not been allowed to own our bodies, feelings, attitudes, behaviors, thoughts, abilities, choices, wants, and limits, we are injured, and we will have boundary disturbances. In addition, we ourselves wish to avoid taking responsibility for ourselves. We *naturally* resist taking responsibility so, when we suffer injury, taking responsibility is that much more difficult.

Usually injury occurs when others refuse to allow us to take responsibility for our own lives. If, for example, our parents did not allow us to own our own choices and made us feel responsible for their choices or the choices of others, that would be a specific injury to our ability to set boundaries. For example, Sandy had grown up with a mother who interfered in Sandy's ability to set boundaries. Sandy had to go through a process of reclaiming what was hers, namely her choices, and giving back to her mother what was her mother's, that is, her mother's choices and responsibility.

Each person has to look at the specific way in which his or her boundaries were not allowed to grow. Abuse, control, and guilt manipulation all stunt the growth of boundaries. In addition, if our boundaries are not fully developed because of past injury, we get injured all the more. It is no wonder that seeing the crowds, Jesus "had compassion on them, because they were harassed and helpless like sheep without a shepherd" (Matt. 9:36). God realizes how lost we really are, and he wishes to help us rebuild our boundaries and the sense of identity we lost at the Fall.

Distorted Thinking

As a result of injuries and fallenness, we distort God's reality. Just as we need to clear up distorted thinking in the area of bonding, we need to clear it up in the area of responsibility. Again, distorted thinking falls into three categories. This is only a partial list of how people can distort themselves, others, and God.

Our View of Ourselves

"I am bad for having boundaries."

Probably the biggest problem to work through in terms of boundaries is the guilt we may feel in realizing freedom to own our own life. Many people have been taught that they are selfish and bad for not being responsible for others' feelings, behaviors, and choices. This teaching keeps codependent behavior going. People with boundary problems invariably feel bad when they are honest about their limits and wishes because they have an inordinate sense of responsibility for others. Their lack of freedom leads to feelings of badness, and vice versa.

"I am selfish for owning my own life."

The people who make this remark may have been told, "You are selfish if you do not give me what is yours." When people are vulnerable to control, they feel that they are selfish for deciding what to do with their own property. In reality, deciding for ourselves is the only way we can ever have true love, for then we are giving freely.

"My wants are not important."

This statement denies one's life in an unbiblical way. We are told in the Bible to deny ourselves, but we can only do this if we first own ourselves. People who do not own their own lives cannot give them away, for they aren't theirs to give! We must be good stewards of our lives before we can give to others.

"My wants are the only ones that are important."

This is the distortion in the other direction. When we do not have boundaries on ourselves, we tend to take over the lives of others and not see them as separate people. The real meaning of selfishness is denying the needs and feelings of others.

"I must have everything I want."

This distortion of the self is very destructive, for it puts us out of control. Putting boundaries on our wants allows us to give to others, as well as tolerate deprivation. Not getting things is often good for us; it builds boundaries. Saying no to some demands of children helps them learn to contain themselves.

"I am responsible for others."

This belief keeps others in an immature position. The truth is that we need to be responsible *to* others, not *for* them. We have a real responsibility to those in need; however, we must require responsibility from the able-bodied. To not do that is to enable them to remain immature.

"I must do whatever anyone wants of me."

This feeling comes from being enslaved to or owned by another. If we feel this way, we can't decide to give, and we are being irresponsible. God has given us finite amounts of whatever we have to give, and we must be intentional about that giving. If we let others dictate what we will give, we are not answering to God.

"Whatever goes wrong is my fault."

People with boundary problems have an inordinate sense of fault. They feel responsible, for example, if someone is driving to their house and has a wreck. They feel responsible if they can draw any connection between themselves and the behavior of others. Then they blame themselves for the others' behavior.

Parents also may blame themselves entirely for their children's failure. They deny the responsibility of others and leave their children impotent. They are sayng that their children have no power over their own lives; parents have it all.

"Nothing is my fault."

This statement indicates the failure to own responsibility in whatever we do. It is not realizing what is within our property line and not taking responsibility for our actions. Blaming is a classic example of this, as well as not owning our part in another's pain. Some parents will not own their part in their children's struggles, which is just as wrong as taking all the blame. It is possible to cause another to sin (Matt. 18:6).

Our View of Others

"They will hate me for saying no."

If we have learned that we are responsible for others'

disappointments, we will fear resentment and hatred for owning what is ours. We will imagine that other people will always reject us for setting limits on what we will and will not do for them. In actuality, research and life experience show that people who can say no are the best liked people by far.

"People will leave me for having my own boundaries."

Sometimes love is withdrawn when children begin to own their own life and create a separate self. They learn from this that they will always be left if they own themselves. Again, this is the opposite of the truth. Boundaryless people are abandoned more often.

"People are controlling and want to manipulate me."

People who do not have a strong sense of will fear manipulation and control. They are always on the lookout for how others are going to control them, and they fear getting involved. Good boundaries give one a sense of not being able to be manipulated and controlled.

"Others will resent my assertiveness and requests."

Some people have been raised in settings in which direct expression of one's wants was resented or considered selfish. They have learned to be passive about their wants for fear of resentment and judgment from others. They are afraid of being seen as pushy by their loved ones. On the contrary, direct people have the clearest and best relationships. It is difficult to feel close to passive persons, for we always have to guess what they want.

"They will leave me if I don't keep them happy."

People who have learned that they are responsible for others' feelings fear losing that person if they don't take responsibility for his or her happiness. They may have lost someone this way, but the real distortion comes when they make a general conclusion based on that experience.

"Others are responsible for me."

In the same way that others feel that way toward us, we tend to cross their boundaries as well. We tend to see others as responsible for our feelings, attitudes, and choices, and do not view them as free people with their own lives.

"People are selfish if they do not do what I want."

We may not realize how our sense of crossed boundaries is projected onto others, and we judge them for their freedom. We resent their no.

"People are unloving if they say no to me."

Often, if we have a split between love and limits, we take others' no as rejection and feel unloved. This is a distortion of them and a lack of respect for how they choose to love us. We tend to see them as mean if they have limits.

"People expect me to be compliant to their wishes."

Often we do not realize how much freedom others give us to own our own lives. If we grew up in a controlling situation, we expect others to give us no personal freedom.

"Others are responsible for my behaviors."

If people have always taken responsibility for us, we will continue to see others as responsible for our own behavior and consequences. Thus, we may not realize the law of cause and effect in our lives and wish to always be bailed out. One secretary I know has a sign on her desk that reads, "Poor planning on your part does not constitute an emergency on my part." In essence, she is saying she is not responsible for someone else's behavior.

Our View of God

"God doesn't want me to own my life."

Many people with boundary problems think that God's commands to deny ourselves and to give our lives to him mean that we don't have ownership for our own lives. This is untrue. We *must* own our own lives before we can give them to God, or they are not ours to give. The Bible and experience show that we must realize all the above components of being a person so that we can freely submit to God as bond servants. Bond servants are freed slaves who, having control over their own lives, can voluntarily give them to a master.

God wants a relationship with us, and relationship requires two free people. When Jesus was in the Garden of Gethsemane, he submitted to the will of the Father, but he was acutely aware of his own wishes. "Let this cup pass" expressed his own desire, which he later surrendered to the Father. He was owning and expressing his wishes. All the great saints of the Bible, including Job, David, and Paul, had a similar relationship with God. They freely expressed their desires to God. God wants us to be real people and own what is ours. Only then we can freely choose to give it away.

"God doesn't want me to have anything of my own."

People with boundary problems feel guilty about having wishes and desires. The Bible is full of examples of God telling us to ask so that he can bless us and we can share what we have. Some believe that God frowns on

their having their desires met. This is the opposite of
what God wants. He wants to bless us, but he wants us to
see him as the source of our blessings: "Command those
who are rich in this present world not to be arrogant nor
to put their hope in wealth, which is so uncertain, but to
put their hope in God, who richly provides us with
everything for our enjoyment. Command them to do
good, to be rich in good deeds, and to be generous and
willing to share (1 Tim. 6:17–18).

God has richly supplied us with blessings to enjoy and
to share. A guilty asceticism is not biblical. It is a distorted view of God, the blessing giver.

"God wants me to have everything I want."

Other people suppose that their wish is God's command and that he has no limits to his giving. This idea is
equally unbiblical, for God often says no to us, and he
does not owe us any explanation. In the parable of the
workers in the vineyard, the landowner was free to do
what he wanted with what was his (Matt. 20:15). The
"name it and claim it" gospel makes God into our servant
and denies his boundaries and choices. God often says no
for reasons we may not understand; his refusal to grant
our wish doesn't mean that we do not have enough faith.
Ask Jesus in the Garden.

"God thinks I'm selfish when I say no to others."

God loves for us to share and to give out of freedom,
not compulsion. The other side of freely giving is saying
no when we don't choose to give. He supports our sense
of boundaries, for he created them. As a result, we can be
intentional, not compliant givers.

In addition, we help God bring people to maturity
when we say no to their irresponsibility. Paul says, "If
anyone does not obey our instruction in this letter, take

special note of him. Do not associate with him, in order that he may feel ashamed. Yet do not regard him as an enemy, but warn him as a brother" (2 Thess. 3:14–15). When we say no to either abusive or enabling behavior, we are serving as God's hand of discipline in someone's life. We are helping them realize their own boundaries.

"God wants me to allow others to do whatever they want to me or to others."

This is a similar distortion. God tells us many times to rebuke others (Matt. 18:15–18; Lev. 19:17; Prov. 27:5–6; Eph. 4:25–26; 1 Cor. 5:9, 13; Gal. 6:1; 2 Cor. 2:5–11; 1 Cor. 5:1–5). To not do so is to give people only grace and no truth. It enables people to remain immature. God is very serious about his people growing up in him. He does not want us to help others stay immature.

"God doesn't want me to pursue what I want."

Many people feel guilty about owning their talents and goals. God has created us with talents, and he wants us to work with him on how best to use them. We are to make plans, but we always have to be aware that God may revise them. "In his heart a man plans his course, but the Lord determines his steps" (Prov. 16:9). "Delight yourself in the Lord and he will give you the desires of your heart. Commit your way to the Lord; trust in him and he will do this: He will make your righteousness shine like the dawn, the justice of your cause like the noonday sun" (Ps. 37:4–6).

"God is totally sovereign and in control; therefore I have no responsibility."

This boundary problem denies our ownership in life. God gives us much responsibility and freedom to manage our lives; he even restricts his boundaries so that we have our own wills and choices. He did not create robots who will do his every command. We are responsible for our choices and will one day have to give an account. As a result, we have a lot of say-so in the direction our lives take.

"God is a 'hands-off' God and is not involved in my life."

This boundary problem denies God's ownership in our lives. God is very active in bringing about our growth. Both God and we have responsibility in our growing up. "Work out your salvation with fear and trembling, for it is God who works in you to will and to act according to his good purpose" (Phil. 2:12–13). We are co-laborers together with God.

"If God says no to me, he doesn't love me."

God is free to limit his giving for his purposes and ours. It is not unloving for God to say no, even to our healing. He knows that sometimes we need to work out our healing instead of his doing it for us. For example, if I am depressed because I don't bond with others, for God to "heal" my depression would prohibit me from learning how to bond and becoming loved. He may then say no to my prayer for healing from depression for my benefit. We, like Job, must trust God's no and his timing. It does not mean that he doesn't love us. It may mean that he wants something better for us.

"God is forgiving and won't discipline me for my sin."

This statement denies God's limits. He will not allow evil to take over. He wants a clean house, and since he has invited us to live with him, he wants us to take our shoes off if they have mud on them! He will discipline us for our own good. He is interested in our developing righteousness because it is not good for us to remain immature.

"God is all limits and no love."

God has many compassionate feelings and much forgiveness, and we must allow him to own them. To see him as the big disciplinarian without compassion is to deny his nature (Ps. 103).

Chapter ℰ℣10

Learning to Set Boundaries

WE'VE SEEN THE IMPORTANCE OF SETTING boundaries in our lives. We've looked at a number of people who suffered pain because they did not learn how to set boundaries when they were growing up.

Stephen was burned out and on the verge of losing his job because he could never say no to people's requests for help. Sandy was unhappy and out of control of her life because she couldn't say no to her mother. Jane suffered panic attacks because she couldn't say no to her husband's drinking. Jim was unhappy because he could never say no to his wife's requests to work around the house. Peter was suicidal because he couldn't say no to his mother's request that he stay home for the rest of his life. Donna was angry because she couldn't say no to her family's excessive expectations of her. Robert was jobless because he wasn't taking responsibility for his own mistaken attitudes about how the world worked. Harold was angry because he couldn't say no to his daughter. All of these people could use some lessons in how to set boundaries and how to keep people from crossing them.

Let's look at some of the skills necessary for setting boundaries and learning to say no when someone tries to cross those boundaries.

Skills for Setting Boundaries

Gain Awareness

Since setting boundaries is merely taking ownership of what is yours, your first step is gaining awareness of who you are. Become aware of your body, feelings, attitudes, behaviors, thoughts, abilities, choices, wants, and limits. Take inventory of where you have come from, where you are now, and where you are going. The Study Guide on Setting Boundaries at the back of this book will help.

Enlist others in taking inventory. You need feedback from others because you do not often see what you have disowned. You may even benefit from professional help. Proverbs 15:22 says, "Plans fail for lack of counsel, but with many advisers they succeed."

Define Who You Are

Just as God defines himself, you need to assert yourself. Begin to say what you feel, what you like, what you want, what you will do, and what you think. Carve out an identity and say, "This is who I am."

Define Who You Are Not

You must also say who you are not. Say what is "not you," as well as what is you. Say what you don't agree with, don't like, won't do, and so on. People with boundary problems often do not stand against anything. They take everything in. This is very destructive. In Proverbs 6, God calls us to stand against and hate some things.

Develop the "No" Muscle

A child learns to set boundaries by saying no. Many of us have eliminated this word from our vocabulary, and we need to rediscover it. Strengthen your no muscle. Begin with little exercises, such as saying no to dining at a certain restaurant that you don't want to go to, and work your way up to more demanding ones, such as saying no to lovemaking when you don't feel loving. Learning to say no is probably the most important and difficult task in creating boundaries, especially saying no to parents.

Stop Blaming Others

Taking responsibility for your own pain and not blaming others is a major move out of bondage and into health. Stop blaming others for your trouble, and deal with it. This does not mean that others did not cause it; it just means that you have to deal with it. Blaming others is a dead-end street.

Stop Playing Victim

As an adult, you have choices. Begin to take responsibility for those choices and own them. If you are giving something, you are making a choice to give and you need to stop acting as if someone is making you. As an adult, you are choosing. If you are working somewhere that you don't like, take responsibility for finding something else. If you are being criticized over and over by a friend, take responsibility to set up a meeting with him or her. You are responsible for what you choose to do. Taking this responsibility will change your life.

Persevere

God commands us to persevere, or to continue on in spite of difficulty or opposition. "Let us run with perseverance the race marked out for us. Let us fix our eyes on Jesus, the author and perfecter of our faith, who for the joy set before him endured the cross, scorning its shame, and sat down at the right hand of God. Consider him who endured such opposition from sinful men, so that you will not grow weary and lose heart" (Heb. 12:1–3).

Create goals for yourself and set about accomplishing them with continued, patient effort. Perseverance creates discipline and responsibility. Perseverance creates character. "Suffering produces perseverance; perseverance, character; and character, hope" (Rom. 5:3–4).

Become Active, Not Reactive

People with boundary problems often see themselves not as initiators, but as reactors. They make choices by passively reacting to others. *Choose* to love and to give, don't just love and give when it is required. Choose to work and accomplish, don't just do it when it is required. This develops character. It develops a sense of "I will."

Set Limits

One of the most important tasks is setting limits on others' abusive behavior. Stop enabling others to be self-centered and irresponsible. Put limits on the ways that their substance abuse or physical abuse affects you. In addition, put limits on more subtle emotional abuse, such as criticism and blaming.

Begin to realize your limits of time, money, and energy. If you sow sparingly, you will reap sparingly; but if you sow more than you have, you will be bankrupt. Get with God and others to find what is reasonable for you at this time.

Choose Values

Define who you want to be and where you want to go. Like Joshua, choose for yourself this day whom you are going to serve. Decide what your values are going to be and work toward your goals. Other Christians may try to tell you what your values should be, but they are not perfect. You must take responsibility for your own choices.

Practice Self-Control

Set limits on your wishes. You can't have everything you want. Be careful not to go to the other extreme and put too many limits on your wishes, thereby controlling yourself out of having a "me." Strike a balance between satisfying your desires and controlling them.

Accept Others

Learn to love and accept others for who they are. If you don't, you are intruding on their boundaries and taking control of something that's not yours—their person. If you want to feel accepted, accept. If you want others to respect your no, respect their no. If you resent others for saying no to you, you will be confused about your own no and will be trying to control them. Love people when they say no, and relish their freedom. Only then will you yourself be free.

Realize Your Separateness

Develop time and interests separate from the time and interests of those you love. Realize that separateness is good and will add to your relationship. Time apart enhances the relationship by creating longing. Otherwise you are clones. Counting the ways you are different from, as well as like, your loved ones will help your sense of identity.

Be Honest

Be honest with one another. Many people will not be honest because they fear loss of intimacy and togetherness. In reality, honesty brings people closer together, for it will strengthen their identities. The more you realize your separate identities, the closer you can become. Telling loved ones what is really on your mind, and telling others what you really think, is the foundation of love.

Challenge Distorted Thinking

Jesus taught that truth sets us free. Identify your distortions and act in accordance with the truth; you will learn new ways of being and will produce a different kind of fruit. This is hard work, and requires the help of friends and God's Spirit to lead you into the truth about yourself and about his world.

In looking at boundaries, we cannot escape one main point: responsibility. Our boundaries basically define our sense of responsibility for us. They tell us what our lives consist of and what we are responsible for. We must own our body, feelings, attitudes, behaviors, thoughts, abilities, choices, desires, and limits.

If we were to stop there, behind carefully guarded fences, we would live a very safe, but very unbiblical existence. This would fall short of love, the goal of life. The biblical concept of love involves loving and laying down our life for others. However, it is impossible to give away what we do not have, and boundaries are our way of "having" the self that we can then choose to give away.

Owning our own lives is the essence of freedom, and there is no love without freedom. Freedom realizes oneself, and love motivates us to give that self to others. When we give before we are free and truly own ourselves, we have fallen short of servanthood and into slavery. Realize what you own, and then share yourself with others. This is to fulfill the law of Christ.

Stephen

The story of Stephen at the beginning of this section illustrates what happens when a person has trouble with his sense of boundaries. Because he was spread so thin, he found it difficult to get anything done. He was resentful of others, irresponsible, and burned out.

"I know everyone's angry with me," he told me. "I keep letting them all down—my wife *and* the church. But I can't keep up with them! The more I do, the more they demand of me. I've been trying to make everybody happy, but all I get is grief."

Stephen believed he was responsible for the lives and feelings of others. Because his father had died at an early age, he learned to take responsibility for his mother, a controlling and self-centered person. As a result, he forgot how to look after his own concerns.

When I introduced Stephen to the concept of boundaries, he saw immediately where his problem lay. I showed him how to recognize when he was giving "out of compulsion and obligation," and I showed him how to discern the "purpose in his heart." As he gained control of himself, he stopped giving to others merely because he felt responsible for them.

"Just say no" was the toughest lesson for Stephen to learn. He hated the disappointed looks and the accusing glances when he had to turn down an opportunity to help someone. Often he was tempted to give in begrudgingly. But, as time went on, he learned to give to others only when he chose to.

Stephen's wife, who was used to being in control of him, fought tooth and nail against his new resolve. However, he stood up to her, took charge of his own life, and as a result, became a more defined person, one who took charge of himself. Over time, she came to accept him when she saw that she could trust him to follow through on his promises. He was becoming dependable.

In his ministry, too, Stephen began to say no. He learned to offer his thoughts and opinions as he discovered what God had created him to be. There were some rocky times, but his sense of purpose returned, and his church sensed that they were working with a person of character and commitment.

Stephen also learned how to set goals for himself. Instead of always responding to events, he began to initiate things and follow them through to completion. Encouraged by his successes, he discovered more and more what he really enjoyed doing, and said no to everything else.

By tending to the tree, Stephen's fruit changed. If he had focused only on the bad fruits—the symptoms of burnout, fatigue, and victimization—he would never have been healed. But when he focused on the developmental issue of boundaries, he was able to grow in the image of God, becoming a clearly defined and responsible person.

Part IV
Sorting Out Good and Bad

Chapter ❧11

What Is the Problem?

TED HAD ALWAYS HAD THE MIDAS TOUCH; everything he touched turned to gold. As a teenager, he excelled in every arena, academically, athletically, and socially. Even his college years—paid for by a prestigious athletic scholarship—were unblemished by failure.

After college he continued to enjoy success after success. By age thirty he was a millionaire. Respected in his community, he had married the "most beautiful girl in the world" and had two "perfect" children. He seemed to have the world by the tail.

Then, little by little, his success began to erode. Lawsuits plagued his subsidiaries. His popularity began to wane. Within a few short years, he had virtually lost his fame and his family. Filled with despair and unable to cope, Ted tried to commit suicide.

At the hospital, Ted went through days in a stupor,

barely able to talk. He refused to see any of his old friends. He did not want them to see their "hero" in a mental health unit.

As Ted began to open up about his pain, it became clear that he could not handle any failure or loss. Any threat to his ideal picture of himself only drove him to further accomplishment, thus building a house of mirrors that covered his disappointment and pain. And he had a lot of hurt to cover up, hurt that went all the way back to his youth in a broken home.

Ted dealt with the bad in himself, his family, or his surroundings by working to create more good. Unable to deal with an imperfect world, he became a ticking time bomb. And at age thirty-eight, he exploded.

Ted had tried to build an image and a life that was all good. When the bad came, the fall was crippling. He felt immediately and hopelessly all bad.

The world around us is good and bad. The people around us are good and bad. We are good and bad.

Our natural tendency is to try and resolve the problem of good and evil by *keeping the good and the bad separated.* We want, by nature, to experience the good me, the good other, and the good world as "all good." To do this, we see the bad me, the bad other, and the bad world as "all bad." This creates a split in our experience of ourselves, others, and the world around us—a split that is not based on reality and cannot stand the test of time and real life.

This splitting results in an inability to tolerate badness, weakness, and failure in ourselves and others. It leads to two basic problems: sometimes we deny the existence of bad; at other times, we deny the existence of good. We feel like we are all bad when we fail, or we think we are all good when we are doing well.

In addition, we blame and punish others for failing to be the all-good person we want them to be. At other times, we deny the real badness they exhibit and end up with an unreal relationship with them that ultimately fails.

In the world around us, we require perfection, and we devalue any church, group, or job that fails our expectations. Either we withdraw from the church, group, or job, only to move to another imperfect and disappointing situation, or we idealize situations in a way that blinds us to their bad points. In short, *if we do not have the ability to tolerate and deal with the simultaneous existence of good and bad, we cannot successfully deal with and live in this world, for the world and we are precisely that: good and bad.*

A Biblical Perspective of Good and Bad

It was not always this way. There was a time on planet Earth when everything was "all good." God had painted a picture on the canvas of reality, and the reality of his picture was perfection. The creation, including humans, was without blemish. We were without sin.

We can sometimes move close to seeing perfection. We can sometimes see it as we gaze at a beautiful sunset. It is evident in some people's physical beauty. Some musical performances challenge us to find a mistake. Some athletes surprise us with perfect performances of grace and beauty. Moments of intimacy between lovers bring heaven close to earth.

It is at times like these that we have little problem imagining an ideal world. We can get lost in the fantasy of what a creation must have been like without evil. It was for this world that we were created. We were never made to live where we live now; that was a mistake. We have been delivered to the wrong address. God created us for perfection, and we find ourselves living somewhere else.

We were not prepared to live in an imperfect world. We were not made to deal with the effects of the Fall. There were to be no cavities in our teeth, no thorns and thistles puncturing our soft feet. We were not made to have to defend ourselves against each other; our spirits are much too tender to live in a world of hurtful people. We were made for perfect relationship with perfect people; instead, the people with whom we find ourselves invariably hurt us. They lie or are unfaithful; sometimes they are just mean.

We were not prepared to be imperfect. We don't have enough grace inside to anesthetize us against the pain of our own badness. It is horrible enough to feel sin; but the guilt of the sin is even worse. We feel hatred and separation instead of love and connection; we feel others' envy instead of their appreciation and gratitude; we feel sad and angry instead of joyous; we panic and worry instead of feeling safe and secure; we feel shame and self-hatred instead of love and self-confidence; and finally, we feel utter fear and terror of God, instead of overwhelming awe and love. All of these feelings touch on issues of good and bad; to be emotionally and spiritually successful, we must be able to deal with them. If we can't co-exist with good and bad, we will have a hard time living in this world.

When we swing back and forth from seeing things as either all good or all bad, we can't have a consistent relationship with ourselves, others, or the world around us. People will sometimes go from friend to friend, spouse to spouse, church to church, or job to job. They think for a while everything is okay, but as soon as badness appears, they can't deal with it. They demand perfection; whatever is not perfect is "all bad" and therefore rejected. They are riding a roller coaster.

Perhaps you have a relationship where you thought everything was okay, and then you didn't call home when you were going to be late. Your partner treated you like you had leprosy. This is an example of someone who can't deal with badness or imperfection in others.

Or, maybe you thought you were doing pretty well in golf, and then played a rotten game and felt enormous hatred for yourself. It felt as if you were a total failure, all bad. Or, maybe you were excited about buying the car of your dreams. And then, it got dented, and lost its perfection. If it's not perfect, it's all bad. Or, you were preparing that special welcoming meal for your new neighbors. The cake falls, and "it ruins the whole evening."

These are all problems of sorting out issues of good and bad. If we are to negotiate life very well, we must find a way to live in a world that has both.

The Ideal Self

We all have a distant memory of what we were meant to be. We can all imagine what a perfect "me" would be like. Think for a second about the perfect you. Think about the possibility of doing perfectly everything you can do. When you force yourself to think about that, you can begin to see the tension between what you imagine and what is real.

Deep down inside, we all realize the difference between our ideal self, the imagined perfection, and our real self, the one that truly is. If these two battle each other, we will be in constant conflict. What we wish were true and what really is true will war with one another.

The ideal self is the one we can imagine and want to be. If you look at your particular abilities, you can imagine what their perfection would be like. For instance, I am a golfer. There are days when I am able to hit a few shots that approach the way I would like ideally to hit every shot. The swing feels as if it could get no better, and the ball flies exactly like I want it to. I can begin to imagine the ideal drive on every hole, and strive for it. The ideal self is the imagined ideal me who hits every shot the way it is supposed to be hit. It is a wonderful fantasy and a wonderful goal.

Or, if you are an attorney, you can have days when the law opens up before you in a way that amazes you. You see every possible angle on your case, and you interpret the law clearly. At the same time, you dream of defending your client in court in a way that the competition hasn't a chance. The clarity and airtightness of your case cannot be challenged, and your presence in the courtroom is a holy protection for your defendant. You begin to tap into talents and potentials you did not even know you had.

Or, if you are a teacher, you build a bridge between your students and the subject matter that allows them to march into greater understanding than you thought possible. You are able to discern instantly what the need of the moment is and to help them work through their knowledge blocks. You begin to dream of creative ways that will aid future classes in leaping over conventional expectations of learning.

Or, if you are a parent, you can imagine what it would be like to know every need of your child and to be able to respond to them appropriately every time. You can see yourself as the model your child looks up to and becomes like, and you envision a wonderful relationship between the two of you.

If you are in business, then you can see the success of your company as you would ideally imagine it to be. You can see yourself amassing the information and expertise you need and can see new branches opening up all over the nation.

Having ideal wishes about aspects of our lives is a part of being human. Those wishes are the lost potentials of the image of God within. We can imagine what an ideal woman would be like, if we are a woman (Prov. 31) or what an ideal man would be, if we are a man (Eph. 4:14–15). In every area of our existence, we can imagine the ideal, and we long for it.

Romans 8 says it this way: "We know that the whole creation has been groaning as in the pains of childbirth right up to the present time. Not only so, but we ourselves, who have the firstfruits of the Spirit, groan inwardly as we wait eagerly for our adoption as sons, the redemption of our bodies. For in this hope we were saved. But hope that is seen is no hope at all. Who hopes for what he already has? But if we hope for what we do not yet have, we wait for it patiently" (vv. 22–25).

We are eager to have our lost ideal recovered; that longing is built into the very nature of who we are. It is who we were and who we will be one day.

The Real Self

The real self is the one that we truly are, not the one we wish to be. The real self is not ideal, no matter how much we wish it were. The reality of our situation is that our real self has fallen; the ideal has been lost. We are beset with weakness and fallenness; we are broken and not what we would like to be. Paul puts it this way: "But I am unspiritual, sold as a slave to sin" (Rom. 7:14).

In addition to our sinful aspects, we are weak. Sometimes we represent our weakness as if it were bad. We don't think it's okay to be weak. Our ideal self would not be weak.

We are also broken. We have been injured in many ways, and our real self houses all of the evidences of those injuries. The pain, the brokenness, and the emotional underdevelopment we all possess is part of who we really are. Brokenness and immaturity are parts of our real selves.

We naturally value the ideal self more than the real. It works better, looks better, functions better, and needs less maintenance. In short, it is a better model than the real thing. The problem is *it's a fantasy*. It's not real. It can't be embraced or related to. It doesn't exist.

We need to look at the relationship between the ideal self and the real self. If they are in conflict, there is going to be a perpetual war inside for center stage. Whenever the real self becomes apparent, the ideal self will judge it, and try to make it hide. And when we are hiding, we are not in relationship with God and others.

If we demand perfection from ourselves, we are not living in the real world. The real self is not perfect—a reality we all must come to grips with. Many people give lip service to this reality, but their actions speak more loudly. Their actions betray a strong belief that they should be ideal and that no imperfection should live in them. We all have many imperfections, weaknesses, and immaturities that are not our ideal. That is reality.

The Relationship Between the Ideal and the Real

The inherent problem in the relationship between the ideal and the real is that the ideal judges the real as unacceptable and brings down condemnation and wrath on the real. This sets up an adversarial relationship between the two, and like all adversaries, they move further and further apart.

Richard, a forty-six-year-old businessman, came to the hospital because he was preoccupied with frightening, uncontrollable thoughts. Sometimes, when he was with his wife, he would picture beating her up. At other times, he would fantasize about being very angry with his children. He would try hard to get those fantasies out of his head, but they would always return, more strongly than before. He tried praying and reading his Bible, but he was still unable to control his thoughts.

Richard would always preface his fantasies with remarks such as "I know I shouldn't have those thoughts, but . . ." or "It's really awful that I think this, but . . ." He would always state the ideal; that is, he would always say that the ideal Richard wouldn't have these kinds of thoughts. But, the truth was that he really did have them.

Richard had an obsessive-compulsive disorder. He would try to get the thoughts out of his head using various compulsive behaviors, yet they would remain. He had decided that he was hopelessly evil.

During his hospital stay, Richard learned that he was very angry at his wife for many things he had never told her about. He thought that he *shouldn't* be angry so he had denied and repressed all his anger. In addition, Richard learned that he felt very angry at his own child-likeness, so he hated the weakness and inabilities of his children.

The problem was not that he was angry, or childlike. Both of those are a part of life. The problem was that he did not accept these parts of himself; his ideal self had decided that they should not be a part of him. Therefore, they were beginning to control him. The "badness" he was denying was coming out in destructive, obsessive thoughts.

As Richard began to understand the demands of his ideal self, and began to accept his real self, he was able to work through his anger at both himself and his wife. As he did this, the obsessions went away.

This split between the ideal and the real is one of the major reasons Christians struggle. The church often stresses such high ideals that many people feel they can't be human and still be Christian—an incredible belief when one thinks of why they came to Christ in the first place. They came because they were sinners in need of forgiveness and acceptance.

Judgmental vs. Accepting Tone

An important aspect of the relationship between the ideal and the real is its emotional tone. If we adopt a judgmental tone, one of condemnation and wrath toward what is real, then we have a divided house. Our ideals will judge and condemn our real self into nonexistence. We will use shame, guilt, hiding, denial, splitting, and other defenses to hide the real self. Whatever we do not accept in grace will be under judgment and condemnation, and we will hide it behind a psychological fig leaf.

If we adopt a loving and accepting tone toward our real self, there is hope for transformation. If we are able to accept the parts of ourselves we do not feel are ideal, then those parts will be loved and healed. They can begin to grow in ways never before imagined. Acceptance is the answer to the dilemma of the ideal versus the real. That is grace.

We can see this in Paul's struggle in Romans 7: "I do not understand what I do. For what I want to do I do not do, but what I hate I do. And if I do what I do not want to do, I agree that the law is good. As it is, it is no longer I myself who do it, but it is sin living in me. I know that nothing good lives in me, that is, in my sinful nature. For I have the desire to do what is good, but I cannot carry it out. For what I do is not the good I want to do; no, the evil I do not want to do—this I keep on doing" (vv. 15–19). He wishes for one thing, and finds the painful reality of another.

Our natural tendency is to try harder to meet the ideal, but Paul has the real answer: acceptance. "Therefore, there is now no condemnation for those who are in Christ Jesus" (Rom. 8:1). The demands of the ideal have been met, and Paul is no longer condemned for not being perfect. God sent his son "in order that the righteous requirements of the law might be fully met in us" (v. 4). When we can get to a point of "no condemnation" for the true self as it really is, we can confess what is wrong and be in relationship just as we are, with no pressure to be ideal. This acceptance can lead to incredible growth and spiritual power.

The nature of the relationship, then, between the ideal and the real needs to be one of grace, of unconditional love and acceptance. If this is true, our house isn't divided. The ideal and the real are not fighting each other, and good relationship can begin. Good relationship involves holding on to the ideal and lovingly accepting the real. If the real is loved and accepted, it can be encouraged to grow toward the ideal. The Teacher in Ecclesiastes puts it this way:

> In this meaningless life of mine I have seen both of these: a righteous man perishing in his righteousness, and a wicked man living long in his wickedness. Do not be overrighteous, neither be overwise—why destroy yourself? Do not be overwicked, and do not be a fool—why die before your time? It is good to grasp the one and not let go of the other. The man who fears God will avoid all extremes. (7:15–18)

In other words, to demand perfection will ruin our life. We all know perfectionists who do not enjoy life in the least and who make others' lives miserable too. On the other hand, to let go of standards and ideals will get us

killed. The God-fearing person avoids both legalism and
license and leads a balanced life. In a life where standards
are accepted and cherished as goals and our true self is
accepted and loved, there will be peace and growth. We
can be real people.

This view of ourselves is consistent with God's view.
He says we are incredibly wonderful, extremely sinful,
beset with all sorts of weakness, and overflowing with
talents. Try to think of all of that at one time! It is a real
exercise in the task of resolving good and bad. Let's look
at some of the Bible's "conflicting" statements:

> What are human beings that you are mindful of
> them, mortals that you care for them? Yet you have
> made them a little lower than God, and crowned
> them with glory and honor. You have given them
> dominion over the works of your hands; you have
> put all things under their feet. (Ps. 8:4–6 NRSV)

> "There is no one righteous, not even one." (Rom.
> 3:10)

> For he knows how we are formed, he remembers
> that we are dust. (Ps. 103:14)

The Bible teaches two themes throughout: the first is
that we are created in the image of God and that we
have incredible value. The second is that we are sinful
and broken. There is the ideal, and there is the real.
Both are true, and both need to be reconciled into a
grace-giving relationship with God and others.

Distortions of the Ideal

What some people think is ideal was never really part
of the ideal human God created. For example, God cre-

ated us to have needs for relationship with other people. "It is not good for man to be alone" (Gen. 2:18). But some people think that ideally they should not need other people. Other people have created an ideal self that denies sexual feelings. Still others envision an ideal self that doesn't get angry or sad. These ideal selves are distortions of the image of God in which we were created. They were never intended.

Some people feel like their ideal self would not need to work or complete tasks. They think that they should be happy just being a doormat and not using their talents. Yet, God created us to have dominion over the earth.

Distortions people create in their ideal self are either part of what was lost (perfection), or part of what never was (non-humanness). Either way, they are not real, and we must confront the demands of our ideal self and accept what is true.

Our perception of the ideal self comes largely from our upbringing. What was valued in our family we internalize into the ideal; whatever is not "up to snuff" we assign a slot elsewhere in the darkness of our souls. We judge the latter as bad, whether or not it really is. Some people feel bad about good things that were not accepted in their family. The ideal self may condemn these aspects of the true self as someone else might condemn murder. For example, in our culture many men get the message from their family that it is bad to have weak and needy feelings. They are told to be macho and to suppress their sad and weak feelings.

The ideal self is not necessarily inerrant! It is a system of internalized values from our upbringing as well as our own wishes for ourselves. The important point is that whatever is true, but not acceptable to the ideal, gets judged and dismissed in some way or another.

When Patrick came into therapy, he had been to see

about fifteen or twenty doctors for his "disease." He had also been to several emergency rooms, thinking he was suffering from a heart attack, a stroke, cancer, and so on. But not one of the doctors could find anything wrong. Finally, his internist told him to seek psychological help.

Patrick was the chief executive officer of a major corporation. His goal in life had always been to rise above everything with his intellect. He had done very well. He just couldn't accept it when his doctors said that there was nothing wrong with him. And he was right. There was something desperately wrong, but it wasn't physical. It was emotional. Patrick was suffering because he had denied several aspects of himself that had not fit into his ideal self.

Patrick's ideal self was composed of a picture of his father, a "strong man" who never showed emotions. Patrick grew up thinking that to be a man meant to never show feeling, as well as to be as different from his mother as possible. He described his mother as "an emotional wreck." Patrick had denied any weakness because he judged it as "bad."

Over time this tough stance began to catch up with him. He began to have various phobias and fears, mostly of physical illness. His "weaknesses" came out as physical illness because this was acceptable to the ideal. He could be sick as long as he was not emotionally weak or sad.

In therapy, he reclaimed the sad, feeling part of his real self. As he reclaimed his feelings, he became much more human and his fears and phobias went away. He no longer ran from emergency room to emergency room, fearing that he was dying.

Another common example of distorting the content of the ideal self is calling boundary setting bad. Many people have had to repress their natural tendency to set limits on others because this was not acceptable in their family.

Dealing with the Good and Bad Conflict

We deal with the conflict between the good and the bad in our lives in four different ways, three of which always fail.

Denial of the Bad

Denial is the way some people handle the bad in their lives. Richard denied his anger at his wife, because anger was judged and condemned. Sandy denied her drive to set boundaries. Setting limits was not encouraged by the family she grew up in.

Other people deny feelings that are not part of their ideal self. Sometimes people who have been taught that their emotions are not acceptable deny sadness. Denial of emotions leads to depression because sadness is God's way of dealing with hurt and loss.

Some deny sinful feelings such as lust, envy, or bitterness. They think that Christians shouldn't have these feelings, so they deny their existence.

I remember one client who, in the midst of the breakup of her twenty-year marriage, was planning vacations and parties. She said that she felt no pain over the separation. She had totally denied it.

The Bible sometimes speaks harshly about our tendency to deny our badness, for it is the sin of pride. Listen to Jesus speak to the Pharisees. "Woe to you, teachers of the law and Pharisees, you hypocrites! You clean the outside of the cup and dish, but inside they are full of greed and self-indulgence. Blind Pharisee! First clean the inside of the cup and dish, and then the outside also will be clean. Woe to you, teachers of the law and Pharisees, you hypocrites! You are like whitewashed tombs, which look beautiful on the outside but on the inside are full of dead men's bones and everything unclean" (Matt. 23:25–27).

The Scriptures strongly urge people not to deny the badness that they have inside. The Bible also urges people not to set people on pedestals. Sometimes people deny the bad in others and see them as all good. They idolize them. They see other humans as perfect, instead of being equal sinners (Rom. 3:23).

Ruth came into therapy for depression. She continually put herself down for petty matters like being tired or serving dinner a few minutes late. I couldn't get to the bottom of what was bothering her. She seemed to be under a terrible burden, but when I asked about her life, she said that things were okay.

When I asked her how her husband responded to her depression, she said that he was very supportive. He sent her flowers, and helped with the cooking. He took her out to dinner when neither felt like cooking, and he was the one who called the plumber or the carpenter when something needed fixing. I was thankful that such a depressed person had such a supportive mate!

It was only when she brought her husband with her to a therapy session that I understood. Although her husband was easygoing and friendly, he spent the entire session putting Ruth down. Her hair was not fixed right, and she was slouching. He contradicted almost everything she said.

Though her husband was critical and demanding, for years Ruth had denied his badness and had been the brunt of his sin. It was no wonder that she was depressed and that they weren't able to resolve their problems. She was stomaching all of the problems. She was all bad, and he was all good.

Denial of the Good

Some people do just the opposite. They deny the good. People who feel so under the pile of the ideal demands do away with standards altogether. As a result, they live in the badness, without any realization that it is bad. The "hardened sinner" has decided there is no ideal standard to live up to. Whatever is, is (Rom. 1:18–23).

In the same way that we can split the good and bad in ourselves and get out of touch with the good, we can do that to others as well.

John, twenty-six and recently married, came to see me for help "with his marriage." He described how critical and demanding his new wife was and how "she never does anything around the house." Since they had married, Lynn "had let herself go," he said, and she was not attractive anymore because of her weight. I requested that he bring her with him to the next session.

When John's wife walked through the door of my office the following week, I was stunned. Lynn was tall and slender and moved with an air of confidence. After talking with her for a few moments, I realized that John was placing some incredible, perfectionistic standards on Lynn, making her seem all bad. In response, Lynn had tried to please him even more, a strategy that never works with a perfectionist. He could not tolerate her being less than ideal, and he was judging her harshly. The truth was that her performance was very good, just not perfect, and he denied the good.

Attack and Judge

Attacking and judging is the most common way of dealing with the bad. The "normal" conscience judges and condemns, saying things like, "I'm so stupid, or worthless, or bad." This angry attack on the real self is condemning and hurtful. The Bible calls this "worldly sorrow." "Godly sorrow brings repentance that leads to salvation and leaves no regret, but worldly sorrow brings death" (2 Cor. 7:10). Sadness over badness that turns to

repentance is godly sorrow. Attack and condemnation is
the worldly way of dealing with badness. Judas and Peter
illustrate this difference. Judas condemned himself and
committed suicide. Peter felt sorry for denying Jesus but
his tears turned to repentance. Judgment never cures
anything. The law judges without mercy.

Many people can see both good and bad, but they
attack the badness in others.

Phil was a very loving husband to his wife. He saw her
good points and supported her faithfully. He praised her
when she did well, and let her know how much he appreciated her. But whenever she made a mistake or did
things differently than he would have, he would get
angry and yell at her, saying very mean things. He would
judge and criticize her, trying to make her feel guilty and
ashamed of whatever she did that he didn't like.

He denied neither the good nor the bad, but he
attacked and judged harshly what he saw as bad. He gave
her truth without grace.

Acceptance

Acceptance of good and bad is the biblical alternative.
It is called grace and truth. In this alternative, we deny
neither the ideal nor the bad. We accept and forgive the
bad, while clinging to the ideal as an unrealized goal that
we strive for in an atmosphere of full acceptance. We
stand in grace. This strategy does not split the good and
the bad, nor does it get angry and condemning, but it
grasps onto both the good and the bad at the same time.

Just as we accept the bad and good in ourselves, we
need to accept them in others. "Be kind and compassionate to one another, forgiving each other, just as in Christ
God forgave you" (Eph. 4:32). "As God's chosen people,
holy and dearly loved, clothe yourselves with compassion, kindness, humility, gentleness and patience. Bear

with each other and forgive whatever grievances you may have against one another" (Col. 3:12–13). "Accept one another, then, just as Christ accepted you, in order to bring praise to God" (Rom. 15:7).

In all these passages, the combination of grace and truth is apparent. We must face and deal with the truth, but we must accept, not reject; we must be kind, not angry. "He who covers over an offense promotes love, but whoever repeats the matter separates close friends" (Prov. 17:9).

A Developmental Perspective

If not resolving issues of good and bad is so destructive, then why don't we just do it? What's the big deal about acknowledging the existence of both of them? Why don't we just accept the bad and value the good?

.   To understand this process, we have to remember the nature of the Fall. We were never intended to handle the co-existence of good and bad. God tried to protect us from it. But we sinned anyway and found ourselves in a tough spot.

The reason is this: *Having been born without knowledge of grace, we need to internalize grace in order to learn how to accept the bad without rejecting relationship.*

The Bible says that we are born without relationship and we must be invited into relationship. As this happens, we begin to internalize love and forgiveness. The scriptural principle is that we love and forgive because we have been loved and forgiven.

Jesus was having dinner at Simon the Pharisee's house. When he was reclining at the table, a woman "who had lived a sinful life" wiped Jesus' feet with her hair and poured perfume on them. The Pharisee thought that if Jesus were a prophet he would realize what kind of

woman was touching him. Jesus told a story to illustrate
the scriptural principle:

> "Two men owed money to a certain moneylender.
> One owed him five hundred denarii, and the other
> fifty. Neither of them had the money to pay him
> back, so he canceled the debts of both. Now which
> of them will love him more?"
>
> Simon replied, "I suppose the one who had the
> bigger debt canceled."
>
> "You have judged correctly," Jesus said. He con-
> cluded by saying, "Therefore, I tell you, her many
> sins have been forgiven—for she loved much. But
> he who has been forgiven little loves little." (Luke
> 7:36–47)

We do not come into the world as forgivers, for we
have never been forgiven. The Bible teaches that to the
extent we have been forgiven, we will forgive. We must
realize our own forgiveness in order to forgive and not
split people off as "all bad," thus losing our connection
with them.

So when a child comes into the world, she is unconscious of being forgiven. As a result, she herself is unforgiving. Grace and truth, or love and limits, are split
apart. She loves if she is happy; she hates if she is dis-
tressed. These two states form two very distinct categories in her head: the good guys and the bad guys, as
well as the good me and the bad me. Good and bad are
totally separated, for the deep fear is that the bad will
wipe out the good.

This way of experiencing and thinking is very perva-
sive for a child. If children are nurtured and get their
needs met, the world is a good place, Mommy is a good
mommy, and they feel happy. They seem to be saying,

"All is well." Children show no shades of gray; things are all good when they are getting what they want.

On the other side, when children are frustrated, everybody is bad. Mommy is a bad mommy, Daddy is a bad daddy, and the world is a bad place to live. A child cannot understand that the same mommy who is three minutes late for feeding was the one who comforted her and made life wonderful the night before!

When Mommy finally comes and gives her what she wants, she is all good again. No one in the world would be able to convince her that she is not perfect at that moment. She is with the "all-good mommy."

Over time, when the mother continues to minister to her needs and the child internalizes this love, and she forgives her attacks, she slowly begins to realize that she is not all good or all bad. Goodness has withstood the frustration. She learns that the same person who loves her frustrates her. The same mother who plays with her sometimes makes her wait to play. If there is enough good, she is able to tolerate the bad.

On the one hand, if there is not enough good and enough forgiveness, then the good and the bad never come together. Children from these kinds of homes continue to split their world into good guys and bad guys—they love people who gratify them and hate people who don't, love jobs that gratify them and leave jobs that don't, love wives who gratify them and leave those who don't, for the bad guys are all bad.

On the other hand, children who are never frustrated can become unforgiving children as well. If getting the good and the bad together depends on a dance between frustration and gratification, and one is never frustrated, one never learns to forgive the source of frustration. We all have seen very pampered people who make the world all bad as soon as they have to wait five minutes in a line for a movie. They are unable to put good and bad together.

In either case, when good and bad are not tolerated together, one sees people as good if they are gratifying and bad if they are not. Such people are not able to forgive the "good guy" who also makes mistakes.

Later in development, as children get more mobile, the ideal self comes into play. They begin to feel as if they can do anything; they feel very grandiose and superhuman with their newfound "power." They can talk, explore, and run. They have not yet had enough falling-down experiences. The ideal is at its height, and they wish to be seen as ideal. This is the elated period of "Look, Mommy." We all go through a stage where we want to be appreciated and made a big deal over.

Gradually, however, the grandiose ideal self should give way to reality. Children learn that falling down is a part of life and that they are not invincible. When our frailties are understood and loved by others, we learn to accept them into our picture of ourselves and to value the *real* self, which is not perfect, grandiose, or ideal. We learn to have what Paul calls "sober judgment" in thinking about ourselves (Rom. 12:3). We learn to not see ourselves so grandiosely, and we learn to value the real self with its frailties, as well as forgive and accept the real self of others with their limitations.

Then, later, as we begin to perform in life, we learn not only that we are good and bad, but also that we succeed and fail. We work on the relationship between our expectations and our performance. At this point it is possible to develop an attacking and judging relationship to the real. This kind of relationship develops when our failures are not lovingly forgiven, but harshly judged. Failures should be confessed, discussed, and forgiven.

Parents need to accept failure the same way God does.

He does not deny failures, nor does he beat us up for them. He convicts us—he shows us the truth—but he gives us tender love and compassion as well, for "God's kindness leads you toward repentance" (Rom. 2:4). God's kindness and compassion tenderly lead us to deal with failure and badness, not heavy-handed judgment and condemnation. If this were everyone's parenting style, we would have very few people feeling that their failures were too big to handle or that they were the only ones who had ever failed.

Love and Acceptance

Love is the solution and resolution to all problems of good and bad. When we were in the Garden of Eden, perfectly loved and accepted, good and bad was not an issue. When we disobeyed, good and bad became a paramount issue.

If we have enough love with limits, or grace with truth, we begin to experience the way God relates to us and to learn that we are standing in grace (Rom. 5:2), where judgment and condemnation don't come into the picture. We experience badness and failure as a sad thing, for it causes us to miss out on loving someone. If we aren't worried about condemnation when we sin, we have more energy to be worried about the one we hurt. That is godly sorrow instead of crippling guilt.

In the first chapter on bonding, I told about how I sometimes ask seminar participants, "If I handed you a baseball bat and gave you permission to bash my face in, would you do it?" People who say they would not hit me with the baseball bat because "That is a bad thing to do" are not basing their statements on the highest Christian morality. Since condemnation is out of the picture for the Christian, the real reason is the one based on love: "No, because it would hurt you." Jesus says this when he says the whole law could be summed up in the law of love. When we see our failures and sin as a lack of love for another person, instead of "badness," then we have moved to a more mature way of seeing issues of good and bad.

This is true of ourselves as well. If, when we sin, we can see how our sin hurts us, instead of calling ourselves "bad people," we can begin to get out of the slavery of the "law of sin and death." Only when we get a picture of the self-destructive nature of our sin do we begin to change. Guilt manipulation does not work; it only makes us sin all the more. "The law was added so that the trespass might increase. But where sin increased, grace increased all the more" (Rom. 5:20).

This is the simple truth of the gospel: only grace sets us free. "Who will rescue me from this body of death?" Paul asks when he is struggling with repeated sin (Rom. 7:24). He goes on to say, "Therefore, there is now no condemnation for those who are in Christ Jesus" (Rom. 8:1). It is only when we are no longer condemned for the bad that we can let go of it. Because we have been set free from that law, we can walk after the Spirit.

But, if we still see our badness as something that incurs condemnation and guilt, the sin cycle will continue. This cycle is easy to see in people struggling with addictions or compulsive behavior. They act out. They feel terrible and unlovable. Then they act out again to get relief from feeling unlovable. Lee is a good example of this.

Lee checked into the hospital for depression, which was secondary to his enormous guilt for sexual addiction. His "sin cycle" went this way. When he began to feel lonely, he would want to see a prostitute. He felt bad for this desire, but he would go anyway. Afterward, he would feel so guilty that it would take weeks for him to shake it off. In the meantime, because of the guilt, he would feel more and more unlovable and he would withdraw. Withdrawal from friends and family would increase his "need," and the compulsion to release the tension, pain, and loneliness would return. He would then visit another prostitute, and the guilt would return, thus setting up the cycle again.

When he began to talk about his addiction in a small support group, he found that he was not condemned. He found that people were not surprised at his "badness" and that they loved him in spite of his acting out. He tried over and over to resist that love and acceptance and to hide from it. But gradually he learned that "no condemnation" was a state that he could not lose and that he would not be condemned if he sinned again. His standing did not change with his performance.

In a state of "no condemnation," Lee learned that his "badness" and guilt was not the issue at all; these had been taken care of at the cross. The real issue was the way he was selling himself short of real love. This is what was killing him. But he could not get to the reality of the destructiveness of his sin until he could get off the guilt cycle. It is only through "no condemnation" that sin loses its power.

Accept the Sinner, Hate the Sin

Badness is never an issue for the Christian, for that has been taken away; we are accepted "in the One he loves" (Eph. 1:6). The real issue is the sin, not the sinner. We are not to be on a merry-go-round of feeling as if we are good when we do good things to feeling as if we are bad when we sin. We are in a constant position of being loved.

Hebrews goes to great pains to point out that the issue of guilty versus not guilty, or good versus bad has been dealt with: "By one sacrifice he has made perfect forever those who are being made holy. The Holy Spirit also testifies to us about this: 'Their sins and lawless acts I will remember no more'" (Heb. 10:14–15, 17).

Many Christians stay on the old merry-go-round, where they think they go from a forgiven state to a guilty state, back to a forgiven state, and so on. They never feel secure in their acceptance. They do not realize that Jesus "is able to save completely those who come to God through him, because he always lives to intercede for them. Unlike the other high priests, he does not need to offer sacrifices day after day, first for his own sins, and then for the sins of the people. He sacrificed for their sins once for all when he offered himself" (Heb. 7:25, 27). Jesus has made us acceptable "once for all." This is not something we lose, slipping into a "bad" state with God. The question is not, "Are we good or bad?" but the question is, "What are we doing?"

If we are hurting someone, God, or ourselves, this sin will grieve us if we do not focus on our guilt. That grief, called godly sorrow, will move us not to punish ourselves or anyone else but to take care of the one being hurt. This is the essence of a love-based morality, instead of a fear-and-punishment-based morality prescribed by the law.

It is a powerful thing, this "no condemnation." It transforms lives. When someone can get to a point where they do not feel condemned, no matter what they do, they are well on the way to being more and more loving, for "he who is forgiven much, loves much." This is the nature of the relationship between the ideal and the real—one of correction toward a goal of love, instead of one of anger and attack toward the real self who fails.

Chapter 12

When We Fail to Accept Good and Bad

LIKE IT OR NOT, WE LIVE IN AN IMPERFECT world. As we all know, the world is not purely "good." Fortunately, however, the world is not purely "bad" either. Rather, the world is a sometimes confusing mixture of good and bad. People who can't deal with that fact develop some of the following problems.

Perfectionism

Perfectionism is an extreme or excessive striving for perfection of self, others, and the world. Everything must be without flaw, or it is not good. We can see this in work, relationships, hobbies, and feelings. Perfectionism is the demand for a pre-Fall existence and the rejection of any person or thing not perfect.

Idealism

This romantic version of perfectionism is an inability

to see the bad that is really there. Idealists look at the world through rose-colored glasses. Everything is "made perfect" in the eyes of the beholder. Idealists can get into some very bad situations, for the bad they deny from the outset can later come up and get them. For example, a woman might idealize her lover to such an extent that she is blind to some serious character problems.

Inability to Tolerate Badness

This is the rejection of anything "not holy." This pharisaical personality is averse to human badness. In this "holier than thou" syndrome, badness can't be tolerated, much less accepted.

Inability to Tolerate Weakness

Human weakness is rejected because it isn't ideal. Based in the wish to be god-like, this symptom is a very cruel sort of splitting. It leads to all sorts of relational difficulties and hates vulnerability and inability of any sort. This is an arrogant stance, because we all are weak, and in that weakness, God's strength is made manifest.

Inability to Tolerate Negative Feelings

This avoidance of negative emotions shows itself in two ways: these people move away from uncomfortable feelings, like anger, sadness, and disappointment, in other people, and they deny these feelings altogether in themselves.

Affective Problems

Affective problems are problems that relate to feelings or emotions. Depression and excessive moodiness can result from the inability to handle negative feelings. If people can't process sadness and anger, they will invariably experience a mood problem of some sort.

Self-Image Problems

The only way people can feel good about themselves, can have a good self-image, is to have the real self loved unconditionally. People who can't deal with good and bad can't bring the less-than-ideal parts of themselves into relationship and have them accepted. If this happens, they can't have a positive self-image because they are too afraid of the bad.

Anxiety and Panic

Anxiety and panic can arise from the possible discovery of any negative. People get anxious when they feel a negative feeling coming into consciousness, or they panic if they think that someone else will see some negative aspect of them. Some people have panic attacks because of a spot on their clothes.

Eating and Substance Problems

Eating disorders and substance abuse problems can be ways of dealing with unresolved negative emotions. People eat or use drugs or alcohol to numb painful negative emotions. For instance, instead of processing sadness over some loss or failure, they may avoid these negative feelings through alcohol.

Narcissism

Narcissism is, simply speaking, self-love, or an excessive interest in one's own appearance, comfort, importance, or abilities. Narcissists are preoccupied with an idealized image of themselves. They focus so strongly on themselves and the image they portray that they lose their real self. Life is a series of events organized to support this idealized image. Love is out of the picture. Admiration is all that counts.

Guilt

If people can't admit their faults, they can't bring their real self into a confessional relationship with God and others. They can never resolve their critical conscience, and they can never emotionally reach the state of "no condemnation." They have never experienced "total acceptance." Consequently, guilt plagues them. They are preoccupied with issues of their own goodness and badness, instead of their love relationship with Christ and others.

Sexual Addiction

Many people who compulsively act out sexually are running from lost ideals and from unprocessed pain. They are looking for sexual idealism, or trying to use sex as a way to deal with pain.

Broken Relationships

A series of broken relationships with people, jobs, careers, or spouses signals a severe problem with issues of goodness and badness. In the beginning, something looks good to these people, but when negative aspects rear up, they break off the relationship, or quit the job, or change the career, or divorce the spouse. They can't perceive good *and* bad in a person or a situation. They see people as all good *or* all bad.

Excessive Rage

People who split good and bad have problems with excessive rage. Their frustration threshold is low. When something bad happens, there is no good to counteract it. The person they are dealing with has all of a sudden turned into their worst enemy, and their emotions are all negative. There is no love to temper the anger.

All-Bad Me

Sometimes people believe they are "all bad." They are unable to see their strengths as well as their weaknesses.

All-Good Me

All-good people are defensive about taking responsibility for any fault. They may globally assent to the fact that they are "sinners," but they do not own specific faults.

Barriers to Resolving Good and Bad

Certain barriers block us from resolving issues of good and bad. We distort our view of ourselves, others, and God.

Distorted Thinking

<u>Our View of Self</u>

"I am really not worth loving."

People who have been unable to risk showing their real self to others may still think that they are unlovable, a belief they built in childhood. They don't realize that our "lovability" rests on the ability of the one doing the loving, not on our merit.

A man in a support group said about the other group members, "I don't deserve their love." I told him he was right. None of us deserves love that comes our way; we don't earn love. It is given to us. Approval can be earned, but love can't.

"My badness is worse than anyone else's."

Many people who have not had experience opening up to fellow strugglers believe this. They have not found the community of strugglers the Bible describes. They feel as if they are the only ones with the feelings Jesus mentions in Mark 7:21–22: "Out of men's hearts come evil thoughts, sexual immorality, theft, murder, adultery, greed, malice, deceit, lewdness, envy, slander, arrogance, and folly." They feel as if everyone else is somehow less fallen than they.

"I have unacceptable feelings."

Some people condemn themselves for their "less-than-ideal" feelings, such as neediness, sadness, sex, and weakness. These human feelings are not sinful in themselves, but have been judged as bad by the ideal self.

"I should be better than I am."

People who hold this belief underestimate the effects of the Fall. They have not yet seen how deeply the Fall has affected us. Somehow they think they should have missed it.

"I am ideal."

People rarely state this view so blatantly, but many believe it. These people think that they really are special and that normal badness doesn't apply to them. They are somehow above it.

"I am unforgivable."

These people think they have committed some unpardonable sin. To them, their badness exceeds that of the human race and the limits of God's forgiveness. They don't know that the only way they can be unforgivable is to not want forgiveness.

"I can't stand an imperfect world."

This distorted view keeps many people slaves to perfectionism. They think they cannot be happy in a less-than-ideal world. They become so disappointed that they reject whatever is less than ideal and miss out on the real.

"I have no strengths or talents."

Some people think they have been born without any goodness whatsoever. The Bible teaches that we are fallen, but that we all have strengths and talents. Some fears and distortions convince some people that they have none, so they give up and don't look.

Our View of Others

"They will dislike me for my badness."

People who struggle with good and bad have learned that their badness will be hated or disliked. They view others as rejecting parents, quick to judge and slow to love. Because this fear keeps them from opening up, it cannot be disproven without new experiences. For this reason, confession to others is important.

"They will attack me for my weakness."

Some think that their vulnerability will bring down the heavy hand of the law. It's as if there is some presence ready to pounce on their weaknesses and judge them the way their parents did.

"They don't have feelings like this."

Often people will idealize others, thinking that the one with whom they are speaking is perfect. They fear that they will be less than perfect. Learning that others are sinners too makes life a lot easier.

"They will leave me if they find out . . ."

A fear of abandonment underlies many attempts to be

perfect. These people believe their connection with other people is so shaky that a mistake or flaw will sever it. Actually, opening up about our weaknesses serves to cement relationships and bonding. Keeping them hidden keeps the connection weak. This happens in a lot of marriages.

"They will not like me if I am not all bad."

Some people develop the all-bad position as a defense against the envy of others. They try to hide their strengths from other people, fearing that they can only be liked without good parts, without talents. They fear people will resent their achievements, so they hide them.

"They will respect my Christian walk only if I am perfect."

This is a major heresy. People are supposed to respect Christ, not us. Nothing is less attractive than a Pharisee. We need to show others that Jesus is the Savior of imperfect people like us so they can be led to grace instead of spiritual narcissism. The Bible lists many failures of spiritual leaders to show the grace and strength of God, not people. The wish for "spiritual respect" is the refusal to fall on our face and beg for mercy and forgiveness.

Our View of God

"God expects me to be all good."

Nothing could be further from the truth, but no distortion is more common than this one. God has said repeatedly that we are sinners, and he expects us to fall over and over again. He knows our frame, says the psalmist (Ps. 103:14). We must comprehend the way in which God sees us, both to be humbled away from our perfectionism and to be awestruck by his grace.

"God accepts me when I am good and rejects me when
I am bad. Then he will accept me again when I am
good."

This roller-coaster view of God does not realize the
once-and-for-all aspect of the salvation God provides.
We truly are in a safe standing with him; therefore, we
can reveal our weaknesses.

"God is shocked at times by me."

Some people cringe at times at what they think and
do. The truth is that God knew it all before we were
even born. He knew that sin or that weakness, and he
still loved and saved us. Nothing we can think or do will
ever shock him.

"God will reject me if I do . . ."

The Bible teaches that the Christian can never be
rejected. Some people have been loved so conditionally
that they cannot imagine another person who will
"never drive them away" (John 6:37). They live in fear of
losing their relationship with God.

"God is keeping track of my badness."

While it is true that God is watching us and keeping a
record of our lives, he doesn't do it to punish us. He has
put our sins as far as the east is from the west. "Christ,
having been offered once to bear the sins of many, will
appear a second time, not to deal with sin, but to save
those who are eagerly waiting for him" (Heb. 9:28).

"God thinks immaturity is bad."

People who believe this forget that God understands
the growth process, and that it takes time. He does not
excuse things; he takes them into account. He looks at us
as a father looks at a child. We are growing, and he does

not expect perfection. Jesus predicted Peter's failure and recovery. He knew it was coming. Immaturity is not a moral question. Young is not bad; it is young.

"God cannot understand my struggle."

People sometimes think that because God is God he cannot understand human badness and weakness. That is why Jesus became man. He is a high priest who can "sympathize with our weaknesses" (Heb. 4:15). He has felt everything that we can ever feel, yet without sin.

These distortions form the prison that houses the real self. Satan has always tried to trick us into believing lies, and he steals lives through these lies and distortions. We need to confront the lies and see where they came from, rebuking them in the mighty name of Jesus.

All of these distortions were learned in the context of relationship, and it is in the context of relationship that they need to be unlearned. We internalize how we are treated, and we must put ourselves into situations where God's ways of relating to us are learned instead of our old ways of relating. Again, as in the other stages, this is not done without risk and pain. However, real healing and spiritual power can be found if one can get into a confessing, safe relationship, where the darkness can be made light and the "dark parts" can find forgiveness and acceptance.

Chapter ✌13

Learning to Accept
Both Good and Bad

THE PLACE WHERE WE ALL NEED TO LIVE IN
relation to the issue of good and bad is one of "no condemnation." But, how do we get there emotionally?

A first step is to look at the emotional nature of our
relationship between the ideal and the real. If this relationship is one of loving acceptance and correction
toward a loving goal, then we will see our failures as
something to learn from. If the relationship is one of
splitting good and bad, anger, condemnation and punishment, we will see our failures as something to hide.

Why We Split Good and Bad

A wrong relationship between the real and the ideal
comes from two sources: nature and nurture.

We are all born with a sinful nature. We are born with

a "wish to be like God" (Gen. 3:6–7; Isa. 14:13–14). We want to be more than we are. This is part of the reason we have such a lofty view of the ideal self. Also, we are born under the law; we are born with a fallen conscience that punishes us for failing in any way. "For whoever keeps the whole law and yet stumbles at just one point is guilty of breaking all of it" (James 2:10).

In addition, we are nurtured by imperfect people who relate to us imperfectly, and they often act "wrathfully" toward us when we fail, reinforcing our condemning conscience. We internalize our parents' critical natures into a self-evaluating system that we call our conscience, and it speaks to us in much the same way that our parents did. If they were loving and accepting, our conscience is loving and accepting. If they were harsh and critical, our conscience is harsh and critical.

How We Get Good and Bad Back Together

We can be forgiven out of this unloved state. We can learn forgiveness in relationships of grace. This is one of the tasks of the body of Christ. We are to accept and love each other in spite of our failures and gently correct each other toward a goal of love.

Forgiving relationships within the church can cure the problem of splitting good and bad. The two most important medicines for curing this problem are confession and forgiveness. A third is integrating negative emotions.

Confess

"Confess your sins to each other and pray for each other so that you may be healed" (James 5:16). Christians know they need to confess their sins to God. But this is only half the issue. They need to confess their sins to *each other*. Much pain comes from our inability both to confess our sins to other people and to feel loved and forgiven by them. In order to feel God's forgiveness, we need acceptance from his people. If we confess our offenses to one another and are accepted in spite of them, our relationship to the ideal changes. We begin to internalize the acceptance we feel from others, and our conscience changes: it becomes more loving.

At the same time, the badness that was in the darkness (1 John 1:5) comes into the light, and Jesus transforms it. Confession is the only way that our problems with good and bad can be transformed. What was buried in the darkness comes into the light and gets loved both by God and others.

The Fall separated us from God, ourselves, and others. As a result, aspects of ourselves are hidden "in the darkness." We hide them from God, ourselves, and others, and they get worse. Outside of relationship, they get darker and darker. In addition, our attitudes and behaviors are separated from grace, truth, and time, and therefore are not growing and changing.

When we confess to God, this buried part comes into relationship with him, and he can begin to cleanse and heal it. When we confess to others, they can begin to accept us and heal our isolation. We move into a loved position.

But many of us have a problem with confessing to others. We think of excuses like, "Don't share it until it is a victory." This directly contradicts the Word. The Bible commands us to confess to one another. Anything short of this is pride. We do not want to reveal our real self because we want to appear to be perfect, or all good. We use excuses such as trying to be a "good witness," but the real issue is pride. A "good witness" is a sinner who "witnesses" not to show how victorious he is, but how forgiving God is.

This does not mean that we are to confess to just anyone. This is dangerous. We need to confess to those who love us and can offer us the grace of God as his incarnational ambassadors. This will transform our split between good and bad, for he who has been forgiven much, loves much.

The sad thing is that many people confess shallow things, such as lack of quiet times, impatience, and swearing, instead of the cancers that kill our souls (Mark 7:21–22). If we were confessing these soul-killers to God and others, and felt absolutely no condemnation for them, our personality would be integrated. Hiding those aspects of ourselves causes them to go into the darkness and take on a life of their own. This is how the roller-coaster Christian experience often happens. A whole host of hatred and grief is covered up (in Jesus' words "dark parts"), and they come out in all sorts of psychological problems and dysfunctions.

Realizing our forgiveness through confessing our real self to others in grace and truth is the key to changes that heal. We integrate what is in the darkness, as well as change the relationship between the ideal and the real. As condemnation goes out of that relationship, greater and greater peace grows, and the person becomes less and less divided between the ideal and the real. The ideal self can become a goal and not a demand, and the true self can be loved along the way. Al is a good example.

Al came into the hospital because of explosive rage. At unexpected intervals, he would explode at anyone who made a mistake. The anger that would pour forth scared everyone, especially his children.

In therapy he confessed his intense hatred for his father. He had felt that, as a Christian, he "shouldn't" hate his father. He had denied his feelings and had become two people. On the one hand, he was the

Christian "nice" guy; on the other hand, he was hiding his hatred. As he learned that the Bible did not condemn him for his hatred, he was able to confess it to others and to God and to find the real reason for it.

In a small support group, he was able to gain both understanding for the injuries that had caused the rage and forgiveness for wanting to get back at his father. As he was free to confess in an atmosphere of no condemnation, his "dark parts" began to get forgiven and healed. This is very different from mere catharsis, or eliminating a problem by bringing it to consciousness and expressing it; it is allowing the Light to touch the dark wounded places and doing away with the laws that force "unacceptable" aspects into hiding.

As this process continued, Al began to accept and forgive others when they failed. The way that his father had sinned against him was being transformed through confession.

Forgive

A second important ingredient in curing the good-bad split is forgiving others. Jesus said that "if you do not forgive others, neither will your Father forgive your trespasses" (Matt. 6:15 NRSV). Since we are forgiven when we accept Christ, Jesus must mean that if we don't forgive others, we have not allowed his grace to touch us and bear fruit.

Matthew 18:29 hints at this interpretation. The servant who owed a great debt says to his master, "Be patient with me, and I will pay back everything." The master took pity on him, canceled his debt, and let him go. The servant then goes out and demands repayment from a fellow servant who owed him a very small debt. In effect, the servant never experienced grace. He was still trying to repay his master, so he demanded repayment from others as well. Usually this is the reason people are unforgiving: they have never truly received grace for themselves. They are still trying to repay God, and earn their ideal standing. They are still under the law.

Some who have received grace still want repayment from others. We must forgive others' debts in order to be healed. If we don't, we are handcuffing ourselves to the one who hurt us. Forgiveness is the knife that will cut through those handcuffs. Letting someone off the hook for what they have done to you is freeing yourself from that abusive relationship. Bitterness and holding a grudge will forever connect you to your abuser. When we can sever that tie through forgiveness, and then accept those who have hurt us as God has accepted us, then we are free to integrate our own "bad" and unforgiven parts. No part of us that is tied to others by revenge will love and be loved. We must confess and forsake hatred.

Integrate Negative Emotions

Many people conceal their negative feelings of anger, sadness, and fear. These people are unable to cope with good and bad because they have never processed these negative feelings, and they suffer from many problems, such as fear of relationships, depression, and anxiety as a result. Negative feelings are valid, and they must be dealt with so they won't cause problems.

Anger

Anger, our most basic negative emotion, tells us that something is wrong. We tend to protect the good we don't want to lose. Anger is a signal that we are in danger of losing something that matters to us.

When people are taught to suppress their anger, they are taught to be out of touch with what matters to them. Ephesians 4:26, citing Psalm 4:4, says, "In your anger do not sin: Do not let the sun go down while you are still angry, and do not give the devil a foothold." It is good to feel angry because anger warns us of danger and shows us what needs protecting. But, we are not to sin in our attempt to resolve the problem. This would mean to resolve it in some unloving way and would ultimately hurt us as well as the other.

Major consequences for denying our angry feelings range all the way from psychophysiological disorders, such as headaches and ulcers, to character disorders, such as passive-aggression, to the inability to work, to serious depression and panic. Any way you look at it, denying anger keeps one from getting problems solved.

Another problem with denying anger is that it turns into bitterness and leads to a critical and unforgiving spirit: "See to it that no one misses the grace of God and that no bitter root grows up to cause trouble and defile many" (Heb. 12:15). Bitterness leaves the door open for Satan to come in and take control.

Instead of denying anger, we must own it and find its source. As we examine our anger, we can find out what we are trying to protect. Anger may be protecting an injured vulnerability or a will that was controlled. We may be under condemnation from someone and need to get out from under perfectionism. Whatever the source, anger tells you there is a problem, and it should never be denied.

We may discover that our anger is protecting something bad, such as pride, omnipotence, control, or perfectionism. Maybe we feel angry because we are losing control of another person. In either case, if we deny our anger, we can't get to the source. Anger, then, is helpful because it is a sign something is being protected, either good or bad.

Sadness

Sadness signals hurt and loss. We live in a world where we get hurt and lose things and people. Sadness helps us grieve and let go. If we repress and deny sadness, we will inevitably become depressed. Unresolved sadness leads to depression and often to a whole host of other symptoms.

The Teacher in Ecclesiastes says, "Sorrow is better than laughter, because a sad face is good for the heart. The heart of the wise is in the house of mourning" (7:3–4). Psalm 30:5 says that "weeping may remain for a night, but rejoicing comes in the morning." Sadness is always the path to joy, because sadness signals a hurt that needs to be processed.

When people deny their sad feelings, they "harden" their heart and lose touch with the tender, grace-giving aspects of the image of God. The New American Standard Bible describes these people as "callous" (Eph. 4:19); other versions describe them as "being past feeling" (NKJV) or "having lost all sensitivity" (NIV). They become unable to love and be tender, or to feel grief over their sin. This state leads them to become very insensitive people.

In addition, suppressing grief leads to all sorts of symptoms, including depression, physiological problems, substance abuse, and eating disorders.

Susan was in her mid-twenties when she began to have panic attacks. She would wake up in the middle of the night and fear that she was dying. If she saw anything on television about death or read about death in the newspaper, she would cease functioning. The panic and dread of death would overwhelm her. Finally, when the panic attacks rendered her unable to work, someone referred her to me.

"I feel ashamed that I'm so afraid to die," she said in our first meeting. "I'm a Christian. I shouldn't be so afraid. My friends keep telling me to memorize verses on death, but it doesn't help." Susan was feeling confused and hopeless because her friends' answers hadn't worked. She didn't know what else to do.

Susan had grown up very isolated in her family. Her parents were very nonrelational people. The only person she felt close to was her sister, Rebecca, who was a few years older than she. One morning, when she was fifteen, she tried wake Rebecca, to no avail. Her sister had died during the night.

Her grief was overwhelming. But her father told the family that day, "There will be no more discussion of Rebecca's death. We must all be strong. Let's forget the past and go on."

Understandably, Susan had many unresolved grief feelings about her sister. Very sad that Rebecca was gone and unable to work through her grief, Susan had a very deep wish to be with Rebecca, her only source of love. This wish registered in her conscious mind as a fear; in reality, it was what she wanted—to be with her sister.

As we began to talk about this loss, Susan began to grieve for her sister. She was able to talk through all of the feelings she had been denying for years and years. Over a period of months, she went through a normal grief cycle, letting go of her sister. This should have happened when she was fifteen, but it was delayed by her family's rule against sadness and weakness.

As she processed this sadness, she lost her fear of dying, as well as the vague depression she had experienced off and on for years.

An important aspect to sadness is tenderness. One of the major aspects of the image of God, our sadness must be protected at all costs. If we can't feel sad, we get cold-hearted.

Fear

Fear is another negative emotion that signals danger.

The danger may be real or imaginary, but we must be aware of our fear to work through it.

The Bible often tells us, usually in the context of not properly placing our trust in God and his provision, to "fear not" because God will protect us. It is an important choice to make. However, if we are not aware of our fear, we cannot make this choice to trust in God, and thus stay even further away. And sometimes, the root of the fear is something other than a lack of trust.

In addition, some who deny their fear turn into cold, insensitive people, who are proud and combative. If we are not afraid and we are not trusting in God, the only other option is to trust in our own ability to win in every situation.

Denying fear keeps us out of touch with our humble position in the universe and keeps us away from God. It is our fear and lack of control over much of life that leads us to our heavenly Father; we must be in touch with our fears to get to a position of need.

If people are out of touch with their fears of abandonment, for example, they will be out of touch with their need for other people and treat them very insensitively. This happens often in marriage when one partner is not in touch with the fear of being left. This partner takes the other "for granted." Fear gets us in touch with our very real vulnerability, and it gets us in touch with our need for others and God. Many times people treat others very insensitively because they are warding off their fears of being vulnerable.

Other Skills Needed to Integrate Good and Bad

Growth does not come without effort. Many skills must be learned and practiced in order to resolve issues of the good and the bad. Here are some.

Pray

Besides confessing your sins, ask God to make you aware of things you may be ignoring. David prayed, "Search me, O God, and know my heart; test me and know my anxious thoughts. See if there is any offensive way in me, and lead me in the way everlasting" (Ps. 139:23–24).

Ask God to shine his light into your soul and reveal anything that you are unaware of. Then ask his forgiveness for it.

Rework the Ideal

Much of the content of our ideal self is false; it is not what an ideal person would be. Check out what needs to be eliminated from your picture of what an ideal you would be. You may need to delete some ideals that come from your family or the culture, instead of from God.

Rework Distortions

Challenge your distorted views of God, yourself, and others. These strongly held beliefs don't give way easily, but in new relationships, you can unlearn them. Study the Scriptures to see what they say about our ideal, our reality, and what God and salvation are really like.

Monitor the Relationship Between the Ideal and the Real

Listen to the way you respond to the less than ideal. Do you deny it? Do you deny the good? Do you attack and judge? Do you accept and forgive? Many people are stunned to find out how much they attack themselves and others.

Practice Loving the Less than Ideal in Others

Learning to accept badness and weakness in others

brings healing in the split of the good and bad. Stay connected to others when they are less than ideal, and you will begin to value real relationship and stop demanding idealism. In this way, attachment increases, and your ability to love grows. The less than ideal begins to matter more than the ideal because you have a real relationship.

Do Not Discard Others When They Are Less Than Perfect

If you have had trouble with going from friend to friend, spouse to spouse, church to church, because you find some little flaw and make them all bad, work on staying in connection and working out the problem. Actively see the good as well as the bad, and love the whole person. Make reality your friend instead of your enemy.

Process and Value Negative Feelings

When you are committed to reality, to both the good and the bad, you will begin to see negative feelings as a part of life. If you fear them less, you can then process them as they arise and avoid all the problems listed in the last chapter. Most problems with negative feelings come from a fear about them. They really are not as bad as you fear they are. Negative feelings will not kill you, but avoiding them may.

Expect Badness and Weakness from Everyone

I'm not suggesting you turn into a pessimist. I'm saying, "Be a realist." Everyone you know, including yourself, has good and bad, strengths and weaknesses. Therefore, expect to see them in action. When the faults come, embrace them and love them so that you can overcome your splitting of good and bad as well as feel closer to others.

Expect Faults from the Creation

Because the world is real, not ideal, everything can eventually break down. Every holiday you plan can potentially get rained out. Every plant you grow will have some dead leaves. Expect things to go wrong, and you will not be surprised. You will be able to value that less-than-ideal car, house, city that you have or live in. It may not be ideal, but it's probably good enough.

Ted

Remember Ted? He had set himself up for a breakdown, pursuing success after success to cover up the hurt of his early family life.

Ted's parents had had many problems, and they too had tried to cover them up with their successes. Uncomfortable with imperfection, they criticized any aspect of Ted or the other children that did not fit their perfect image. The children had to be perfect in school, sports, manners, and everything else.

"My father was very domineering," Ted told me. "He'd attack any weakness in me. I could never show when I felt bad, and I could *never* cry in front of him!"

Ted soon learned not to show his hurts and weaknesses. Because he could not share these negative parts of himself with others, he began to hide them even from himself.

When his parents divorced, he was devastated. "Even though my father sounds like a cold person, I loved him," he said. "And I loved my mother as well."

The divorce left Ted full of unresolved, unexpressed hurt and anger. For years he buried his feelings. Using his parents' method of dealing with bad situations, he pursued one accomplishment after another. Yet none of his achievements was able to erase his pain.

When his accomplishments were threatened with business failure and marital problems, he had nowhere to turn. He had never been accepted for his real self. He had never had someone love him even when he had failed. He could not conceive of love apart from performance, or friendship apart from admiration.

Luckily for Ted, others could conceive of it. His friends rallied around him, showing him that they loved him for himself, not his accomplishments. They told him of their own failures, and he learned that failure was not the end of the world, and that success was not what love was built on. He began to open up about his hurts and fears.

Loved back to health by his friends, Ted slowly began to give up on pursuing his "ideal self." Instead, he began to show people his real self with all its hurts, sinfulness, weakness, and immaturity. Liberated from his ideal self, he later started support groups for people in the same situation.

Ted did not give up the pursuit of excellence; he put it into perspective. Instead of working for admiration, he worked out of a foundation of love. Failure did not phase him, and success did not define his existence. He loved his work, but he loved the people in his life even more. Having found love, he no longer needed the ideal.

Part V

Becoming an
Adult

Chapter ❧14

What Is Adulthood?

SARA WAS ANXIOUS ABOUT EVERYTHING. "I'M never able to relax," she admitted to me at her first counseling session, "no matter how well things are going or how successful I am. I always think something's going to go wrong, or that I haven't done quite enough."

She worried most about what other people thought of her. Constantly on her guard, she did everything she could to make sure her superiors approved of her work.

In addition, Sara always had an older woman in her life whom she looked up to but could somehow never please. From her early twenties till her late thirties she was tormented by these women, who were always proper, sweet, and concerned, but who had a critical streak in them a mile wide. "Your living room would look warmer if you changed the color of your drapes," they'd say. Or, "If you were more strict in your discipline, your children would obey you more readily." Whatever their opinion, she would faithfully comply and await their approval. When they didn't approve, she would feel enormously guilty, but when they did approve, she could get only short-lived satisfaction.

Not only was Sara striving to please these women, she also labored to please her husband. She sought his approval and felt horrible if she did not receive it. Sexually, she was uneasy and unfulfilled, always wondering if she had performed "well enough," and never feeling satisfied herself. Over the years, she had steadily lost interest in sex, but she did not like her husband to see her as cold.

Poor Sara. She was just a little person trying to make it in a big person's world. What was she doing wrong?

Sara was one-down in all her important relationships. Her husband and these women were above her, and it was her task to gain their acceptance and approval in order to feel like she was okay. Like a child, she continually sought parental approval. She was a "little person in a big person's world."

Sara was not able to enjoy peer relationships with other adults. The freedom that adults have—to make their own decisions without permission from others, to evaluate and judge their own performance, to choose their own values and opinions, to disagree with others freely, and to enjoy sexual relations with an equal spouse—somehow had escaped her.

The Nature of the Problem

Everyone who has ever lived has encountered a particular problem: being born a little person in a big person's world and being given the task of becoming a big person over time. We are all born children under adult authority, and over time we are to become authorities ourselves and be in charge of our lives.

This section will explore the problem of coming out from under a one-down relationship to the adult world and assuming one's role as an adult equal with other adults. *Becoming an adult is the process of moving out of a "one-up/one-down" relationship and into a peer relationship to other adults.* Becoming an adult is assuming the authority position of life, an important part of the image of God.

Authority has a number of different facets: power, expertise, office, influence, and submission. Adults have the *power* or right to give commands, enforce obedience, take action, or make final decisions. Adults often derive authority from their *expertise* or knowledge. They also have authority because of their *office*, or the position they hold. Parents, for example, have authority over children because they are parents. In addition, adults have *influence* in the arena in which they operate. What they do affects other people. A final part of being an authority is to be able to give up rights and serve others in submission.

In terms of functioning in the image of God, we need to have command over our lives and the domain God has given us, officiate a role or office when asked, influence out of real ownership of something, have expertise, and submit to the authority of God and others without conflict. No wonder growing up is so hard to do. Many forces and circumstances interfere with the process; nevertheless, we must accomplish the task to function successfully as real image bearers. If we don't attain this position of adulthood, if we stay a child in our adult years, we will suffer significant psychological and emotional distress.

Adults who have not yet become "big people" feel one-down to their contemporaries, or they defensively take the position of being one-up on everyone else. In either case, the developmental task of establishing equality with other adults is imperative if guilt, anxiety, depression, sexual dysfunction, talent development, and spiritual bond servanthood are to be worked through. The developmental process is one of starting life from a position of one-down to the adult world, and gradually growing in stature and wisdom (Luke 2:52) to the point of being an adult in an adult's world.

Becoming an adult is a process of taking on more and more power and responsibility as we become old enough to handle them. Adults identify with the adult role enough to be able to do grown-up things without conflict, including developing a career, engaging in sexuality, establishing mutual friendships, treating other adults as peers, and having opinions. Adults establish a sense of competency over their lives.

This process of starting as little people and becoming equal with big people begins with bonding, having boundaries and separateness, and resolving good and bad, but ultimately has to do with *coming out from under the one-down relationship that a child has to parents and other adults and coming into an equal standing as an adult on his or her own*. This is the final step of development so that one can exercise the gifts and responsibilities God has given. It is a big leap into adulthood, but we are supposed to become equal with other adults. Then we can all be siblings—brothers and sisters—under the fatherhood of God.

Jesus calls us out of the one-down relationship to other people but encourages us to have respect for the role of authority at the same time:

> "The teachers of the law and the Pharisees sit in Moses' seat. So you must obey them and do every-

thing they tell you. But do not do what they do, for they do not practice what they preach. They tie up heavy loads and put them on men's shoulders, but they themselves are not willing to lift a finger to move them.

"Everything they do is done for men to see. They love to be greeted in the marketplaces and to have men call them 'Rabbi.'

"But you are not to be called 'Rabbi,' for you have only one Master and you are all brothers. And do not call anyone on earth 'father,' for you have one Father, and he is in heaven. Nor are you to be called 'teacher,' for you have one Teacher, the Christ." (Matt. 23:2–5, 7–10)

He says to do what Moses commanded, but not to consider other people as above us. Do not see them as fathers, for God is the father of Christian adults, and adults are all brothers and sisters. Do not see others as the leader, for Christ is the leader. He is calling us to the mutual equality of believers, but he is not doing away with the offices others hold. We are to respect the offices of the church. We are to think of other people as equal siblings with us under God, even if they have an office. *To submit to them is to submit to God, not to people.*

People who believe others are above them are still relating from a child's position of being under a person, not under God. This belief makes the difference in one's ability to follow God and to seek God's approval instead of what people want. People who are stuck in this "people-pleasing" stage can't take charge of their lives as God commands. "Many even of the rulers believed in Him, but because of the Pharisees they were not confessing Him, lest they should be put out of the synagogue; for they *loved the approval of men rather than the approval of*

God" (John 12:42–43 NASB, italics mine). These believers could not exercise their faith because they needed approval from human authority. They had not grown up.

Compare this to the statement about Jesus in Mark 12:14. "Teacher, we know you are a man of integrity. You aren't swayed by men, because you pay no attention to who they are; but you teach the way of God in accordance with the truth." Jesus did not fear men; neither did he need their approval as parent figures. As a result, he could speak the truth to them and let them worry about whether or not they liked it.

In fact, Jesus implied that we are doing something wrong if everyone likes us: "Woe to you when all men speak well of you, for that is how their fathers treated the false prophets" (Luke 6:26). There has to be some sort of people-pleasing going on when everyone speaks well of us! We have to be speaking from both sides of our mouth. People-pleasing can even keep one from seeing what is true from God: "How can you believe if you accept praise from one another, yet make no effort to obtain the praise that comes from the only God?" (John 5:44).

Paul also talked about getting out from under the "approval-of-men" trap: "We speak as men approved by God to be entrusted with the gospel. We are not trying to please men but God, who tests our hearts" (1 Thess. 2:4). Both Jesus and Paul realized that to do the authoritative work of adulthood, one could not be seeking the approval of other adults. That is what children do, and children cannot do adults' jobs! Therefore, seeking the approval of God and not trying to please others is an important aspect of growing into adulthood.

Adults make decisions, have opinions, establish values not subject to approval or disapproval from parents or parental figures, and incur legal consequences for their actions. Along with adulthood comes enormous freedom and responsibility, but the main theme is this: adults don't need "permission" from some other person to think, feel, or act. And adults are accountable for the consequences of the things they think, feel, and do.

Sara is a good example of someone who has not become an adult. She does not have the internal "permission" from herself, as the manager of her life, to do and think as she sees fit; she invariably needs approval and permission from some parental figure in her life. She will be burdened by enormous and unending anxiety until she is able to come out from under the pharisaical domination of others.

Becoming an adult is a process of gaining authority over our lives. You can probably think of people who have "taken charge" of their lives, who function as adults. They know what they believe, think through things for themselves, make decisions, do not depend on the approval of others for survival, and have an area or areas of real expertise. One gets a sense from being around these people that they are authoritative. They have become adults.

You probably also know people who seem wishy-washy, who look for other people to tell them what to think and believe, blindly following whatever the last "authority figure" has said. They are easily swayed by the thoughts and opinions of others. Others can make them change direction with a word. Others have too strong an influence over their identity, leaving them with strong feelings of guilt and anxiety. They have not become adults.

These are all issues of becoming one's own adult so that one can submit to the authority of God by choice. Let's look at the biblical basis for authority.

The Biblical Basis for Authority

In the beginning, God made a glorious creation and entrusted it to human beings to govern and rule. He placed Adam and Eve in a position of authority over the creation:

> "Let us make man in our image, in our likeness, and let them *rule* over the fish of the sea and the birds of the air, over the livestock, over all the earth, and over all the creatures that move along the ground."
>
> God blessed them and said to them, "Be fruitful and increase in number; fill the earth and subdue it. Rule over the fish of the sea and the birds of the air and over every living creature that moves on the ground." (Gen. 1:26, 28, italics mine)

Inherent in this lofty position of authority was the power to determine the entire course of the creation. God gave humankind freedom to be a real authority over creation, with real responsibility and real consequences. This was no dress rehearsal. "Now the Lord God had formed out of the ground all the beasts of the field and all the birds of the air. He *brought them to the man to see what he would name them; and whatever the man called each living creature, that was its name*." (Gen. 2:19, italics mine). Listen to the incredible delegation of power and autonomy in this phrase, "whatever the man called each living creature, that was its name."

The one condition to this lofty position of authority was submission to a higher authority: God. God told Adam and Eve to do all that was delegated to them freely, but they needed to stay within the parameters God gave them. They were not to usurp the authority of

God by eating "from the tree of the knowledge of good and evil" (Gen. 2:17). God warned them against trying to function past their given authority. If they did that, they would die.

This is the model. God grants us a lofty position of rulership and authority, of adulthood and responsibility, of freedom to be "in charge" of our lives. Along with this comes the responsibility of submitting to God's authority and the accountability if we fail. Note three aspects of "being in charge": authority, responsibility, and accountability.

The enormity of this trust is evident in the nature of the Fall. When Adam and Eve defied the authority of God, the consequences were grave. We all suffer for the movement the first couple made out from under the authority of God. We also feel the individual consequences when we fail to take authority over our own lives. In short, when we act like children with our adult responsibilities, we run into trouble. This is what Adam and Eve did. They listened to what a serpent said without even questioning and with disastrous results.

Maybe you can feel the individual consequences of your failure to take authority over the domain God has given you to manage. Maybe your finances are a wreck, or you don't know what you believe about certain doctrines, or your children are out of control, or your talents are undeveloped. Whatever the area, when we do not take charge of whatever God has given us to do, we fall from the position God has given, with serious results. This is not punishment from God; it is a validation of the amount of trust and responsibility he has given us.

This is the authoritative position God first gave to us. But after the Fall of Adam and Eve, we were no longer in a free position to take authority over life. Instead, we became slaves, with sin having authority over us. The entire book of Romans is dedicated to the theme of how we lost our freedom and became slaves to sin and how through grace we are returned to freedom and can now be servants of righteousness (Rom. 6:17–18).

Redemption is a reversal of the effects of the Fall—a return to the freedom and authority we had in the beginning. We are now in a position where we can be united with the "new Adam," who is Jesus, and it is impossible for him to rebel against God! This last Adam became "a life-giving spirit" (1 Cor. 15:45). Therefore, to be united with Jesus is to be restored to a real position of authority that cannot fail. So great a salvation!

Our task of regaining our authority over life, then, is directly related to how much we walk "in him" (Col. 3:3; 1 John 2:4–6; 1 John 1:5–7; Col. 2:6). He cannot fail in his task as the second Adam, and the more we identify with him, the more we become like him, the less we fail in taking authority over our lives.

Authority has existed from the beginning, with God being the ultimate authority over all. As God is an authority, we are to be authorities as his image bearers.

In the Old Testament, God placed many people in positions of authority over others. "Choose some wise, understanding and respected men from each of your tribes, and I will set them over you" (Deut. 1:13). He always wanted his kings and leaders to walk with him, however, and to lead his people to him and his ways. There were lines of authority in the law and authority structures in individual families. The three principles present in the Garden of Eden remained: authority, responsibility, and accountability.

Parents, for example, were placed in authority over children, to teach them about God and to lead them in his ways. "These commandments that I give you today are to be upon your hearts. Impress them on your children. Talk about them when you sit at home and when you walk along the road, when you lie down and when you get up" (Deut. 6:6–7). Parents are God's representatives of authority in the child's life, so that the child could later be turned over to the direct fatherhood of God and his authority.

As children gain this direction from their parents, they internalize these things into an obedient heart and are prepared to follow their heavenly Father in the same way as their earthly father. "Honor your father and your mother, as the Lord your God has commanded you, so that you may live long and that it may go well with you in the land the Lord your God is giving you" (Deut. 5:16). As children are nurtured and raised in the things of the Lord, they identify through obedience with the statutes and ways of God. In the Old Testament this ensured wisdom and good tribal relations that would allow them to do well for the rest of their lives. If they learned the right way to live and could get along with the extended relatives, they could have a smooth road ahead of them.

The role of authority in the Old Testament is an important aspect of the image of God. It started with God's delegating authority to Adam and Eve, then to Moses and the patriarchs, then to the different judges and kings, until the prophets began telling of the coming of Christ. At that time, the real King would come, the One to whom all authority is given. He would set up his own kingdom and have authority over it.

Then, as he established this authority, everything would be in subjection to him. From this position of authority, he would submit to the Father, and *would reestablish God's ultimate authority*. Paul tells us of this in 1 Cor. 15:22–28:

For as in Adam all die, so in Christ all will be made
alive. But each in his own turn: Christ, the firstfruits; then, when he comes, those who belong to
him. Then the end will come, when he hands over
the kingdom to God the Father after he has
destroyed all dominion, authority and power. For
he must reign until he has put all his enemies
under his feet. The last enemy to be destroyed is
death. For he "has put everything under his feet."
Now when it says that "everything" has been put
under him, it is clear that this does not include
God himself, who put everything under Christ.
When he has done this, then the Son himself will
be made subject to him who put everything under
him, so that God may be all in all.

This is the plan of redemption. Christ would get back
what God lost by taking authority; then he would give it
back to God, submitting to his authority. His ability to
be authoritative would enable him to recapture what was
lost and give it back to God, who gave him the authority
to do that. What an awesome plan!

The same thing God did with him, Jesus does with us.
He gives us authority in him to take back what was lost,
to reclaim it, then give it back to him, and he can give it
back to the Father. In a real way, God is allowing us to
take part in the war to regain what was lost. To do that
we must do the two things Jesus did.

First, we must submit to authority and learn obedience. "In the days of His flesh, when He offered up both
prayers and supplications with loud crying and tears to
Him who was able to save Him from death, and who was
heard because of His piety, although He was a Son, He
learned obedience from the things which He suffered"
(Heb. 5:7–8 NASB). We must learn to obey first from par-

ents, then from the Lord. This allows us to be perfected through discipline. "And having been made perfect, He became to all those who obey Him the source of eternal salvation" (Heb. 5:9 NASB). We must be able to submit to the authority of God in Christ and to internalize his likeness.

Second, we must take authority over what is delegated to us and redeem what has been lost, so we can give it back to him. We must take the role of authoritative ruler in the domains of our lives and follow his example in order to be agents of redemption. Then, we will reign forever with him as a joint heir.

In the New Testament, Jesus takes authority over situations and asks us to do the same. Let's look at a few aspects of authority that Jesus exercised so that we understand how much authority we have been commanded to take.

Power

The people were all so amazed that they asked each other, "What is this? A new teaching—and with authority! He even gives orders to evil spirits and they obey Him." (Mark 1:27)

He replied, "You of little faith, why are you so afraid?" Then he got up and rebuked the winds and the waves, and it was completely calm. The men were amazed and asked, "What kind of man is this? Even the winds and the waves obey him!" (Matt. 8:26–27)

Jesus showed that he had power to do things. He proved his authority by exercising power over certain situations.

Expertise

> When Jesus had finished saying these things, the
> crowds were amazed at his teaching, because he
> taught as one who had authority, and not as their
> teachers of the law. (Matt. 7:28–29)

Jesus had knowledge of God's Word and skill in inter-
preting it. His listeners sensed his authority.

Office

> For as the Father has life in himself, so he has
> granted the Son to have life in himself. And he
> has given him authority to judge because he is the
> Son of Man. (John 5:26–27)

Delegated authority is authority that is given to
someone. Jesus receives his authority from the Father.

Influence

After Jesus drove an evil spirit out of a man in the
synagogues, "news about him spread quickly over the
whole region of Galilee." (Mark 1:27)

Through the exercise of his gifts, Jesus gained influence with people. People who are respected for their
skills, knowledge, and talents have earned influence, and
can use it for good.

Submission

> Jesus called them together and said, "You know
> that the rulers of the Gentiles lord it over them,
> and their high officials exercise authority over
> them. Not so with you. Instead whoever wants to

become great among you must be your servant, and
whoever wants to be first must be your slave—just
as the Son of Man did not come to be served, but
to serve, and to give his life a ransom for many."
(Matt. 20:25–28)

An important part of being an authority like Jesus is
to be able to give up rights and serve others. He submitted to the cross and to his Father. We are to model
Jesus' submission; it is an important aspect of authority
resolution.

> Your attitude should be the same
> as that of Christ Jesus:
> Who, being in very nature God,
>   did not consider equality with God
>   something to be grasped,
> but made himself nothing,
>   taking the very nature of a servant,
>   being made in human likeness.
> And being found in appearance as a man,
>   he humbled himself
>   and became obedient to death—
>   even death on a cross! (Phil. 2:5–8)

Just as Jesus became an authority in these different
aspects, we are to grow up and become an authority in
exercising power, holding the offices he has given us,
developing expertise, using earned influence, and submitting to others. Jesus led the way. He was a person
like us, just without all the mistakes! (Heb. 4:15).
Therefore, he can be our model, who was tempted in
all of the problems of growing up, but made it nevertheless. He can help us become an authority over our
lives.

A Developmental Perspective

If becoming an adult is a task that requires power and expertise, it's easy to see why it is so difficult. When we are born, we have very little of either. All of the power and the expertise is in other people, and we are so very much smaller than they are.

As we continue to grow, however, and increase in wisdom and stature, we gain more ability and expertise to do things through the processes of internalization and identification. We internalize aspects of our parents and begin to identify with them as role models. Through this identification with authority figures, we learn to take in their roles and become like them. This path to adulthood lasts about eighteen years or so.

The Early Years

In the beginning stages, the main internalization is love. Learning that the big person who takes care of us is loving builds a bond that allows us to internalize aspects of them. If this goes well, parents put limits on us, and after some conflict, we eventually learn that limits really are a good thing.

Gradually, we develop more and more expertise, and our parents delegate more and more tasks to us, in respect for our budding abilities. If we do those well, then more and bigger ones are given, and we become more and more able to handle more and more responsibility. Expertise, delegation, power, and accountability are all increasing. First, the child is allowed to ride his bike down the street; later, at age sixteen he may be allowed to drive the car to a neighboring city. "Whoever can be trusted with very little can also be trusted with much" (Luke 16:10).

As we get even older, around ages four to six, more

specific identifications begin to take place, such as sex-role typing and sexuality development. The little boy identifies with his dad as a man, and the little girl identifies with her mom as a woman. In turn, they both identify with that parent's relationship with the opposite sex. The boy wants a "girl just like the girl that married dear old dad," and the girl wants a boy just like the boy that married dear old mom. They have taken one more step in the identification process that paves the way for later adult functioning.

Around this same time, children begin to internalize some of the standards of their parents, and performance becomes very important. Parental approval is the only way out of guilt at this time, so children increasingly repress their rebellious and competitive feelings toward their parents, even though these feelings are increasing. The guilt of wanting to usurp the same-sex parent being too strong to fight, the child identifies with the competition and becomes like them.

Between ages seven and twelve, mastery of tasks and work roles become very important. School-age children are increasingly industrious and into skill development; play is like a job, learning the ways of the world. Childhood chums are very important at this time also.

The Role of Parents

While all their children are growing into adults, parents can help or harm their children's identification with authority in each of its aspects.

Power

The power a child needs to live out his adult responsibilities later comes from an early identification with authority. If the nature of a parent's power is gentle, warm, and loving, as well as firm, the child will sense that personal power is a good thing. If a parent exercises power either passively or harshly, the child will get a mixed-up notion of power.

On the one hand, if a child's model is passive, she doesn't learn a sense of personal power, and this can be disastrous. Jesus has called us to be able to stand, but if a child has no picture of a "standing" adult, how can he learn? He feels as strong as the adult, and that's a weak view of power. (This power is the power inherent in the parent's personality, not the power attributed to the office of parent. In this interpretation of power, the child feels as if he is with a passive person, a domineering person, or a healthy person with a good sense of personal power.)

On the other hand, if a parent uses power harshly and cruelly, the child develops a hate relationship with power and can't internalize it without conflict. The New Testament gives us two clear passages on this dynamic:

> Children, obey your parents in the Lord, for this is right. "Honor your father and mother"—which is the first commandment with a promise—"that it may go well with you and that you may enjoy long life on the earth." *Fathers, do not exasperate your children*; instead, bring them up in the training and instruction of the Lord. (Eph. 6:1–4, italics mine)
> Children, obey your parents in everything, for this pleases the Lord. Fathers, do not embitter your children, or they will become discouraged. (Col. 3:20–21)

These two passages give us a clear picture of the two roles of child and parent. The child is to obey, and the parent is to not inspire wrath, or discourage the child. A child can't identify with someone he hates. The child needs to develop power, expertise, and influence for adulthood, but if the child hates the source of those things, he will have conflict. He will have a difficult time both developing his own authority and later submitting to God's.

Ralph was twenty-eight when he came in for counseling. He had been fired from almost every job he had had.

"Why does this happen?" I asked him.

"Well, those guys always order me around like I'm a nobody. I can't stand to be talked to like that. So, I decide, 'I'll show them,' and then I do."

"But it always costs you your job. Is it worth it?" I asked.

"Every time," he said, definitively. "I'll never bow down to them that way. Nobody will ever do that to me again."

"Do what?" I asked.

Ralph began to shake with anger. As we talked further, he described years and years of angry abuse at the hand of his authoritarian father. Hating all authority figures with a passion, he had not been able to learn to submit to them or act authoritatively in his own life. He was still an angry little boy in a power struggle with his father.

After a considerable amount of hard work, Ralph was able to work through his problem with authority. He first had to deal with his overwhelming anger toward his father, then find some older men as mentors. With God's help, he became an adult and took charge of his life.

Mike had the opposite reaction to an exasperating father. He had always passively succumbed to his father and had almost totally rejected his own sense of power. Whenever any male figure told him what to do, he would just fold his cards. His life drifted by until he was well into his thirties, and he was plagued by feelings of insecurity and confusion. He had truly lost heart.

He joined a therapy group, in which he met some powerful, as well as supportive, men. For about a year, he avoided conflict with the other men, but gradually he began to challenge them. He found out he was capable of fighting back, without being crushed as he had been as a child.

He took them up on their challenges in sports activities and reached a place where competition was fun again. He wasn't as afraid of winning as he had been in the past. He had found men whose egos could stand it. This newfound self-confidence carried over into the work world, and he gradually tried new risks and jobs. Through the mentoring and his challenging of these other authority figures, he overcame his fear of male authority.

Mike's passive solution was as disastrous as Ralph's aggressive one. Neither one had been able to get their adult authority roles in order because their fathers had disobeyed God's command. One had provoked his son to anger; the other had discouraged his son.

Expertise

In growing up, a child should have ample opportunity to learn more and more expertise, and the parents should support this process. In addition, the parents need to be models of expertise for the child to get a picture of the value of work and industriousness. Children can identify with these positive role models and learn that "a desire accomplished is sweet to the soul." They need to look up to their parents in order to learn how to strive for excellence, to develop self-esteem, and to worship someone other than themselves.

A child develops expertise as his individual strengths and talents are recognized and built up by his parents. One young man who came to see me described how he would spend hours and hours practicing baseball, only to have his father walk by and say nothing. When he wanted to try a new project, his father would throw cold water on the idea. In early adulthood, when he needed to go out and take on the world, he suffered major depression at the thought. He was totally overwhelmed: he had no picture of an encouraging parent figure to cheer him on and believe in him. No parent had built up his expertise.

As a child develops ability, opportunity needs to accompany it. A child needs to get a sense of being good at trying and learning. Parents should reward effort by getting their children the resources necessary to develop to the next level. For example, a boy learning to play baseball doesn't need the best baseball bat in the store, but it would help to have some sort of bat available when the child is ready. If someone has the opportunity to *learn that they can learn*, the rest of life is a cinch. They develop basic belief in their ability to tackle any task. This is becoming an adult.

Correction

As we have seen earlier, the relationship of the ideal to the real needs to be loving and accepting, while prodding onward. Good parenting follows this guideline, as God does with us. A child who is treated harshly for failure becomes afraid of trying. Fear of failure often comes from an authority figure's harsh reprimand for a mistake.

God's attitude toward us as we learn things is quite different. Hebrews 5:14 says that we learn through practice, or "constant use"; therefore, God works with us as we are learning and gaining experience. Parents need to treat their children with understanding and patience as they practice new skills. If parents do this, their children will love trying new things.

The book of Hebrews describes an authority who is very loving toward the process of growing up:

> For we do not have a high priest who is unable to sympathize with our weaknesses, but one who has been tempted in every way, just as we are—yet was without sin. Let us then approach the throne of grace with confidence, so that we may receive mercy and find grace to help in time of need. Every high priest is selected from among men and is appointed to represent them in matters related to God, to offer gifts and sacrifices for sins. He is able to deal gently with those who are ignorant and are going astray, since he himself is subject to weakness. (Heb. 4:15–5:2)

Our High Priest (Jesus) corrects gently, for he empathizes with our weakness. If parents follow his lead, learning will be a joyful experience.

The Power of the Office

An office is a position of authority or trust. Because they hold the *office* of parent, parents have authority to enforce consequences. They are role models for their children as those children try to identify with authority.

In the story of Adam and Eve, God held an office as their authority. In addition, he gave them the office of steward. When their behavior was out of line, he showed the power of his office to enforce the consequences of their behavior. This instilled a basic view of the authority of God in the universe for eons to come. Human beings and the heavenly hosts learned that when God said something, he meant it.

Children who are raised in situations where authority has no power learn neither to respect authority nor to identify with it. According to researchers, models with these characteristics are more likely emulated: they are warm and loving; they possess some similarity to the person following them; they not perfect, but are coping with life; and they have perceived power.

Thus, children in the developmental process need parent figures who are authoritative and who possess the power of their *office of parent*. The respect gained enables the child to follow the parents out of a healthy "fear"—a fear based in love. Loving power is the best power to identify with, and some of this power has to come not only from the personality of the parent but from his or her office of parent. Developing respect for this office lays a basis for the child's later respecting of the law, governing authorities, and church authorities (Rom. 13:1).

This will also give them the ability to execute with authority whatever role they later play, whether it be homemaker, church leader, factory worker, or company president. They have a model in their head of what it means to take a role or office and execute it with authority.

Adolescence

If all of these processes go well, the stage is set for a healthy twelve-year-old to go crazy. Adolescence is the beginning of the undoing of the yoke of slavery called childhood. It is the beginning of stepping into an equal role with the adult world, and like every other overthrow of government, it usually doesn't occur without a rebellion.

The Bible compares childhood to slavery, because a child does not yet legally own his or her own life.

> What I am saying is that as long as the heir is a child, he is no different from a slave, although he owns the whole estate. He is subject to guardians and trustees until the time set by his father. So also,

> when we were children, we were in slavery under
> the basic principles of the world. But when the
> time had fully come, God sent his Son, born of a
> woman, born under the law, to redeem those under
> law, that we might receive the full rights of sons.
> (Gal. 4:1–5)

From this slavery, the child rebels until he recognizes his freedom as an adult and can reidentify with this role. And that, my friends, can be a stormy process. During adolescence a little person is becoming a big person and trying to take the power over her life, but is not quite there. The child, or near-adult, has one foot in each camp, and she is in the process of overthrowing authority and becoming her own person.

Adolescence is the time of questioning authorities and choosing things for oneself. In a real sense, parental *control* has vanished in favor of parental *influence*. If parents have built up a good relationship with their child over the years, they can try to exert their influence over the child during this time period. But they will have little control. By this time, the child is big enough and mobile enough to do pretty much what he or she wants to do. They can enforce limits and consequences, but it is very difficult to control another adult. They can only control themselves and how they respond.

In this wonderful time of life, all sorts of things prepare one for adulthood proper. The adolescent experiences power different from earlier times. He has real mobility and can often get work that pays more than babysitting. He has buying power, as well as intellectual power to begin to figure the world out and deal with it. The often-heard cry is, "Let me do it. You always treat me like a child!" The adolescent is testing his own power to run his life.

Also, a shift in office occurs. Parents lose a lot of respect at this time, and the adolescent listens to other authority figures outside the home. She learns that Mom and Dad are not the only ones that know anything. Youth leaders, teachers, and coaches become valuable sources of influence; their influence is even greater if they differ from parents! Heeding others' advice gives the child a feeling of independence from parents, which is the chief task of adolescence.

In addition, the peer group becomes the main attachment. As adolescents move into adulthood, they need the support of community and friends, in addition to that of their parents. This move is healthy. By establishing strong peer relationships, they will have the ability to create support networks for the rest of their lives. Many people in their early thirties have never emotionally left home. When they try to separate from parents, they don't have the skills to build real support networks, and their move to adulthood doesn't work. They are stuck as children because they cannot depend on friends instead of parents.

Adolescents begin to recognize their real skills and talents so that they can take authority in this area. They pursue many activities and get the idea whether or not they like sports, academia, social concerns, or the arts. They aren't ready to pick a career, but they are discovering their basic interests and talents. They often run into problems with parents, for their interests may not be what the parents want for them. Parents need to lose this battle, or they will lose worse in the end. Children begin to make choices, and their choices need to be respected.

As they realize the bents God has given them, they pursue things outside of home to nurture those talents. Sports teams, school clubs, service organizations, church groups, and explorer groups are invaluable for the teen to learn more about the world. Work should become more important, and the teens should earn money in some substantial way. They also need to have the freedom to decide how they will spend it. If parents remember that adolescence is a boot camp for adulthood, they begin to ask this question, "What will help them prepare for when they will not be living here and have me around?" This takes much of the power struggle out of parent-adolescent relationships.

The teen years are a wonderful time of learning about the opposite sex and how to relate more intimately. They discover their bodies and feel things they have never felt before. They learn to relate in a deeper way, risking romantic attachment in a way that is much deeper than puppy love. They throw off the repression of the last decade of their lives, and they become a factory of impulses they have difficulty controlling. They also have difficulty understanding why they need to control them.

They need sound guidance from parents and other authority figures that upholds the value of sex and gives proper guidelines and limits without being repressive. Most parents find this difficult because they fear their teen's sexuality. On the one hand, they do not want to destroy their view of sex; on the other hand, they want to set appropriate limits. Good youth leaders are very important here.

Teens also struggle with values. For the first time, they are in a position to question what their parents have taught them to be true. They need to question the things Mom and Dad believe and come up with their own reasons for faith and other values. If their faith does not become their own, they will lose it later, or become Pharisees. Exposure to good youth groups and leaders is so important, for it allows opportunity to take doubts and questions to someone other than parents. Their friends will be giving them answers as well, so it is good to have solid youth leaders and peers to relate to and go through the "valley of the shadow of death of the childhood faith" with. The Bible provides many examples of people who have gone through this questioning period, including the prodigal son and the two sons in the vineyard.

Teens overthrow parental standards and select their own standards and values for life. Don't get me wrong; parents are significant in this process, but teens need freedom to think and choose, to question and doubt, especially later in adolescence and early adulthood. In these times, other adults are very important in their lives.

If this process goes well, the people who come out the other end can be called adults. They are their own person, responsible for themselves, leaving home and establishing a life of their own with their own talents, direction, purpose, power, office, influence, and expertise. This is the process of becoming an adult, and one can see why it is not an easy one.

By this time, however, they need to have a good beginning in personal power, expertise, influence, office, and healthy submission. It's not complete at this time, just started down the right road. If good seeds are planted, as well as good experiences, they are prepared to dive into adulthood with all of its trials and victories. By this time they have begun to think for themselves, stand on their own two feet, disagree with authority figures and stand with their own opinions. They have the tools to be released from parents to the authority of God and the brotherhood of humankind.

The main issue here is that they feel adequate enough in those areas to come out from under the one-down position to adults they have had all their life. They feel more of an eye-to-eye equality to other adults, *are no longer looking to other adults to perform parental functions for*

them. If they have reached adulthood, they do not look
up to other adults for parental functions, such as thinking for them, telling them how to live, and what to
believe. Other adults are looked to as experts to whom
they can turn to get advice and input, but each person is
responsible for his or her own life. This is adulthood.

The Spiritual Implications of the Adolescent Passage

It is essential to make the connection between this
step of maturity and its spiritual implications. The adolescent passage is when we overthrow the legalistic structures that interfere with our relationship with God. We
need to chisel away at the authority of our parents as
godlike figures so that God can be our parent. In short,
we need to put aside our parents, so that we can be
adopted by God. If we have never gone through that process, we will suffer from spiritual childhood and not be
able to get out from under the law and the slavery of
rules.

Paul equates these parental structures with the law, as
we saw above. Looking again at Galatians 4:1–7 will help
us to understand many spiritual problems people have.

Paul compares childhood to slavery (Gal. 4:1) and
talks about children being "in slavery *under the basic principles of the world.*" These basic principles, referred to
elsewhere as the rules of religion, are worthless in creating real maturity:

> Since you died with Christ to the basic principles
> of this world, why, as though you still belonged to
> it, do you submit to its rules: "Do not handle! Do
> not taste! Do not touch!"? These are all destined to
> perish with use, because they are based on human
> commands and teachings. Such regulations indeed

have an appearance of wisdom, with their self-imposed worship, their false humility and their harsh treatment of the body, but they lack any value in restraining sensual indulgence. (Col. 2:20–23)

Basically Paul says that we are to be freed from rules and adopted as sons and daughters of God. This freedom from parental structures leads us to a love relationship with God and an obedience to his principles of love. It moves us from a rule-based way of thinking to a love-based way of thinking and enables us to work according to *principles* instead of rules.

However, if we have never questioned the authority of our earthly parents, the givers of the first law, we can't question the authority of the law itself and reject its ability to save us. This is why authority-bound people like the Pharisees are always so legalistic. They are always trying to be "good enough" to be accepted by their legalistic consciences. Listen to Paul's words:

Before this faith came, we were *held prisoners* by the law, locked up until faith should be revealed. So the law was put in charge to lead us to Christ that we might be justified by faith. Now that faith has come, we are *no longer under the supervision of the law.* (Gal. 3:23–25, italics mine)

We have to come out from under the law, for its supervision is over. We are to be adopted by our new parent, God himself! Like Paul, we must reject the notion that, by obeying parental structures, we can save ourselves: "no one will be declared righteous in his sight by observing the law" (Rom. 3:20). This puts us into a direct relationship to God as parent, and out of the slavery of the legal mentality: "So you are no longer a slave, but a son; and since you are a son, God has made you also an heir" (Gal. 4:7). This is a calling to the freedom of bond servanthood with God, as opposed to a childhood system of rules. We have to move past the system of rules and parental governing of behavior to reach a place of freedom and obedience to the Spirit.

Paul speaks of the nature of this freedom: "You, my brothers, were called to be free. But do not use your freedom to indulge the sinful nature; rather, serve one another in love. The entire law is summed up in a single command: "Love your neighbor as yourself" (Gal. 5:13–14). He echoes Jesus' statements to the Pharisees, the authority-bound people of his time. Jesus called them to get out from under their parental-based rules and elementary ways of seeing and move toward love. They apparently had never gone through the adolescent questioning of their elders and fathers and coming up with their own beliefs:

> The Pharisees and some of the teachers of the law who had come from Jerusalem gathered around Jesus and saw some of his disciples eating food with hands that were "unclean," that is, unwashed. (The Pharisees and all the Jews do not eat unless they give their hands a ceremonial washing, holding to the *traditions of the elders*. When they come from the marketplace, they do not eat unless they wash. And they observe many other traditions, such as the washing of cups, pitchers and kettles.)
>
> So the Pharisees and teachers of the law asked Jesus, "Why don't your disciples live according to the tradition of the elders instead of eating their food with 'unclean' hands?"
>
> He replied, "Isaiah was right when he prophesied about you hypocrites; as it is written,

    " 'These people honor me with their lips,
        but their hearts are far from me.
    They worship me in vain;
        their teachings are but rules taught by men.'
    "You have let go of the commands of God and are
        holding on to the traditions of men."
    (Mark 7:1–8, italics mine)

The Pharisees' questioning of Jesus and judgment of his disciples came from their fusion with their parental figures and parental structures, "the traditions of the elders." They were not free enough from them to see the truth.

Jesus also accused the Pharisees of thinking it was more important to please parent figures than to please God. Again, another fusion with the ways of their fathers:

> "Woe to you, because you build tombs for the prophets, and it was your forefathers who killed them. So you testify that you approve of what your forefathers did; they killed the prophets, and you build their tombs." (Luke 11:47–48)

Here Jesus says that to approve the evil deeds of our parents and parent figures is to become like them. He calls us to question our fusion with authority, leave that allegiance, and give our allegiance to Jesus (Matt. 10:34–37). Allegiance to him must be stronger than our earthly parent-child relationship, for our parental relationship must be to God.

How Jesus dealt with his parents when he began to assert his independence and purpose is also very instructive. Up until a certain age, Jesus was under his parents' authority, as was commanded in the law. But, in adulthood, things began to change. When Jesus was twelve, his parents noticed that he had separated from them to go to the temple. When they told him that they had been worried about him, Jesus answered, "Why were you searching for me? Didn't you know I had to be in my Father's house?" (Luke 2:49).

Another time he made it clear that he needed to obey God, not his mother: "Dear woman, why do you involve me? My time has not yet come" (John 2:4). Jesus was growing up and transferring his parental allegiance to God, just as we all must do.

In all of these examples, Jesus makes two points. First, we need to come out from under our parents' authority and give our allegiance to God. Second, when this happens, our thinking needs to shift from rules to principles.

Remember when the Pharisees criticized Jesus' disciples for picking grain on the Sabbath? He answered them, "Haven't you read what David did when he and his companions were hungry? He entered the house of God, and he and his companions ate the consecrated bread—which was not lawful for them to do, but only for the priests. Or haven't you read in the Law that on the Sabbath the priests in the temple desecrate the day and yet are innocent? I tell you that one greater than the temple is here. If you had known what these words mean, 'I desire mercy, not sacrifice,' you would not have condemned the innocent. *For the Son of Man is Lord of the Sabbath*" (Matt. 12:3–8, italics mine).

When Jesus says that the Son of Man is Lord of the Sabbath, he places himself above the rules. The rules were made to serve his agenda, and that agenda is love. Thinking has shifted from being rule-based black-and-white thinking to principle-based thinking that must be interpreted in light of love. Our obedience to Jesus must supersede our obedience to traditions of our parental figures.

Rigid, pharisaical people can't tolerate this teaching. If they don't have a strict rule to handle every situation, they are lost, and they will invent one, as the Pharisees did. The Bible tells us to love, and if we have to upset a "tradition of the elders" to love, so be it. The Pharisees' theology wasn't big enough to allow for the need of the person, be it hunger or healing (Matt. 12:10–12). Anytime someone's theology will not allow them to help someone who is hurting, their theology is not big enough to hold the love of God. They "condemned the innocent" (v. 7).

A spiritual leader once told me that if the only way an autistic child could be helped was through the intervention of therapy, it must be God's will for this child to suffer! He said he could not see therapy condoned in the Scriptures, and if this were what the child needed, it must be God's will for the child to stay cut off from love and relationship! His theology was not big enough for love to fit in. He was not free to "heal on the Sabbath" and he was condemning the innocent.

When people separate from these legalistic "principles of the world," changes take place both in their reasoning and in their ability to love. Their thinking changes from rigid and concrete to principle-based and symbolic. They begin to understand the mysteries of God and relate to him in love, applying his truth in wisdom and love, instead of hiding behind strict, legalistic formulas. The gospel becomes more of a relationship between God and people than a system of rules designed to keep people in control.

The ways people think about situations change, and they reason in the light of love. Paul, in the great love chapter, says the following: "When I was a child, I talked like a child, I thought like a child, I reasoned like a child. When I became a man, I put childish ways behind me. Now we see but a poor reflection as in a mirror, then we

shall see face to face. Now I know in part; then I shall
know fully, even as I am fully known. And now these
three remain: faith, hope and love. But the greatest of
these is love" (1 Cor. 13:11–13, italics mine).

When people begin to reason as adults, and not as black-
and-white-thinking children, mystery and ambiguity
become more acceptable, and love becomes most important. People who have not gone through the adolescent
passage of coming out from under parental rules do not
think they are seeing "but a poor reflection" or "in part."
They think they have the "absolute" answer for everything.

When we become spiritual adolescents, we find ourselves clinging much more closely to God, our Father, for
we need his direction through the fog. We are not so sure
of everything, and our theology does not have an answer
for every situation. We find ourselves needing a relationship with him, not just a system of rules. We go through
our own Gethsemane, trying to submit to the will of God
in the midst of the pain (Luke 22:42). There is no simple
theological answer to pain; the answer is a relationship
with God in the midst of pain. Those who need things in
neat little black-and-white packages cannot tolerate such
a faith.

People who make this transition let go of rules and get
to a real, adopted relationship with God the Father.
Their reasoning changes to principle thinking instead of
black-and-white rule thinking. Their theology changes
from being based on the law, to being based on love, and
their faith changes from an ethical system to a relationship with God. Rejecting the "traditions" of people and
looking inside to find the real, impulsive adolescent self
that at times resembles utter chaos is the only way to a
real relationship of needing a Father.

When we let go of the rules that "keep things in
check," we find ourselves "poor in spirit" (Matt. 5:3) and

in need of a Father. This is what being adopted is all about. This is redemption and spiritual adolescence. We must become aware of the rebellion underneath outward compliance, confess it, and be welcomed home by the gracious Father. That is faith that saves.

Coming out from under the parental bondage allowed spiritual greats, such as John the Baptist, to accomplish their work. John the Baptist stood against the parent figures of the day, calling them a "brood of vipers" (Matt. 3:7). Martin Luther stood up against the religious authorities of his time, who said that we could not have a direct relationship with God without intermediary interpretation.

It takes someone who feels equal to other adults to be able to do the things God asks us to do. We must own our lives and not need parental approval so that we can walk "not as pleasing men but God, who examines our hearts" (1 Thess. 2:4 NASB). The next chapter shows what happens when we don't.

Chapter 15

When We Fail to Grow Up

MY FRIEND HAD ONE OF THOSE LOOKS ON HER face that people sometimes have when they discover the truly profound. This was no exception. She said something I'll never forget: "You know something. Life is upside down."

"What do you mean?" I asked.

"We should be adults first, and then children. It's too hard the other way around."

Symptoms of an Inability to Become an Adult

Everyone who has ever lived (except Adam and Eve) has encountered the problem of being born a little person is a big person's world and being given the task of becoming a big person over time. We are all born children under adult authority, and over time we are expected to become adults ourselves and to take charge of our lives. This task, as my friend observed, is not easy. Some of us never accomplish it. We try to live adulthood from the one-down child position. Following are signs of this inability to achieve adulthood.

Inordinate Needs for Approval

People who struggle with taking charge of their lives often cannot function independently of the approval of others. They strive constantly to gain the approval of some "significant other," whether it be their boss, their spouse, their friend, their pastor, or their coworker.

This kind of approval is different than the normal affirmation we all need for our work. We all need praise for a job well done. Approval becomes problematic when people don't feel good about themselves or the work until someone tells them that the work is good. They wait until an "authority" figure pronounces it good before they know that it is (and they are) good. If the authority figure pronounces it good, their entire self-image changes. The other's opinion carries far too much weight and has taken on the role of judge and jury, or parent, for the person.

Fear of Disapproval

Fear of disapproval goes along with the need for approval. Often people are inordinately anxious whenever an authority figure is around. Their anxiety interferes with their ability to do the job well. Every time their work is to be evaluated, their fear is activated, or they have a constant fear of being evaluated.

One young graduate student would begin to have panic attacks near the end of every semester. Everything would be going well until three weeks before semester's end. At that time he would go into a state of tension that would increase to panic. He would lose sight of the tasks at hand and begin to focus on whether or not his professors would like his papers.

His history revealed a perfectionistic father who would criticize his work harshly. Fearing his father, he had remained a submissive little boy well into his twenties. Because he had never come out from under his father's rule, adult authority figures still had the role of judge in his life. They had the power to approve or disapprove of him, and exam time gave a platform for this dynamic.

Gradually, as he began to challenge the professors, he learned they weren't so powerful after all, and he eventually got to feel as if he were their equal. He got to where he could enter an exam without excessive anxiety. He had gone through a "rite of passage" of becoming equal with his father figures. He was a peer and no longer feared being judged.

Guilt

Guilt always has as a component the loss of parental approval. Therefore, wherever one struggles with guilt, one still feels "under" the parental voice. The internal parent has not been dethroned so that it can't punish.

Guilt keeps the focus off the consequences. An adult conscience lives life according to real consequences, not guilt. If adults get a traffic ticket, for example, they feel bad about the money for the fine, and may be sad because they violated a value. People in the child position feel more guilt than consequences.

People who have not grown up also feel pressured by credit card balances, bills, deadlines, assignments, and tasks. The demand itself is perceived like a parent; they feel pressure to comply, or they are "bad." This comply-resist dynamic often ends up in a guilt-procrastination battle that makes them spend more.

Sexual Struggles

People who feel one-down to authority more often than not have sexual difficulty. The reason is simple: they have not gone through the adolescent passage of disagreeing with their parents and therefore overcoming guilt and repression. Sexuality is still a "no-no" to them because psychologically they are children who "shouldn't think about such things." Since children don't have sex, their thinking interferes with their sexual functioning. They can suffer from inhibition (which is usually fear of parental criticism), lack of orgasm, guilt, loss of desire, or performance anxiety.

When people feel like adults with other adults, their bodies are their own to give away to their spouses and enjoy as they please. Only then can there be mutual giving and receiving.

When Sally got married, she suffered a complete loss of sexual desire. Sexuality had intrigued her before marriage, but after the wedding, the desire disappeared. After months of trying to regain the desire, she came into therapy.

As she began to unravel the problem, it became clear that she was still "Daddy's little girl." Her father was overinvolved in her marriage, and she was still experiencing a strong desire to please him as best she could. In a real sense, she had not left home.

Since she had not come out from under his authority, she was still a child inside, and children do not have sex. Since her main attachment was still to her father, not her husband, any sexual wishes were too incestuous to handle. Consequently, she repressed her entire sexuality.

She worked hard to let go of her relationship with her father, and her wish to please him. She even wrote him a letter, resigning from the job of making him happy. As she moved through this process, she moved from being a repressed little girl to being a sexual woman. Because she let go of her parent, her adolescent function of sexuality was able to emerge. She began to enjoy sex very much, and was more and more uninhibited.

Fear of Failure

People still under their parent's domain fear failure because they fear the disapproval of their rule-bound conscience (Gal. 4:3; Col. 2:20). They internally feel that their actions will be judged and disapproved. In biblical terms, they haven't been released from "the supervision of the law" (Gal. 3:25).

When they realize that they stand in grace "in Christ," the dynamic of being "under" a judge and waiting for a stamp of approval is changed (Gal. 5:1). They are free to practice without fear of failure and to learn without guilt and anxiety.

Need for Permission

Many struggle with an inordinate need for permission. They invariably think they need to get clearance from someone before they can proceed. They often ask, "May I say something?" in the middle of a conversation, when it's unnecessary to ask permission to speak. They are speaking from an internal state of bondage to a parental authority.

They hesitate to test the limits of any system or organization to find out what is okay and what isn't. Their bosses are often bothered by how much supervision and direction they need to make decisions because of their fear of "getting into trouble." It's as though they live in the small basement room of a large mansion. They are afraid to venture out and discover how big their living space really is.

"You Can't Do That" Syndrome

Authority-bound people tend to stifle creativity. Someone may come up with a new way of doing something, and the authority-bound person will say, "You can't do that," or "It'll never work." They appear to have prison bars around anything creative or new. They are pessimistic about trying new things, preferring the "tried and true."

They overidentify with their limiting and punitive parent, always giving restrictions and rules. They haven't thrown off their parents' restrictions and found their own. They are like robots who do whatever their parents say, even at age forty.

Inventors and entrepreneurs hate people with authority problems and call them "tunnel visioned" or "myopic." Everyone who has ever started a new business has heard discouraging messages from scared observers.

Feelings of Inferiority

The word *inferior* comes from a word that means "low" or "below." It is easy to see, then, how people who have been put down or held down by authority figures feel inferior. Often their parents have not treated them with respect as people in their own right so they invariably look up to others and feel lower than them. They tend to think that someone else is always better in some way, or always is a model for them. They never feel equal.

Martin's life was marked by feelings of inferiority. He felt one-down to most people he had contact with. A successful businessman, he had done well when he was in the servant position in business transactions as a subcontractor to the "big cheese contractor." He worked hard at pleasing the person he was working for, and as a result, was rewarded.

At the same time, however, he suffered panic attacks

when he had to work directly with contractors. He vacillated between fearing their disapproval of his ideas to being terrified that they would think he was too smart and resent him. He was in a bind that made his work life a wreck.

Competitiveness

Since getting to an equal stance with others means competing with our parents for the role of "boss," people who have never established equality with their parents act out unresolved competitive issues, often with people of the same sex.

Our earliest form of competition comes from same-sex parents. If we do not resolve this competition by identifying with our same-sex parent, lingering competitive struggles can follow us for a long time.

Competitive people are always trying to usurp the position of the "one-up" person. They cannot stand for anyone to win "over" them, for it puts them in a one-down position in their head. Instead of saying, "I lost the game," they say, "I am an inferior person." Therefore, they *must* win in order to not be inferior to anyone. They are often still trying to feel equal to Mom or Dad, so they see every situation competitively.

Loss of Power

Those who have not become an adult either repeatedly give away power in relationships or feel that they are losing power. On the one hand, these people do not see a good relationship as one in which two people mutually submit to one another's preferences in love; instead, they give all power to the other person and then obey this person like a parent. Being "in charge" is like a hot potato that needs to be passed along as quickly as possible.

On the other hand, these people lose power to controlling and domineering people. They think what their pastor thinks. They buy the Bible version their spiritual leader has. They go where their friend tells them to go. To a ridiculous extent, they give the adult functions of life over to controlling people. Half of the problem is that too many people are willing to play God in other people's lives. Many spiritual leaders think that their job is to parent such "children" and keep them in check instead of to lead them into maturity under the lordship of Christ.

In the Christian world many people do not think for themselves. They do not question teaching or doctrine; it is "right" because "so and so" says it is. If that person is a big-name leader, then it must be right.

Martin Luther rebelled against this attitude, arguing for the priesthood of all believers. Luther felt that everyone could have their own relationship with God and could listen to teachers and decide what they believed, instead of being told what they believe. "As for you, the anointing you received from him remains in you, and you do not need anyone to teach you. But as his anointing teaches you about all things and as that anointing is real, not counterfeit—just as it has taught you, remain in him" (1 John 2:27). Believers can rely on the Holy Spirit and the Word to interpret the interpreters and thus decide for themselves what they believe. John is not ruling out human teachers, but all believers have the capacity to appreciate and appropriate God's truth.

No Equal Differences

People who live in a one-up and one-down world rarely consider differences acceptable. If someone believes or thinks something different, that someone is "wrong." There is no such thing as a difference of opinion or "agreeing to disagree."

These people also tend to treat differences in taste as being right or wrong. If their friends buy a certain car or move their kids to a certain school, they begin questioning themselves, "Do I have the right car?" or "Should I move my kids as well?" People who haven't grown up experience difference as a threat; if two people are doing two different things, someone must be doing the wrong thing.

This attitude can affect very small things such as what sale to go to, or what clothes to buy, or which racquetball racket is "better." These people always ask, "Which is the better of the two?" instead of, "You like that one, and I like this one." The latter is the way two equal adults experience their differences.

These pharisaical minds have such a stringent list of what is "right doctrine" that they miss the real doctrine of "Love your neighbor as yourself." They are so concerned with determining how others are "wrong" that they can't love them. The Pharisees did this over and over again; they saw others as "less than" them, and therefore bad.

Black-and-White Thinking

People who can only see the world as black and white, right or wrong, are stuck in a pre-adult way of thinking. They are thinking like an eleven-year-old. They are unable to think in terms of gray; there are no tough moral dilemmas. Everything is simple. "If the rule says it, do it."

Jesus repeatedly ran into this sort of thinking with the Pharisees, and he tried to lead them past this rigidity to an adult position of love. I wish we all had a nickel for every time he heard the Pharisees ask, "Is it lawful for . . . ?"

They were so preoccupied with the rules and right and wrong that they could not get to wisdom, truth, and love.

People who are stuck here adhere to rules that have an "appearance of wisdom" (Col. 2:23), but are worthless to bring about maturity. Rigorously obeying man-made rules instead of showing God-made love will always cause problems. This is why the adolescent passage of "breaking the rules" is so important.

Judgmentalism

Judgmental people fuse with the parental, legal position and look down on everyone else. They not only resist identifying with the acting-out adolescent inside, they judge it. "But the Pharisees and the teachers of the law who belonged to their sect complained to his disciples, 'Why do you eat and drink with the tax collectors and "sinners"?' Jesus answered them, 'It is not the healthy who need a doctor, but the sick. I have not come to call the righteous, but sinners to repentance'" (Luke 5:30–32).

Judgmental people don't identify themselves as sinners; therefore, they aren't forgiven and can't become loving. Instead, they deny the "sinner within" and act like they are perfect and "above" sin (Matt. 23:27–29).

Anytime we look "down" on someone else, we have "seated [our] selves in the chair of Moses" (Matt. 23:2 NASB) above everyone else, and therefore have not identified with the sinner position within. The essence of the adolescent passage—the confession of the sinner within—puts us in a humble position under God, instead of a proud position with people.

Anxiety Attacks

Both generalized and specific anxiety can be related to authority problems because anxious people fear disapproval externally as well as internally. Generalized anxiety signals something dangerous about to emerge into one's consciousness. People who suffer anxiety attacks often fear disapproval from the parental conscience.

Sam came into therapy for anxiety attacks. He suffered these attacks whenever he was dealing with a parent figure. When he was discussing a negotiation with a "father figure" in the law firm, for example, he became overwhelmed with anxiety.

Sam thought his problem was fear of authority, but in reality he was afraid of his own strengths. His feelings of equality were emerging and threatening the internal demand of his conscience to stay one-down to father figures.

As he gave himself permission to grow up and challenge these parent figures, his conscience gave him permission to be equal and aggressive. His anxiety disappeared, and his ability to close cases increased. Because he had conquered his fears of challenging authority figures, in a few years, his income quadrupled. He was afraid of being equal, not unable to be so.

Impulsiveness and Inhibition

Both license and inhibition can stem from authority problems. On the one hand, some people can be so angry at authority that they completely deny any rules or standards and live lawlessly. These people are often impulsive and do whatever they wish. These out-of-control adolescent adults have done away with authority, even God's.

On the other hand, legalists are so bound up with guilt, they aren't even aware of their impulses. These people are very shy and inhibited, and they often struggle with feelings of embarrassment. Their friends often say, "Let your hair down sometimes." Or in Solomon's words, "Do not be overrighteous, neither be overwise—why

destroy yourself?" (Eccl. 7:16). They don't feel free
enough to enjoy life or their feelings.

Superiority

Superiority is the opposite of inferiority. Some people
always find a way to see themselves as better than everyone else. It can look like narcissism, or idealism, but it is
really one-upmanship.

Parenting Others

Some people who have never grown up think they
know what others "should" do. They are unable to realize
their own limited knowledge of a person's situation, as
well as the person's responsibility or ability to deal with
his or her own problems.

Counselors and teachers who directly tell others what to
do fall into this category. They do not foster maturity in their
clients, but rather make them dependent on them. These
counselors try to justify their omnipotence by aligning themselves with the "authority of Scripture." But they often use
the law like Pharisees, placing themselves in the "seat of
Moses." They pay little attention to the "more important
matters of the law—justice, mercy and faithfulness" (Matt.
23:23). They like to dominate those "under" them.

You can spot parenting people by their overuse of the
term "you should." Much of what they say to others has a
parenting sound; others speak of feeling "crummy," or
"guilty," or "convicted" after being with them. But the
conviction is the type that makes people feel like prisoners instead of being the true conviction of God, which is
tender and graceful.

Hate for Authority Figures

Some people never identify with authority; instead,
they resist it either actively or passively. These adults

are perpetual teenagers, never identifying with the adult position and always taking adolescent cracks at leaders.

Passive resisters constantly criticize people in authority, conveying a subtle feeling that they are superior to their superiors. They undermine the authority's decisions and wisdom, and speak of them behind their back; they find the bad in every leader or pastor.

Active resisters are the rebellious "haters of authority" the Bible speaks about. These people openly resist any authority figure, and generally rebel against authority of any kind, including God's.

The parable of the two sons (Matt. 21:28–32) illustrates these two positions. It was only the son who was aware of his rebellion who could repent and own it.

Depression

This depression stems from a "bad me," self-critical attitude. People who are criticized by their internal parent feel bad and guilty, which leads them to depression. They have not become free from parental structures. When these people get in touch with their anger at their critical parent and use this anger constructively to separate from that parent and become an adult, their one-down depression goes away, and they often find all sorts of creativity in its place.

Dependency

Some people actively avoid taking responsibility for themselves and find someone to parent them. They give executive power of their life to someone else. People who always need someone else to make decisions for them and to do things for them lack self-respect and usually are angry and resentful of the "parent" figures who are keeping them from growing up.

It is not unusual for people to marry out of dependency and then resent their partners for treating them like children. These people usually rebel either actively or passively to get an equal standing with their mate. Sometimes the person gets divorced to get their autonomy from the "parent spouse," acting out their adolescent rebellion toward their spouse and taking a household down with them.

Idealization of Authority

The perception that someone in authority is perfect presupposes a one-down position, because people who have identified with authority realize that authority figures are just like them, with warts and all. Idealized authority figures are not expected to have weaknesses and faults as well as strengths, even though the Scriptures tell us they will. "Every high priest is able to deal gently with those who are ignorant and are going astray, since he himself is subject to weakness" (Heb. 5:1–2).

People who idealize authority need to be reminded of the sins of David, Paul, Moses, and Peter, and shown that being an adult is not as scary as they think. They don't have to be perfect to be an adult. It is really only stepping up to a different kind of childhood, to being children of God (Gal. 4:4–5).

Idealization of Childhood

Because of their conflicts with becoming an adult, some people idealize childhood and see it as the only life worth living. They think that adulthood is full of drudgery and responsibility; it's boring. They avoid becoming adults and devalue it.

Barriers to Becoming an Adult

In the same way that other stages can be stagnated because of convictions about ourselves, others, and God, so can the stage of becoming an adult. These distortions need to be challenged and risked in new relationships other than the ones that they developed in, just like the other stages. Here are several:

Distorted Thinking

Our View of Ourselves

I am bad if they don't approve of me. That proves it.

I am less than others.

I must please others to be liked.

I am bad if I disagree.

My opinions are not as good.

I have no right to my opinions.

I must get permission from others to . . .

I am bad if I fail.

I shouldn't feel so sexual.

Sexual feelings are bad.

My plans will never succeed.

I should defer to their beliefs, even though I disagree.

I need someone else to manage my life. I am not capable enough.

If I differ, I am wrong.

I think they should . . .

I shouldn't let myself feel . . .

I am better than they are.

My group is the right group.

We really have the best theology.

Our ministry is the only real one.

I know what's best for them.
I know better than them.
I could never teach him or her anything.
Adulthood is out of my grasp.

Our View of Others

They are all disapproving and critical.
They are better than me.
They will like me better if I am compliant.
They think that I am wrong or bad for disagreeing.
Their opinions are always right.
They will think I am bad for failing.
They have no weaknesses.
They never fail like I do.
. . . is easy for them.
Their beliefs are better than mine.
They know what's best for me.
They never feel . . .
They know everything.
They are never this afraid, or mad, or sad, or . . .
They will hate me for standing up to them.

Our View of God

God likes for me to be nice to everyone.
God wants me to always defer to my authorities, never questioning.
God does not want me to run my own life. He wants my "leaders" to do that.
God disapproves of me when I fail, just as my parents disapproved.
God does not like me to be aggressive.
God does not like me to disagree with the pastor.
God does not allow me freedom to choose some of my own values. They are all prescribed in the Bible. There are no gray areas.

God thinks others are more (or less) important
    than me.

God wants me to adhere to a bunch of rules.

God likes discipline and sacrifice more than
    compassion, love, and relationship.

Our View of the World

Competition is bad; someone always gets hurt.

Disagreement is bad; someone always gets hurt.

Conflict is bad; someone always loses.

There is no such thing as a "win-win" relation-
    ship.

People who are people-pleasers are liked better
    than people who say what they think.

Everything has a "right answer." Especially
    since we have the Bible.

There is a right and wrong way of seeing every-
    thing. Perspective makes no difference.

Flexibility is license and lawlessness.

Sexuality is evil.

There is a right and a wrong way to do every-
    thing.

It will never work.

These heartfelt convictions about God, self, and others that many of us have learned through experience are
barriers to becoming an adult. Some of them we probably
learned in the family we grew up in; others are just a part
of the pre-adult mind. In any event, they can only be
overcome with work, risk, prayer, relationship, and practice. The next chapter will explore the skills needed to
become an adult.

Chapter 16

Learning to Become Mature Adults

LEARNING TO BECOME AN ADULT IS NOT AN easy task. Perhaps becoming an adult while you're already living in an adult body is even harder. But it is a necessary step to take to get out from under the authority of others.

"I cannot make good choices," wrote Thomas Merton, "unless I develop a mature and prudent conscience that gives me an accurate account of my motives, my intentions, and my moral acts. The word to be stressed here is *mature*. An infant, not having a conscience, is guided in its 'decisions' by the attitude of somebody else. The immature conscience is one that bases its judgments partly, or even entirely, on the way other people seem to be disposed toward its decisions. . . . Even when the immature conscience is not entirely dominated by people outside itself, it nevertheless acts only as a representative of some other conscience. The immature conscience is not its own master."[1] Here are some of the skills you will need to become your own master under God, to become a mature adult.

SKILLS FOR BECOMING AN ADULT

Reevaluate Beliefs

We need to reevaluate what we believe. The time is past for "inherited beliefs"; it is time for an adult faith. We need to look into why we think what we think and why we believe what we believe. Is it because we really believe it, or because someone told us to believe it? We need to recognize what is a belief of "tradition" versus what is a real heartfelt conviction from God, his Word, and our own experience. This questioning period could last a while. But, when we are through, we will have developed a mind of our own.

Disagree with Authority Figures

Be honest about your disagreements with others. Most people have disagreements with authority figures, but they are afraid to admit to themselves how strongly they disagree. And they are afraid to voice their disagreements. If you are in a group where you are not free to have a different opinion on gray issues, be careful. Your group may have cult-like qualities.

Allow yourself freedom of thought, and do not call yourself "bad" for your opinions. No one is right about everything, and we all go through periods of reshaping what we think on any topic. Speak your opinions, and listen to the criticism. Speaking out may help you shape your views, or you may help shape others' views. Critique others' thoughts as well. Disagreement is healthy, and "iron sharpens iron."

See Parents and Authority Figures Realistically

Knock parents and other authority figures off the pedestal you've put them on. See their weaknesses as well as their strengths. Look at the ways you disagree with what they believe and think. Since no two people agree on everything, search your life for anyone with whom you agree on everything, or who you think has it all together. You may be either unaware of how you disagree, or you may be a flatterer.

Confess the sins of your fathers and then forgive them. If you idealize your parents, you are fusing with their mistakes, and you may become like them. Disagree with bad patterns, call them sin, and be different from the generations that went before.

Think also about the spiritual "heroes" of the Bible and their frailties, as Hebrews points out. They were all human like us.

Make Your Own Decisions

If people in your life are telling you what to think, believe, do, or buy, start making those decisions yourself. You are an adult; learn to think and act for yourself. Who cares if someone disapproves of the purchase you make? It's your money, and how you spend it is between you and God.

Anyone who tells you "you should" buy this and not buy that, or read this and not read that, or attend this and or not attend that, is parenting you. Giving advice or feedback and confronting is good, but parenting other adults is bad. Avoid people who take away your freedom as redeemed and adopted sons and daughters of God and who want to become your parents. Remember the words of Paul: "However at that time, when you did not know God, *you were slaves to those which by nature are no gods*. But now that you have come to know God, or rather be known by God, how is it that you turn back again to the weak and worthless elemental things, to which you desire to be enslaved all over again?" (Gal. 4:8–9 NASB, italics mine).

These legalists, or parent figures, or pushers of rules are "no gods." Therefore, take their opinion as you would another adult; listen, but do not feel compelled to do what they ask. You have only one God. Listen to him.

Practice Disagreeing

If you struggle with these issues, you probably have no shortage of parental types in your life. You have great opportunities to practice what you could not do when you were growing up: disagree and not do what self-appointed human gods tell you to do.

Be aware of the times when someone is parenting you, and say what you are thinking. You do not have to be mean, or even confrontational. Just say, "Well, I see your point, but I look at it differently. I think . . ." This is normal conversation, even though it may feel disrespectful or mean to you if you haven't tried it before. Learn to be equal with those who have assigned themselves as gods in your life, or to whom you have given this exalted position.

Deal With Your Sexuality

If you are prudish or embarrassed by sex, your parents may still be looking down their noses at your sexuality, or at least that's the way you are perceiving it. Work on reeducating yourself about the beauty of sex; desensitize yourself to the "no-no" attitude you have toward it. If you feel ashamed, you may still be in a preadolescent stage regarding sex.

Become familiar with your body and cherish it. You may need to talk with someone you trust in order to get over the "hush-hush" feelings about sex that come from childhood. "Children don't talk about sex," but adults can. Stop whispering!

In addition, become aware more and more of your sexual feelings. This normal adult thing happens around age thirteen. If you are repressing your feelings, you may be keeping other sorts of adult functions from developing as well. All these functions affect one another, and as your repression of your opinions lifts, so will repression of sexuality and creativity.

One client regained her sexual feelings by spending a few weeks becoming aware of her own opinions about her boss! Her repression of her thoughts about this female authority figure served to repress other adult functions as well. You can't repress just one aspect of yourself; it usually affects many areas.

Give Yourself Permission to Be Equal With Your Parents

Many authority problems have as their kernel the inability to assume the role held by the same-sex parent. You either dislike the way this parent functioned in the role, or you are afraid of taking the role over. In either instance, this is the role you were born to assume, the adult role of your gender. Look at the ways that your parent fulfilled this role. Appreciate where your parent succeeded, and choose other role models for where he or she failed. This will help your transition from child to adult.

In addition, look at the ways that you fear usurping their position. Many people fear going through the adolescent passage, for they do not want to dethrone their same-sex parent.

Recognize and Pursue Talents

To become an adult requires that you own and recognize the talents and gifts God has given you. You may be aware of some area that you are gifted in, and God has been telling you to develop it in some way, but you have been burying that talent in the ground.

To develop your expertise, you must take the talents God has given you and do something. This may mean to take a course, or get a mentor, or do some study, or whatever. But the important thing is that you are developing the talents. If you do not know what your talents are, ask God. He will tell you. Also, get some other people's insight. Often we cannot see our strengths.

Practice

This is important to develop whatever skill and expertise you are considering. You can't learn to be an authority and have expertise in an area if you don't have the freedom to practice and learn. Give yourself permission to fail.

No one ever became an expert in any area without trial and error. Whether it's homemaking, basketball, business, personal finance, teaching, Bible exegesis, or child rearing, it takes practice to develop a skill. Practicing is an important aspect of realizing independence and adulthood.

Go out there and fail, and then laugh it off and do it again. Learn to value process more than result. Internalize the substance of the task as well as the product. People who are only results oriented do not often enjoy their talents. Learn to enjoy them; you will be exercising them for a long time.

Recognize the Privileges of Adulthood

When people realize how much freedom their child position is costing them—freedom to develop as God intended without approval from other adults—the one-down position starts to look like prison. Remaining in a child position is safe because others do all the thinking for you; all you have to lose is your self-respect.

Adults have freedom to choose their own talents, values, beliefs, relationship with God, tastes, friends, and church. They also can express God-given aspects of themselves, such as feelings and sexuality, without inhibition and fear, or need for approval from anyone else. They can be themselves. Like Paul says in Galatians 4:1, the child owns everything, but is not free to use it. Adults are.

Discipline Yourself

Adults discipline themselves. Proverbs says to "Go to the ant, O sluggard, Observe her ways and be wise, which *having no chief, officer or ruler,* prepares her food in the summer, and gathers her provision in the harvest" (6:6 NASB, italics mine). The key phrase here is "having no chief, officer or ruler." In other words, the ant is not under another ant's authority, yet takes responsibility for her tasks.

If you lacked discipline when growing up, you may need to learn discipline now. Get a good friend to hold you accountable in this area; agree on something you are going to be disciplined to do, and have some built-in consequences if you don't. Once I agreed to pay a friend a sum of money if I did not follow an exercise program. I needed the consequences to make me act.

Gain Authority Over Evil

The Bible commands us to "resist the devil, and he will flee from you" (James 4:7). Jesus also said that he had given us authority to command the evil spirits. The Word and the power of Jesus' name is enough for you to bind the forces of evil as they present themselves, and if you do not know how to do this, it is probably important at some point to learn about spiritual warfare. We are to take dominion over the evil one.

Submit to Others Out of Freedom

An important aspect of becoming an adult is to learn to submit to others in love, without an authority conflict. This includes government, spouses, friends, evil people, bosses, and God. When we submit in love, we are displaying our freedom; if we submit in compliance, it is not true submission. It's slavery (Rom. 13:1; Eph. 5:21; Matt. 5:39; 1 Peter 2:18–19; Heb. 13:17; James 4:7). Submitting to others as God has ordained is identity-affirming.

Do Good Works

"For we are God's workmanship, created in Christ Jesus to do good works, which God prepared in advance for us to do" (Eph. 2:10). You are God's workmanship; you are a prized possession he has created for a function. In the same way Adam was created to have dominion and exercise good works in the garden, you have been created for a purpose.

As you are working with God to find your talents and develop them, seek him for the good works you are to do. They do not have to be grandiose. Your good work could be being a link between God and a few of your neighbors, using your skills as a homemaker, or it could be using your academic skills to develop relationship with someone in your class. It could be donating some time to an orphanage or to a needy family. The point is this: You have some expertise, and using it for good works will help you realize your adulthood.

If you are in a building time, like Paul, where God has set you aside to heal you and develop you, give him time to do this. Don't think you have to go save the world too quickly!

Become a "Pharisee Buster"

We all have remnants of legalistic thinking and remain under the tutor of parental approval. Try to find ways you may still be operating under the old system of gaining approval in order to be okay. Look for legalism that has crept into your faith and ways that you are being "made for the Sabbath." Let go of the ways you are trying to earn approval; they can only eat away at your soul.

Appreciate Mystery and the Unknown

One of the hallmarks of people with authority problems is their inability to tolerate mystery and the unknown. They need an answer for everything, and everything has to be wrapped up in neat little packages. Jesus kept trying to shake the Pharisees out of this rigidity.

In many ways God is "unfathomable" (Rom. 11:33–34). He is so awesome that the more we know him, the more we realize we don't know. This is where worship begins. It is his very transcendence that we worship. Begin to appreciate the things that you cannot figure out about him, and let them be. This is why we call him "God." If you can know everything about him, then he is no longer God; you are. This is the most serious authority problem of all.

Worship his mystery. Get out of the black-and-white, "we-have-all-the-answers" mentality that keeps God in a box. He is much greater than that.

Love and Appreciate People Who Are Different

People often see other people as not as good because they are still trying to be the better child. When you can appreciate other people who are different from you, you have stopped sibling rivalry—the childhood battle of trying to be the better child to win parental approval—and

have begun to assume an equal stance with your adult
brothers and sisters.

Sara

When Sara came to me, she was filled with anxiety.
Dominated by older peers, fearful of disapproval, and sexually unfulfilled, she had spent her life fruitlessly trying
to please others. Instead of enjoying an equal relationship with her husband and peers, she was always in the
position of the subordinate.

The causes of Sara's problem came clear as she talked
about her early family life. "My parents were very strict,"
she said. "They always wanted me to do my best. My
mother had a very strong personality. She told me what
to do and how to do it. But then when I did things how
she told me to, she would still find things to criticize. I
could never do anything right for her."

Sara's mother had never allowed her to find out what
sorts of things she liked to do, and to practice them at
her own pace. Nor had her mother seen failure as part of
the normal road to achieving expertise. When Sara
became a teenager and tried to broaden her interests, her
mother grew worse, even trying to dictate the clubs and
activities that Sara engaged in.

Meanwhile, Sara's father kept his distance. He did not
contradict her mother's statements, nor did he give much
approval of his own. In fact, he also criticized Sara when
he felt she was not living up to her potential.

Sara became a Christian in college. There she joined a
rigid group of Christians who lived by rules and regula-
tions. Having learned from her parents how to comply,
she did pretty much whatever the spiritual leaders asked.
She never expressed her own thoughts or wishes, espe-

cially when she sensed that they would have disapproved of her.

When Sara got married, she continued to comply. She did everything possible to please her perfectionistic husband. As a result, she grew more and more out of touch with her own feelings and desires.

Because Sara had not been allowed to pursue her own talents and opinions, and because she had never openly disagreed with her mother, she was developmentally still a child. She was unable to have peer relationships with other adults because she had never assumed adulthood.

When Sara began to understand her background, she went to work on herself. She met regularly with friends who had similar problems. Rather than parenting each other, they gave each other feedback and support.

Then Sara went to work on her relationship with her parents. Since they lived nearby, she had ample opportunity to change her approach. Instead of trying to please her mother, she said things like, "I understand that you would do it that way, but I think I'll do it this way instead." For months, her mother could not handle this "disobedient" forty-year-old, but over time she realized that Sara was not going to live to please her anymore.

Sara began to voice her opinions and thoughts in other settings as well. In a couples' Bible study she sometimes disagreed with the leader. She also began to choose clothes which were different from her "spiritual leader's" tastes. When the perfectionistic women around her tried to tell her what to do, she ignored them and went forward with what she thought was best for her. And gradually their power over her lessened. She saw them as imperfect humans, like herself. Even though they gave directions forcefully, she did not have to order her life as they wished.

She battled internal, as well as external, voices. She

learned to talk back to her internal "parent," which drove her to perfection. And she learned to survive the anxiety of being "disobedient." Over time, the parental voices in her head were stilled, and she grew less anxious.

She also began to pursue her own talents and take risks to develop them. When she feared failure, she reminded herself that her parents were not perfect either, nor did they have power over her life. Soon it became easier for her to accept failure as a normal part of the learning process.

She also had to own up to the anger she felt deep inside toward all the parent figures who had controlled her. When she stopped blaming herself for their criticism, she saw the pride disguised behind their comments. As a result, she stopped bowing to their authority, and her anger dissipated.

Finally, her stance of equality with other adults affected her sexual relationship with her husband. She was more direct with him about what she liked and didn't like; she allowed herself to be less inhibited, worrying less about his disapproval. With her new power she forced him to be less demanding, and she herself became much more sexually responsive.

Growing up took quite a bit of time, prayer, and work, but in the end Sara won. Out of a forty-year-old little girl, God grew an adult.

Conclusion

EACH SECTION OF THIS BOOK BEGINS WITH the story of a Christian struggling with bonding, setting boundaries, sorting out issues of good and bad, or becoming an adult. I hope these issues have become clearer to you and that some other things have become clear as well.

First, we all struggle with all four issues. There are no clear-cut lines between the issues. Because of the Fall, we will all be able to see all four issues in our lives. Our sanctification has a lot to do with resolving these issues in God's way.

Second, there is no such thing as either an emotional problem or a spiritual problem. We all have broken relationships with God, others, and ourselves. Because of this brokenness, we develop symptoms that are felt on an emotional level and lived out in our spiritual lives. For that reason, we need a spiritual solution that involves our emotions, and any spiritual solution must be one of love. Relationship reconciliation is at the base of all healing.

In the final analysis, therefore, this is a book about relationship, and the barriers that must be broken down for us to have a real relationship with God, others, and ourselves. Any solution short of a relational one is a solution short of love.

Third, our symptoms are not the problem. For years Christians have focused on the symptoms and not the issues. As a result, healing has been superficial. We must learn to use our symptoms as signs that lead us to issues. Issues can be resolved; symptoms cannot. If we resolve the issues, the symptoms will no longer have a reason to be.

Fourth, meaning, purpose, satisfaction, and fulfillment are fruits of these issues. Meaning comes from love, which flows out of bonding. Purpose comes from direction and truth, which form boundaries. Satisfaction comes from having the less than perfect be "good enough" in the light of God's ideal, and fulfillment comes from the adult ability to exercise talents.

And last, "the greatest of these is love" (1 Cor. 13:13). What I have written about is a model that can help us become functioning human beings. But if that is the final goal, we have sold ourselves short. We were made to love, and the fully functioning person is one who takes his bonded, separate, forgiving, adult self into a world and denies that self for the sake of others. We have seen how this does not mean being without a person inside; it means having such a full one that it can be imparted to others.

Work on your ability to attach to others so that you can have your empty heart filled. Work on setting boundaries so you can own your own life. Work on confessing and receiving forgiveness so you can develop your real personhood. Work on assuming adulthood so you can be an authority. Then, go out and give it to others. Remember, "Greater love has no one than this, that he lay down his life for his friends" (John 15:13). God bless you.

For more information regarding materials, tapes, seminars, or speaking engagements, write or call:

Dr. Henry Cloud
Minirth Meier New Life Clinics West
260 Newport Center Drive, Suite 430
Newport Beach, CA 92660
1-800-877-HOPE.

For information on the treatment programs of the Minirth Meier New Life Clinics West or the Minirth Meier New Life Clinic nearest you, call 1-800-NEW-LIFE.

Study Guide

GROWING UP IN THE RETAIL BUSINESS, I ESPE-
cially remember the time of year when we checked
inventory. Before the days of computers, we had to take
an arduous count of what we really had, in order to see
three things:

1. What did we start with?
2. What do we have now?
3. What do we need to get for the future?

Taking inventory of your life is important as you study
the four essential tasks that will help you make changes
that heal. Have a pen and notebook handy so you can
record your answers to the following questions about your
past, present, and future.

Bonding with Others

The Past

When we take a personal inventory, we need to ask, "What did I start with?" We then look at how we have bonded in the past and what those relationships have been like, not to blame anyone, but to understand the relationship.

When we don't understand a behavior, we tend to repeat it. You have probably heard the story of the mother who, before cooking a beef roast, would cut off the end of the roast. One day her daughter, seeing her do this, asked why. The mother said, "I really don't know why. It's how you're supposed to cook a roast. It's the way my mother did it."

Later, the mother began to wonder about it. She called her mother and asked, "Why did you always cut the end off the roast before cooking it?"

"Well," her mother replied, "that's the way you're supposed to do it."

"I know, but why?" she asked.

The grandmother replied, "I don't really know. It's the way my mother did it when I was growing up."

Determined now to solve the mystery, the first mother called her grandmother, the great-grandmother of the clan, and asked, "Grandmother, why do you cut the end off the roast before you cook it?"

She replied, "I don't anymore. But when your mother was growing up, we had a very small oven, and there wasn't room enough for all the pans. I had to use a small one that wouldn't hold all the meat. So I would always cut the end off."

This silly but true story has a deeper truth in it: when we cling to the "tradition of the elders," we invalidate the truth of God. The sins of the fathers are carried on throughout generations if they are not confessed.

To break free of unhealthy generational patterns, to make changes that heal, we need to discover our rules of attachment and where we learned them, examining not only our family relationships, but also our relationships at church and school. This will help us immensely in a couple of ways.

First, it allows us to understand and reject the negative voices from the past that we have internalized. Most bonding problems arise when a person projects a past relationship onto a present relationship. For example, a wife may describe her husband as uncaring and emotionally unavailable, when the husband is nothing of the sort and she is actually describing her father. By projecting her father's attitude onto her husband, this woman has blocked herself from intimacy with her husband.

A successful marriage counselor will uncover this pattern. The wife in this example, seeing her mistake, might say, "I can see now that my husband is not as bad as I was seeing him. It was my unresolved relationship with Dad that was getting in the way." By understanding her past relationship with her father and correcting her view of her husband, she is able to achieve marital bonding.

Understanding the past allows us to see people in the present more realistically. It also enables us to choose new patterns of relating—patterns based on God's way rather than on past relationships.

Second, examining our past shows us who we need to forgive. No healing can occur without forgiveness, for unforgiveness binds us to the person who originally injured us. To break that hurtful tie, we must forgive the one who hurt us.

Unforgiveness also prevents us from opening up to new love objects. We saw earlier how Paul asked the Corinthians to let go of the old bonds, or "affections," and open up to the new. Unforgiveness keeps us tied to the past so that we can't reach out to the future. But when we forgive, we open ourselves to new, good attachments that replace the old.

Here are some questions that may help you take an inventory of your past. They will help you remember what was good in order to re-create those patterns, and to recognize what was bad so you can avoid those patterns.

1. With whom did I have a good bonding relationship in the past? What were the ingredients of that relationship that allowed me to make a connection?

2. Who hurt my ability to bond and trust? How? Which of their personality traits were hurtful to me?

3. What convictions of the heart did I develop about myself and others from these attachments? What core convictions did I develop about relationships in general?

4. Have I been able to forgive the people who hurt me? What is blocking me from forgiveness? Am I waiting for them to apologize, waiting for them to change, wanting revenge, enjoying punishment of them internally, not admitting how mean they really were, feeling guilty over telling the truth about how bad they were, or feeling angry that no one has ever listened or believed me?

5. Have I been able to realize God's acceptance for the parts that they hurt in me and labeled "bad"? What is blocking that? (Some possible barriers include distortions, lack of vulnerability, and lack of sharing it with someone else to feel acceptance.)

6. What parts of my bonding self did I bury as a result of those bad bonds from the past? Why are they still "buried in the ground"?

The Present

Any good inventory will also take stock of the present. The past allows us to gain insight, forgive ourselves and others, learn where our distortions came from, and express our hurt. But archaeology never built a new building, and the focus of sanctification is to build something new.

Like any builder, if we are building something we must take an inventory of our materials to see if we have what we need. We have identified the ingredients grace, truth, and time. Here are some questions that may help:

1. With whom do I now have a good, bonded relationship? What are the elements that help create that? How can I increase those elements (i.e., be more vulnerable, take more risks, show more need, move toward more)?

2. With whom do I currently have a negative bond? Why am I staying in this relationship and not changing it? What elements of the connection are hurting me and leaving me isolated?

3. How does this negative bond reinforce my distortions about myself and the rest of the world? How is that relationship reinforcing my defenses and injuries?

4. What distortions and barriers am I allowing to dominate my current picture of relationship?

5. Am I showing my real self to someone who can give grace to me?

6. If I believe that time is an element to growth, how much time do I invest in creating these attachments each week? If I devote very little time, why?

7. Who is available that I am not connecting with?

The Future

If we do not make plans to change what has been, it will continue into the future, and that "bad" future will someday be more of a "bad" past. This is what we talked about earlier when we looked at "bad time." Unused time is wasted time, and we are not growing.

If you are going to pursue attachments, you will need to do something different than what you have previously done. The bonding aspects of the self have to come out of hiding and get into relationship with others. This takes some real strategy and commitment to yourself and to God, who commands us to "guard your heart, for it is the wellspring of life" (Prov. 4:23). You need to plan for the future, which begins one second from right now!

Here are some questions that may help in making the future different:

1. As I look "out there," who is available and how am I going to increase my relationship with those persons? What concrete steps am I going to take?

2. What already structured situations can I take advantage of? What are some available support groups, prayer and sharing groups, group therapies, or counselors I could investigate?

3. What specific ways am I going to challenge my distortions and barriers?

4. What difficulties do I envision encountering as I begin to challenge my isolation? How am I going to handle these when they arise, as they most assuredly will?

5. How can I allow God to be a part of ending my isolation?

6. Who will I share my plan with and get review and feedback from? Who can I ask to pray for me?

7. What negative attachments of truth without grace or vice versa do I need to either change or avoid in order to grow?

8. How am I going to set aside the time I need to increase my bonding with others?

9. What am I going to do when my defenses arise?

Setting Boundaries

In looking at boundaries, we also need to look at past hurts, present hurtful patterns, and ways to change in the future.

The Past

When we look at our past handling of boundaries, we first need to examine whether we may have crossed the boundaries of others and repent if we have done so. Then we need to examine whether others have crossed our boundaries and injured us. If so, we will need to forgive those who have sinned against us so that we do not stay stuck in that pattern of relating. Forgiveness will give us a clearer vision of the relationship and break the bondage that person holds over us. Then we will see what has been lacking in our past relationships and show us how to direct our future relationships. Here are some questions to think about.

1. With whom in the past was I able to discover and keep my boundaries? What qualities of that relationship supported my boundaries?

2. Who crossed my boundaries in the past? How did they do that? What were the hurtful qualities of that relationship?

3. What convictions and distortions did I develop in those relationships that need to be challenged and replaced with God's precepts? How would I describe my philosophy of boundaries learned in those significant relationships?

4. Have I been able to forgive those who hurt my sense of boundaries? Have I called what they did to me sin and let them be responsible for it? Am I taking responsibility for what is not mine before God and feeling guilt that does not belong to me? How is unforgiveness a chain that

is binding me to people who have crossed my boundaries? How can I let go?

5. When have I failed to keep my own boundaries when I should have? When have I allowed others to cross my boundaries when I was old enough to know better? When have I tried to let others be responsible for things that I should have taken responsibility for? Do I have a pattern of allowing others to cross my boundaries and limits? What is it?

6. Have I invaded someone else's boundaries and crossed them? Is there a pattern that I need to confess and turn from? To whom do I need to make restitution?

7. How can I change? How can God help?

8. What parts of my fences and boundaries have I taken outside of time, and when did that happen?

The Present

To work on our boundaries, we also need to examine the present to be sure we are not repeating the past. Answer these questions about your present behavior and relationships.

1. With whom do I have a good relationship at present—a relationship where boundaries are not crossed? What components of this relationship allow for mutual responsibility of all other aspects of ownership? How can I increase those elements? How can I respect others' boundaries more?

2. With whom do I now experience crossed boundaries and a lack of boundaries and limits? Why? What are the elements that make it that way? What will it take to change?

3. How do the boundary problems in those present relationships reinforce my original beliefs about boundaries? How are those present relationships injuring my sense of boundaries?

4. What distortions of boundaries and limits are presently dominating me?

5. When am I better at setting and realizing boundaries? Why?

6. What exercises am I doing to bring my boundaries back into time and to get practice so that they can develop?

7. To whom do I have difficulty saying no? Why?

8. Whose "no" do I not respect and try to override?

9. Whose boundaries am I overriding in other aspects? Why?

10. What actions do I need to confess to God and others and receive forgiveness for? Whom do I need to confront in order to resolve some ongoing issue?

The Future

Continuing the past into the present will guarantee us a similar future. Making plans for change will get us back into "good time" and make us more productive.

1. As I evaluate the future in terms of the problems I see in boundaries, what am I going to change? How?

2. Knowing that it takes relationship and truth to change, whose help am I going to get for my plan?

3. In what specific ways am I going to challenge my distortions and barriers?

4. What specific practice activities can I do to strengthen my sense of boundaries?

5. What difficulties do I envision when I begin to create boundaries? How will I negotiate those difficulties?

6. Who will I get to listen, pray, and support my plan?

7. What crossed boundaries with others am I going to confront?

8. What do I expect them to do when I confront them? How will I deal with that?

Sorting Out Good and Bad

Taking an inventory also helps us learn to deal with good and bad. We need to see the unresolved bad in the past, present, and future, and begin to take steps to resolve those tendencies we all have to not deal with issues of good and bad. This can be the essence of the power of forgiveness in our lives.

The Past

In looking at the past, it is important to look at specific patterns of dealing with good and bad in our lives. If people have taught us that we are all good or all bad, we need to reevaluate and forsake those perceptions. We need to often forgive those who injured us. We need to see the patterns we used to deal with good and bad as well as the way that others dealt with us. Here are some questions to help in this process:

1. To whom did I feel safe to confess my badness or weakness to? What qualities made me feel safe to be less than ideal?

2. Who denied my badness in the past and destructively saw me as without fault or weakness? Why did I allow this?

3. Who denied my good parts and saw me as all bad? How did I respond to this?

4. Whose badness in the past did I deny? Do I see it now? Have I faced how bad they actually were, or do I take responsibility for their badness or weaknesses?

5. Have I forgiven them?

6. Whose goodness did I deny and who did I see as all bad? Do I still? Have I forgiven them?

7. When have I tried to appear all good or ideal? How did this affect my relationships? What would I do differently now?

8. When did I hide weakness from accepting people? Why?

9. When did I not take into account my good? What were the results?

10. Is there anyone anywhere I have not forgiven? How is this hurting me?

11. Is there anything that I need forgiveness for? What is keeping me from admitting this to God and to people who love me and bringing it into the light?

The Present

Take a prayerful inventory of the present and see if you are avoiding issues of good and bad.

1. With whom do I have a safe confessional process now? Do I show them my badness and weakness? All of it? What helps me to do that in this relationship?

2. Who denies my badness at present and makes me all good? How is this destructive? Why am I allowing it?

3. Who denies my good parts at present and makes me all bad? Why do I allow that?

4. Who am I seeing as all good? Why?

5. Who am I seeing as all bad? Why?

6. Who am I not forgiving? Why?

7. How and where am I hiding weakness and badness? Why? How is it hurting me?

8. How am I expending energy to appear ideal to others? Why?

The Future

If some things do not change in the future, we will repeat our past. See what sort of plans you can make to become more of your true self with others, and see more of their true self as well.

1. Whose badness do I need to confront? When and how?

2. Whose goodness do I need to appreciate? How will I let them know?

3. With whom can I begin to share my real self? How will I let them know about my badness and weakness? Are they a good choice to let in on those parts of me?

4. How will I take my good parts out of hiding?

5. What aspects of my ideal self will I begin to get in line with a true ideal as God sees it?

6. How will I work on my relationship between the ideal and the real? How will I make it more forgiving?

7. What imperfections in others and in situations can I work on accepting and loving?

Becoming an Adult

You may need to redeem the past, evaluate the present, and be different in the immediate future, before you can become an adult.

The Past

In terms of the past, your attitudes about authority came from somewhere. It is important to see where you got them so that you can actively disagree with their negative aspects and forgive the injury. This process will help get you out of conflict with the adult role so that you can assume it. We can't assume a role we hate.

1. Who was a good authority figure for me in the past? What did I appreciate about them? What kind of modeling do I want to emulate?

2. What negative aspects of authority figures do I disagree with and would like to be different from? Why did I not like these attributes and what sort of feelings did they create in me?

3. What are my parents' strengths and weaknesses? My other early authority figures?

4. How did they injure me and have I forgiven them? Why not? What is the block?

5. What authority figures did I falsely comply with after I was old enough not to do that? Why?

6. What was adolescence like? Have I entered adolescence yet? Why have I resisted becoming an adult and who helped me resist by playing God in my life?

7. What legalists have I succumbed to and what "rule-bound behavior"? Why?

8. What detrimental places and situations have I ended up in because I let some parent figure run my life?

9. What talents have I neglected developing? Why?

10. Where have I fused with the ideas of someone else without thinking for myself?

11. Who have I been afraid to disagree with in my life?

12. Have I come into my own sexual identity since adolescence, or am I still "hush, hush" about sex? Am I still repressed?

The Present

Take a prayerful inventory of the present and ask God to show you what situations are currently hurting you and keeping you from growing up.

1. With whom do I feel one-down right now? In what areas? Why? Is it a good one-down as in mentoring, or is it a bad one-down as in personhood?

2. With whom are you trying to be one-up? Why? Do you realize that you are playing God in their life?

3. Who are you trying to please and get their approval? Why? Is it worth it? Has that pattern ever helped you?

4. What talents and expertise am I not developing at present because of some sort of fear? What am I doing about the fear? Am I getting help? How can I step out in

faith to develop that expertise and allow God to make me into an adult?

5. What role or office am I resisting identifying with because of conflict? Why?

6. What authority roles in my life am I failing to submit to lovingly? (For example, my boss, the police, my board of elders, God, the IRS.) How can this be destructive?

7. With whom am I fusing currently in terms of thoughts and opinions and not stating my own? With whom am I afraid to disagree?

8. In what situations do I hide from my sexual feelings or thoughts? Why? Who is the parent figure there?

9. What "spiritual" group do I act "nice" around? What group of friends are more adolescent? Why am I trying to please this "spiritual" group and then passively rebelling on the side? How is this practice keeping me a child? Which person am I most afraid of being judged by? Why?

10. What doubts and wonderings do I have about God or theology that I am afraid to face and research on my own? What is keeping me from finding out what I believe?

11. What current spiritual leaders do I disagree with? Am I afraid to say my thoughts?

12. How are my spouse or closest friends functioning as parent figures in the negative sense of the term?

The Future

1. What authority figure do I need to go and disagree with? When?

2. What person will I stop hiding from? When?

3. What ideas will I stop fearing to voice and think about? When?

4. Who will I begin to show my real thoughts to? When?

5. How will I get in touch with my adult sexual role? When?

6. What plans will I make to find and develop my expertise and be a good steward of my gifts? When?

7. What role will I do better at assuming authority over? When?

8. What person will I do better at assuming authority over? When?

9. Who will I stop "obeying" that I have no business obeying? How?

10. What siblings (real siblings or siblings in the Lord) will I stop treating as if they were my parents?

11. What will I do the next time I hear "you should"?

12. What am I going to do about my lack of discipline?

Notes

Chapter 1

[1]Frederick Buechner, *Wishful Thinking: A Theological ABC* (New York: Harper, 1973), 33.

Chapter 4

[1]*Webster's Medical Desk Dictionary* (Springfield, Mass.: Merriam-Webster, 1986), 172.
[2]Ibid., 235.
[3]Ibid., 409.

Chapter 16

[1]Thomas Merton, *No Man Is an Island* (New York: Harcourt, 1955, 1983), 27.